SAGE was founded in 1965 by Sara Miller McCune to support the dissemination of usable knowledge by publishing innovative and high-quality research and teaching content. Today, we publish more than 850 journals, including those of more than 300 learned societies, more than 800 new books per year, and a growing range of library products including archives, data, case studies, reports, conference highlights, and video. SAGE remains majority-owned by our founder, and after Sara's lifetime will become owned by a charitable trust that secures our continued independence.

Los Angeles | London | New Delhi | Singapore | Washington DC

COLONIALISM
and the Call to
JIHAD
in
British India

COLONIALISM
and the Call to
JIHAD
in
British India

TARIQ HASAN

⑤SAGE www.sagepublications.com
Los Angeles • London • New Delhi • Singapore • Washington DC

All photographs' courtesy: Aligarh Muslim University

First published in 2015 by

 SAGE Publications India Pvt Ltd
B1/I-1 Mohan Cooperative Industrial Area
Mathura Road, New Delhi 110 044, India
www.sagepub.in

SAGE Publications Inc
2455 Teller Road
Thousand Oaks, California 91320, USA

SAGE Publications Ltd
1 Oliver's Yard, 55 City Road
London EC1Y 1SP, United Kingdom

SAGE Publications Asia-Pacific Pte Ltd
3 Church Street
#10-04 Samsung Hub
Singapore 049483

Published by Vivek Mehra for SAGE Publications India Pvt Ltd, typeset in Century Schoolbook 10/12 by Diligent Typesetter, Delhi and printed at Saurabh Printers Pvt Ltd, New Delhi.

Library of Congress Cataloging-in-Publication Data Available

ISBN: 978-93-515-0261-6 (HB)

The SAGE Team: Supriya Das, Sanghamitra Patowary, Tamanna Tripathi, Anju Saxena and Vinitha Nair

Dedicated to

Raja Mahendra Pratap—Freedom Fighter and
Founder of Religion of Love

and

Dr K.A. Hamied—Pioneering Swadeshi Entrepreneur and
Ardent Nationalist

Thank you for choosing a SAGE product!
If you have any comment, observation or feedback,
I would like to personally hear from you.
Please write to me at **contactceo@sagepub.in**

Vivek Mehra, Managing Director and CEO,
SAGE Publications India Pvt Ltd, New Delhi

Bulk Sales

SAGE India offers special discounts
for purchase of books in bulk.
We also make available special imprints
and excerpts from our books on demand.

For orders and enquiries, write to us at

Marketing Department
SAGE Publications India Pvt Ltd
B1/I-1, Mohan Cooperative Industrial Area
Mathura Road, Post Bag 7
New Delhi 110044, India

E-mail us at **marketing@sagepub.in**

Get to know more about SAGE

Be invited to SAGE events, get on our mailing list.
Write today to **marketing@sagepub.in**

This book is also available as an e-book.

Contents

Contents

List of Photographs

Acknowledgements

This work has been a labour of love for me. I begin by thanking all my friends, especially those from my early years. It is they who largely helped me in shaping my vision and idea of India. This work is my way of offering gratitude to them.

I am deeply indebted to my friend Farhat Hasan of the Department of History, Delhi University. He was very kind to extend his most erudite support whenever sought by me. Similar guidance was extended by Professor Shan Muhammad, the former Head of the Department of Political Science, Aligarh Muslim University (AMU). His work on the role of Muslims in India's freedom struggle is indeed voluminous. He is a great teacher and, what is more, even a better research guide.

I can never fully thank my good friends Ananda Majumdar and Abid Shah—both outstanding fellow scribes—for their invaluable help with the manuscript. Similarly, the help of Shakir Hussain, whose understanding of the Middle East affairs was of critical importance, and cannot be minimised. I would like to thank Manjula Das as well.

Rahat Abrar and his assistant in the Public Relations Department, Shamim Uzzaman, were unflinching in their support whenever I sought their help in procuring any inputs from the Maulana Azad Library, AMU. The latter never refused any help in handling my computer and software-related problems.

I would like to convey very special thanks to my family, especially my wife Habiba, for so painstakingly helping me with my manuscript and inspiring me to carry on with this work for more than half a dozen years. Had there not been any encouragement from them, this work might not have seen the light of the day.

I would also like to thank my cousin, Rajen Khwaja, and uncle, Professor Jamal Khwaja, who have always been an inspiration in my quest for free inquiry.

Introduction: Forgotten Pages from Indian History

Study the past, if you would divine the future.

—Confucius

People who cherish and delve into their past to understand it and introspect in its light are, indeed, fortunate. Even more fortunate are those who draw the right lessons from their history in order to shape a vision for a future—a future course that is shorn of past follies and is tempered with imagination and the yearning for a better world.

With this thought in mind, the present work tries to chronicle the inevitable confrontation between British imperialism and the Muslim clergy in 19th-century India. The narrative recalls some elided narratives from that era. They have largely been purged even from the footnotes of the history textbooks of this land. These accounts are relevant today not just for India, but also for the West because they mirror the larger story of imperialism and its victims. The legacy of the colonial era is somehow far from over. It lingers through to cast its shadow on today's troubled world.

One important outcome of India's national movement in the 20th century is the realisation that ever since India came under the colonial yoke, her historiography was deliberately tampered with to serve the political interests of the British rulers. The 19th-century British historians, liberals, such as James Stuart Mill amongst them, had divided Indian history into Hindu and Muslim periods. This eventually laid the foundation stone of the two-nation theory, so much so that this facilitated Britain's hold on power and tarrying in the subcontinent for half-a-century more before they finally sailed home in 1947. The colonial domination over historiography was a key element of their grand strategy.

The leaders of India's freedom movement were alive to this but took time to realise that imperialism, to a large extent, thrived on a deliberately obfuscated narrative of the country's past.

It was this compelling thought that prompted Professor Mohammad Habib, one of the leading Indian historians of his time, to state, 'Three-fourths of the communal fanaticism we see today is the result of these textbooks; they have misrepresented the Musalmans to the Hindus and the Hindus to the Musalmans and have tried to sap the foundations of India's self-respect'.[1] Professor Habib tried to draw attention to the writings of Sir Henry Elliot, which were mainly politically-laced historiography to suit the tasks the British rulers had set for themselves.

Soon after India became independent in 1947, bringing in the Nehru era, systematic efforts were initiated to undo the grave damage to the country's unity and syncretised culture by Western historians during colonial rule. Thus began a struggle to recover India's past by postcolonial nationalist historians. Their task was, first, to painstakingly identify and then vigorously counter the problematic discourse woven through by colonial historiography of India. An all-India panel, comprising leading historians of the time, was formed. Its members were known for their erudition, scholarship, intellect and integrity, and it included Dr Tarachand, S. Gopal, Mohammad Habib, Nilkant Shastri and D.V. Poddar.

This crucial task of nation building was taken forward despite various setbacks and challenges faced by Jawaharlal Nehru's successors, right up to the year 2000. Sadly, with the beginning of the new millennium, the then government launched a project to undo the good work of nearly half-a-century and to once again tweak, twist and maul history in a manner akin our colonial masters. Only this time, the insidious mechanisms were set rolling by ethnic nationalist and religious fundamentalist Indians themselves. The spirit and practices of Macaulay and James Mill, who spearheaded the brazen efforts to write warped history to benefit the British, were resorted to once again to divide India on the fault lines of faith, religion and belief.

Thus, a distinctly colonial worldview that treated any *difference* as being inferior and requiring assimilation or elimination has undergirded this 21st century move to rewrite Indian history

---

[1] K.A. Nizami (Ed.), *Politics and Society during the Early Medieval Period—Collected Works of Professor Mohammad Habib*, Vol. 1 (New Delhi: People's Publishing House, 1974), p. 8.

for serving the political interests of sectarian radicals merrily donning and flaunting the convenient garb of Hindutva. Besides being at odds with the faith itself, the strident move undertaken in its name was nevertheless detrimental to those whose cause it feigned to espouse. It sought to deny people's modern instincts and consciousness built so assiduously through the Nehru era. What it also did was to set the alarm bells ringing in progressive academic circles. Fortunately for India, the next government which came to power in 2004 stalled this blatant attempt to spread ill will and sectarianism amongst the people of this country. However, the vulnerability of the system had been exposed.

There is strong historical evidence to support the thesis that beginning from the early 19th century, the ulema (Muslim clergy) played a major role in mass nationalist mobilisation in India against colonial rule. It is understandable that prejudiced British historians in the colonial era had tampered with history to underplay, stain and blur the role played by the Muslim clergy in shaping Indian nationalism. After all, the interests of the British rulers were better served by promoting and projecting the separatist Indian Muslim League as the 'true saviours of Indian Muslims'. What is inexplicable is the failure of professional historians in independent India to give the ulema their due in their fight against colonialism. The present work is a small step in shedding light on this aspect. But it does not cover the role of the Indian ulema in the post-Independence era. It is unfortunate that in recent years, they have more than a few times failed the Muslim community in its faltering course of reform and modernisation. For this, the ulema be held accountable to history.

The insurrection of 1857 is a landmark event in Indian history. It has been chronicled extensively by historians, both Western and Indian. This book deals with one crucial facet of the tumultuous event—the role of the Muslim clergy in this clash with 19th century colonialism. It traces the roots of this conflict, beginning with the Mohamadiya Movement—erroneously referred to as the *Wahabi* Movement by the British. It covers the subsequent war waged in the North West Frontier Province (NWFP) of India by Sayid Ahmad Barelvi, a revolutionary Muslim cleric from Rae Bareli, a small town adjoining Lucknow, the capital of the former princely state of Awadh. Barelvi first led a campaign against the Sikh ruler of Punjab, Raja Ranjit Singh. Later, after Barelvi's death, his loyalists turned their attention to the British and fought them for nearly three decades until the late 1860s. Many Western historians refer to him as the spiritual *father* of Afghanistan's modern-day jihadi deviation. The present work seeks to unravel an intermingling of events and ideas which led to a fusion of jihad and Indian nationalism in the 19th century.

The narrative encompasses the entire trajectory of the clash between the colonial West and radical Islam, and seeks to distinguish between *radical Islam* and the *militant strain of 20th century Islam*. From the battlefields of Awadh to the tribal resistance of North West Frontier India, the stage shifts yet again to the dusty plains of the United Provinces (UP). It was here, in a small nondescript town of Deoband, that a battered and bruised section of the Muslim clergy from North India decided to set up a theological school for drawing spiritual sustenance after the traumatic reverses suffered by them in the failed Revolt of 1857. It is important to trace the roots of the Deobandi anti-imperialist movement which was largely accommodating, unlike Wahabi fundamentalism which was disturbingly divisive.

The Deoband School was essentially based on the Hanafi school of thought of Sunni Muslims. It was a revivalist movement which sought to focus on the Hadiths or the original sayings of the Prophet. It also sought to legitimise all the major established schools of Sufi thought. Politically, it was anti-West rather than anti-Christian.

The present work also seeks to remove a certain confusion which arose after the New York twin towers terrorist strike when the name of the Deobandi *madarsas* (schools) of Pakistan cropped up. When the movement for Pakistan was reaching its climax in undivided India in the 1940s, certain clerics broke ranks from the main Deoband seminary and switched loyalties to the Pakistan movement. After partition, they set up the Jamiat Ulema-e-Islam in Pakistan and broke away from the original India-based Jamiat Ulema-e-Hind. Till the 1980s, the Jamiat Ulema-e-Islam remained moderate in its political approach. When America started funding madarsas across Pakistan to wage jihad against the pro-Soviet regime in Afghanistan, these so-called Deobandi madarsas drew ideologically closer to the Wahabi school of thought rooted in Saudi Arabia. Flush with funds from the West and also from certain client states of the West in the Middle East, they became sanctuaries for the militant strain of Islam. Certain Western analysts erroneously linked these madarsas with the original Deoband seminary, which in turn sought in vain to disassociate itself from these deviant schools of Deobandi thought.

The Silk Conspiracy Case

In 1914, a determined band of Muslim clerics plotted to over-throw the British Raj in India. This ambitious venture was supported by the axis powers led by Germany and the Ottoman Empire. In the annals of the British government, this abortive revolt is referred to as the Silk Conspiracy Case. This narrative traces seemingly unconnected events in Asia, Europe and North America, and examines the role of jihad as an instrument for combating colonialism in South Asia.

The Silk Conspiracy or the Reshmi Rumal Movement, as it was referred to by Indian nationalists, ended in failure for its leaders. However, it led to the emergence of yet another charismatic figure on the stage of the 20th century Indian Muslim nationalism—Maulana Hussain Ahmad Madani. British historians have described him as 'one of the most important Muslim figures in 20th century South Asia'. Mahatma Gandhi revered him, and Jawaharlal Nehru held him in high esteem. Jinnah was dismissive of him, and yet feared him. After India's Independence, the Nehru-led government was keen to bestow the highest civilian honour, the Padma Vibhushan, to Maulana. But Maulana politely declined the honour saying the award would make him indebted to the government. In the years following his death, Maulana's sterling contribution to shaping collective Indian consciousness sadly faded away from public memory. The present work tries to identify the factors which have led to the near eclipse of Maulana's role in Indian history textbooks.

Another narrative strand traced by this work is the trajectory of Muslim separatism leading to the creation of Pakistan.

Its main thrust, however, is limited to the role of the Muslim ulema in this decisive play of events. It seeks to emphasise that the majority of Muslim clerics in undivided India were till the bitter end against the move to establish the theocratic state of Pakistan. The overwhelming momentum given to the drive for Pakistan emanated primarily from the upper-class landed aristocracy of Muslims along with the middle class. In any case, 90 per cent of the masses were not voters in the crucial elections of 1945–1946, which were treated as a sort of plebiscite on the issue of Pakistan.

Among the ulemas who strongly advocated partition was Maulana Sayyid Abul Ala Mawdudi, the radical Islamist who founded the Jamaat-e-Islami in 1941, a religious organisation with a pan-Islamist political agenda. He was a strong proponent of Pakistan, but had scant regard for Jinnah's secular concerns. In time, he would become one of the founding ideologues of *Islamic fundamentalism*.

This book examines the role of the ulema in India's freedom struggle through seven main protagonists. These are the 19th-century cleric Sayyid Ahmad Barelvi, the mystic revolutionary Maulvi Ahmadullah Shah, Maulana Mahmoodul Hasan (the founding father of the Silk Conspiracy and later of the Jamia Millia Movement), Maulana Obaidullah Sindhi, Barkatullah Khan and Maulana Hussain Ahmad Madani. All eulogised the ideal of jihad, but this was a call far removed from the present-day notion of this belief which rests entirely on warfare stemming from hatred. This is also the story of a Hindu prince, Raja Mahendra Pratap, whose close association with three of the clerics (mentioned earlier) transcends all commonly accepted barriers of religion and interpretations of jihad.

This work concludes with a brief account of Jinnah's last days shortly after the creation of Pakistan—a state largely conceived and created by him—and is predominantly based on a long lost book, *With the Quaid-e-Azam During His Last Days*. This was written by Lt Colonel Ilahi Baksh, the doctor who first diagnosed that Jinnah was suffering from tuberculosis and treated him in his final days. First published in 1949, the book was heavily censored because the author was then in government service (He was, in fact, the first Pakistani principal of King Edwards Medical College, Lahore). The first edition of this book was quickly sold out, and then it was quietly put under wraps for more than half-a-century.

Obviously, Lt Colonel Baksh was privy to the innermost thoughts and feelings of the creator of Pakistan in his final days. If one carefully scrutinises this critical piece of evidence, then one is bound to arrive at a startling conclusion—the architect of Pakistan died of tuberculosis, but his end was hastened by another major killer, depression. He felt that the Pakistan which he had created was 'departing from the cardinal concepts of what he had visualised'. In his dying days, Jinnah had awakened to the reality that a theocratic state has no place in the modern world.

Why I Chose to Tell This Story

I was born in the North Indian city of Aligarh during the tumultuous months preceding partition. The Muslim family into which I was born was deeply religious. It was, however, not a divisive faith. From childhood, we were taught to honour the holy books of all faiths. Pandit Sundarlal, the noted Gandhian and author of the Gita and the Quran, was a family friend; so also was Raja Mahendra Pratap, one of the protagonists of this work.

Most of my cousins were given Hindu names by my maternal grandfather Abdul Majeed Khwaja, who was a close associate of Mahatma Gandhi. This was not because of some hollow *secularism*, but because my *nana* (grandfather) was of the clear opinion that 'names have nothing to do with religion'. He genuinely subscribed to the notion that 'names should be rooted in the ethos of one's land of birth'.

My earliest memories are, however, not of India but of the battle-scarred cities of London and Vienna, where my father had ventured shortly after my arrival in this world. He had gone to Europe to finish his higher education in modern medicine.

My paternal grandfather belonged to a zamindar family of district Pratapgarh, south of Lucknow. Our ancestral village, Garhi Samdabad, nestles on the banks of the river Ganga. My great-great-grandfather Asad Khan had been an artillery commander in the army of the ruler of Awadh.

Asad Khan had played a valiant role in the Great Revolt of 1857. After the defeat of the rebel-led forces, he narrowly evaded capture by the British, by hiding in a nearby village in the house of a family friend. If captured, it would have meant certain death for him. Subsequently, he took advantage of the general amnesty by surrendering before the British authorities. His estate was confiscated. Later, a small portion of his land holdings was restored to him.

My grandfather Ali Hasan Khan was an enlightened zamindar known all over the district for his nobility and wisdom. Like all members of the landed class in his time, he was a loyal subject of the British Raj. For this loyalty, he was rewarded with the title of Khan Bahadur. During the freedom movement, he initially thought it prudent to remain aloof and concentrate on rebuilding his depleted estate. His priority was to give the best education to his three sons. Thus, sometime in the early 1920s, my adventurous father Ajmal Hasan Khan boarded a steamship and headed for the shores of the imperial metropolis of London, with a little over 20 pounds in his pocket. His two younger brothers, Niaz and Majid, spent their early years studying in the neighbouring city of Allahabad.

My grandfather's loyalty to the government of the day was, however, destined to face some testing times, shortly after my parents' wedding in 1936. My mother, Akhtar Sutan Begum's father, Abdul Majeed Khwaja, was a staunch Gandhian and would never lose any opportunity to display his anti-British sentiments.

Khwaja had studied law at Cambridge and struck up a friendship with Jawaharlal Nehru there, which had been a lifelong one. Unfortunately, this relationship was somewhat marred in his final days. The reason for this was my grandfather's deep worry over the communal riots in the early 1960s, mainly at Jamshedpur, Jabalpur and Aligarh. I suspect that he was disappointed by Prime Minister Nehru's subdued response to what he himself perceived as a grave portent to Hindu–Muslim relations in free India. Angered by the Congress government's failure to swiftly dispense justice to the perpetrators of these riots, one of Khwaja Sahib's sons, my uncle Raveend Khwaja, resigned from the Congress party and joined the newly formed Republican Party of India in 1961. Such happenings must have cast a shadow on Nehru's feelings towards his old friend. Soon the Indo-China war broke out and Nehru was shattered by the setback brought by it. Abdul Majeed Khwaja passed away after a brief illness in December 1962.

In retrospect, I feel that though Nehru was very fond of my grandfather, he would often get impatient with Khwaja's stubborn, and rather simplistic, approach to political issues. Thus, instead of taking Khwaja into his cabinet, he chose the more skilled politician and capable administrator Rafi Ahmad Kidwai.

It was Khwaja's unflinching loyalty to Gandhian ideals which led Gandhi himself to comment just before the country was partitioned that if Indians could learn from 'Badshah Khan [Khan Abdul Ghaffar Khan] and Khwaja Abdul Majeed, then the India of their dreams would emerge'. The exact quote and the context in which the Mahatma had paid tribute to two of his closest associates find detailed elaboration in Gandhi's official biography *Mahatma Gandhi—The Last Phase* by Pyaareylal.

Millions of Hindus and Muslims lost their lives and property during partition. Along the path leading up to partition, ironic as it may appear today, the Muslims of UP and Bihar had played a leading role in the struggle for establishing the Muslim State of Pakistan. Barring Mohammad Ali Jinnah, all the chief protagonists of Pakistan, including Liaqat Ali Khan and Choudhary Khaliquzaman, were from the heartland of U.P. An inexplicable wish for self-destruction apparently engulfed them. Besides the loss of life and property which all the migrants suffered, for the thousands of Muslims from the two states, partition led to a vertical split in their families—brothers separated from brothers, children from parents, wives from husbands.

Ours was a large family—if one counted first cousins, second cousins, uncles and aunts, the figure would cross a hundred. My mother had four other sisters and three brothers; her mother had three sisters and five brothers, and so on. Our family, too, was split equally between India and Pakistan.

Going back to my childhood years, I have vivid memories of small towns in the heartland of North India. On our return to India in 1950, after spending nearly three years in Europe with my parents, my father was posted as Civil Surgeon at Mainpuri district, a town in the badlands of U.P. It was the beginning of a new era. The country's first parliamentary elections were still to be held. The British rulers had left but the *Raj* was still very much a reality. The respect and fear of authority was still palpable.

In the mofussil towns, it was the 'Collector sahib's writ which still ran'. 'Captaan sahib' (superintendent of police), Judge sahib and Civil Surgeon sahib would follow. The district officials lived a life of comfort and were in a way fairly insulated from the common people. The poor were suffering, yet it decidedly was a disciplined society. The justice delivery system was largely intact because corruption was still within limits. The one place where the district officials lowered their guard was at the City Club—a legacy of the Raj. Most top officials played tennis or badminton. There were no bars in such clubs and only soft drinks, suh as Rooh Afza and lemonade, were served. On weekends, those fond of *shikar* (hunting) would go to nearby ponds for duck and partridge shooting.

After a two-year stint at Mainpuri, my father was transferred to the neighbouring district of Etawah—then in the limelight because of the legendary dacoit Maan Singh and his son Tehsildaar Singh. Maan Singh had acquired a reputation for being somewhat of a Robin Hood. He had for years eluded the police of three states. It was during our stay at Etawah that Maan Singh met his end after being lured by a police informer who spiked his glass of milk with poison. His son, the *tehsildaar* revenue administrative officer), was arrested and sent to the district jail at Etawah. Since the district jail was administered by the civil surgeon, my father would often come across Tehsildaar Singh during his daily rounds of the jail. He was always very respectful towards my father. My father would often tell me that the dacoits of the Chambal ravines would refer to themselves as *baghies* (rebels), and had their own code of conduct and sense of honour.

There were no good schools at Etawah, and so I was sent to Bombay (now Mumbai). I was admitted to class one at St Marys High School, where two of my cousins were already studying. My uncle was then the general manager at the newly established pharmaceutical firm Cipla, now world-renowned.

Bombay was even then a truly cosmopolitan city. The ambience was marked by its melting pot culture devoid of any sort of parochialism. At school, in my class, the ethnic mix of students

was like this: In a class of around 50, there were at least four
Jews of European stock, about half a dozen Parsis and at least
15-odd Anglo-Indians. As a child, I do not remember any incident
which smacked of any parochialism or communalism.

My memories of Bombay's high society are, to a large extent,
linked to what I saw at the Colaba residence of my uncle (my
mother's cousin) Dr Khwaja Abdul Hamied, founder of Cipla
Pharmaceuticals. Dr Hamied, then a budding entrepreneur,
was selected to be the sheriff of Bombay, a post more grand then
than today's mayor of such a city. For a Muslim to adorn such
a post in those early years was no mean achievement. But then
Dr Hamied was no ordinary man. After obtaining his doctorate
in chemistry from Germany, instead of taking a cushy teaching
assignment in Europe or India, he chose the difficult task of setting up an indigenous pharmaceutical company in India. From
the very beginning, Hamied took on the giant pharmaceutical
firms of the West, then operating in India. Such was his vision of
swadeshi or indigenous capitalism that when Mahatma Gandhi
visited Bombay, he spent several hours at Cipla just to express
his solidarity and encourage this promising young man who,
he felt, embodied the ideal of young India's new breed of entre-
preneurs. Dr Hamied became a sort of role model for me and
the rest of our extended family. After him, his two sons Yusuf
Hamied and Muku Hamied, led Cipla in playing a heroic role in
confronting the multinational pharmaceutical companies and
their exploitation of Third World countries on the issue of providing cheap medicines to the AIDS-affected millions in Africa.

The one unforgettable memory from that early stage of this
midnight's child revolved around Sunday mornings. Cricket was
a passion for Bombayites. The Times of India Cricket League
Tournament was a favourite event during winters. It was a
league contest in which about 20 top clubs of the city vied for
honours in matches played at about half a dozen grounds spread
all over the city. The most famous destinations, of course, were
Azad Maidan and the Oval. On such Sundays, you could find
most members of India's test team representing some club or
the other. More than half of India's test team was from Bombay.

Cipla, which was hardly known till then, came into the limelight after its team drew laurels in the Cricket League. The
Cipla team, which was led by my uncle Niaz Hasan, included

test stars such as Rusi Surti, Ajit Wadekar and Salim Durrani.
When they played for Cipla, they were still knocking on the
doors of test cricket.

But the real romance of the Bombay of the 1950s was the
magical world of the film industry which was beginning to come
into its own. The golden era of Bombay films had truly begun,
and the whole of India was captivated by the magic of the trio of
Dilip Kumar, Dev Anand and Raj Kapoor. As a starry-eyed eight-
year-old, I along with my cousins would often get an opportunity
to peep into this world of magic when our uncle, Dr Hamied,
would throw lavish parties in which some of the most sought-
after luminaries of the film world were frequently invited.

Winter Dreams

In the month-long winter vacations, the entire family would
congregate at our ancestral village. From different places, such
as Pakistan, Britain and the US, family members would come
in to share the joys of family life. These annual get-togethers
were the bedrock of our existence.

Garhi Samdabad has undergone sea change. And some of it
is for the better. As for us, about a dozen houses, once bustling
with our large extended family, now remain vacant most of the
year. The families have moved to towns, such as Allahabad or
Lucknow. Gone are the annual family gatherings. My cousins,
uncles and aunts, who had migrated to Pakistan, find it impossible to get visas to meet the family and visit the land of their
ancestors' birth.

There is, however, a positive side. There has been a marked
reduction in poverty which had dogged most villagers during
my childhood days. At that time except for our family, the rest
of the village folk lived in mud shacks. For potable water, the
village had a single well. All that has changed now. Except for
an odd hutment here and there, all the residents live in brick
houses. There is electricity, and community hand pumps for all.

I am writing about the life and times of a Muslim zamindar
family in the very heart of the so-called Hindi belt—or cow belt
as many describe it—barely 150 kilometres from the yesteryears'

disputed site of Babri Masjid. Our village is located in Tehsil Kunda where the percentage of Muslims in the population was less than 10 per cent.

Yet, the atmosphere was tranquil. Communal amity, warmth and goodwill permeated our social relations. The biggest temple of that area—the Jwala Devi temple—was managed by our family. According to the temple records, this arrangement had been in place for well over a century. This single fact reflects the traditions which were deeply rooted in this area right from the Mughal era. This was true not just for our village but also to the large swathes of Awadh stretching through several districts. Around 1960, an over-enthusiastic government officer in all his wisdom thought it prudent to wrest control of the management from our family. It was a pointer to the mindset of a system which failed to grasp the simple fact that India could only thrive if its social fabric and pluralistic ethos are nurtured, instead of being subjected to bureaucratic whims and political machinations.

In October 1956, my father was transferred to the cantonment city of Jhansi. Since the place had some excellent missionary schools, I promptly joined my parents and was admitted to class five in Christ the King School. The Catholic priests who managed the school were Irish. I fondly remember our Principal Brother Gannon. I was the favourite pupil of my class teacher Brother Malaky. My views on Christianity were shaped by those pious souls. As a sensitive child, I was never made conscious of my identity as a Muslim.

I can say that in the early 1950s despite the trauma of partition, the 1950s were the golden era of communal amity in the 20th century Independent India. The credit for this, undoubtedly, goes to the founding fathers of India. But with the beginning of the 1960s, sporadic incidents of Hindu–Muslim violence started taking place in North India, such as in Jamshedpur (then in Bihar), Jabalpur in Central India, Aligarh and Meerut in U.P. On hindsight, it can be said that had the Congress government of the time taken remedial steps to introduce constitutional and statutory measures for combating communalism and communal violence, India perhaps would have been saved from some of the most virulent forms of inter religious violence in the decades ahead. But by then, perhaps, Prime Minister Nehru had become too tired and old to take such bold steps.

Life in My Village

My grandfather and his brother lived in a style reminiscent of the zamindari era. The spacious *haveli* (mansion) was surrounded by at least five acres of lush green mango groves. The property included a riverside bungalow which served as a guest house. Throughout the holidays, there were shikar parties, partridge hunts and cricket matches with neighbouring villages and conviviality all around.

There was a large retinue of helpers. Barring two or three Muslim retainers, all were Hindus. Till their old age, they served us with utmost loyalty, honesty and complete dedication.

It was only in the winter of 1991, when the Babri Masjid clash took place, that for the first time it jolted us like never before, mainly because for decades after partition, we had been living in a world where followers of different faiths cohabitated peacefully.

After my father was transferred from Jhansi, I was packed off to a boarding school in Allahabad—St Joseph's Collegiate—in July 1959. It was here that I started becoming aware of my social moorings.

I cannot deny that the India of my childhood was deeply conservative in its social norms. Social interaction between different religious groups was limited. However, there was a certain code of behaviour which was observed in social interaction between Hindus and Muslims.

My experience in school contrasts sharply with what my three children faced in the post-Babri Masjid era of the 1980s. None of my close friends at St Joseph's ever made me conscious of my religious identity. I was quite popular in school as a member of the cricket and hockey teams. It was, above all, an era of idealism and this touched all of us even in school. Politics and politicians were not held in general contempt by the masses. Prime Minister Nehru was a figure of admiration and love for children.

After school, I completed my 12th grade from the Government College, Allahabad and then went to AMU to study engineering. I had no particular aptitude for the subject but in those days, *smart boys* were supposed to study either engineering or medicine.

Aligarh was where I got a reality check. AMU had passed through a very testing period in years following independence.

There was a powerful lobby, which included some members of the ruling Congress party, who were of the opinion that a Muslim university had no reason to exist in secular India after the creation of the Muslim *homeland* of Pakistan. The state of affairs which had prevailed at AMU in the run-up to partition had given strength to their argument. But Gandhiji and Jawaharlal Nehru had different ideas. With the help of Maulana Abul Kalam Azad, the then education minister and Dr Zakir Hussain, AMU was given a new lease of life after being on the very brink of closure. I am privy to first-hand accounts as to what happened in those tumultuous days as my grandfather Abdul Majeed Khwaja was a key figure in the high drama over the university's future.

AMU was a vibrant place in those days. Yet, I could not escape the feeling that at a certain level, the campus had not fully emerged from the hangover of partition. There is a background to this. Since its early days, the Aligarh College while catering predominantly to the Muslims took pride in itself for its open door policy towards other communities. This liberal approach had been the cornerstone of the ideology of its founding fathers in the 1870s. This state of affairs continued right up to 1937, but underwent a drastic change in the last decade or so before India became independent. Between 1940 right up to 1947, Jinnah's Muslim League had succeeded in making the university its stronghold. During this period, anyone who spoke in favour of the Indian National Congress was ostracised. My uncle Raveend Khwaja, then known as Rasheed Bilal Khwaja, a committed Gandhian, was amongst the half-a-dozen Congress activists who were expelled from the university for opposing the Muslim League. It was this turbulent phase that made things very rough for AMU in the early post-Independence years.

My years at AMU gave a new perspective to my identity as an Indian Muslim. Having spent all my school years in missionary schools, I did at times feel uneasy. But during my stay of more than four years at AMU, I do not recollect any incident of *communal prejudice* against Hindu students. Most of my close friends at AMU were Hindus, and I have no hesitation in stating that it has been a life-long association with most of us.

AMU was, however, destined to pass through another turbulent phase which began in the early 1970s and lasted over a decade. It all started in 1969, when the country's highest court questioned the legality of the university's status as a minority institution. The university community and Muslims of North India got deeply exercised over this, as they perceived that they were being deprived of their legitimate right of administering this historic institution and preserving its Muslim identity. There were widespread protests by Muslims. The agitation ultimately subsided after the Indira Gandhi-led Congress government restored what it described as AMU's special historic character in 1981.

Things, however, did not stay calm for long. The rise of the Babri Mosque and Ram Janambhoomi issue—a legacy of the Raj—ensured that the communal cauldron would continue to be on the boil. Aligarh was one of the most inflammable cities during this period. I was covering this city for The Times of India during this critical phase. It was, indeed, a challenging proposition to be objective, truthful and, at the same time, resonant of the concerns of my own community in those days. How far I succeeded in this endeavour is not for me to judge. That is the reader's prerogative.

The post-Babri Mosque demolition violence was one of the most disturbing phases in the history of Independent India. I must confess that for quite a few months after the demolition of the Babri Mosque, I was overcome by great despondency. I was tormented by the fear that the India in which I had lived was gone forever. My fears, however, proved unfounded. Things gradually started returning to normalcy. This state of affairs continued right up to 2002. Then the Gujarat carnage took place in February 2002, one of the worst of its kind.

In the life of a nation, a few years are of little consequence. Ultimately it is only history which will assess the damage which the Gujarat carnage caused to the country's pluralistic ethos. Till it took place, terrorism by Muslim fanatic groups was largely the handiwork of Kashmir-based outfits.

The sad truth about the existing state of Hindu–Muslim relations in India is that 65 years after India gained independence, the discord between the communities and mutual suspicion is dangerously high. The Gujarat violence will remain a dark milestone in the history of Hindu–Muslim relations in post-Independence India. The issue relates not just to the intensity of the violence which occurred, but also to the near-total abdication of authority by the state in rebuilding shattered lives and rehabilitating thousands of victims.

Unlike what happened in the aftermath of the Babri Mosque demolition, this time no substantive initiative to heal wounds and build bridges was undertaken. Instead of attempts to heal, there was a vicious move to spread the venom of communal hatred through the social media. This is one of the most pernicious attempts to strike at the very roots of India's pluralistic ethos.

The most disturbing element in this emerging reality is the glaring gap in the perceptions of the Muslim community as a whole and an influential segment within the majority community. The Muslim community feels increasingly isolated and persecuted, ironically enough, in states ruled by the secular parties. On the other hand, a large section of the majority community insists that the so-called secular parties are appeasing the Muslims. It is an alarming clash of perceptions. The failure of the secular parties to go beyond mere tokenism and address the real issues brings their guilt almost to the same level as those whom they dub as Hindu fundamentalists.

The Emerging Scenario

India is becoming a dangerously intolerant society. The media— the guardians of our conscience—is refusing to take up cudgels for the right to dissent.

The track record of the Congress-led government—which ruled India for 10 years beginning 2004—on the issue of framing innocent Muslim youth on terror charges, does not quite cover them with glory. There is, naturally, a socio-political cost to this.

Meanwhile, a new political dispensation has taken charge in New Delhi, introducing a new element into the power equation. The Bharatiya Janata Party government of Narendra Modi has taken the entire country in its sweep. There has been a radical shift in the power structure, having been triggered by a highly polarising and divisive election campaign. This poses serious questions about the future of Nehruvian pluralism, which ushered India into a new era in 1947.

In the history of a nation, five or 10 years can well be of transitory significance. What matters is the broad direction in which a nation moves. Since the very idea of pluralism and secularism is being questioned by an influential section Indians, it becomes an issue of critical concern and calls for soul searching. No one, not even the preceding secular political dispensations will escape the verdict of history. They too will be held accountable for allowing the concept of secularism to be mauled and belittled when the need was to reinvent and make it a dynamic creed.

As mentioned earlier, the fallout from 9/11 worldwide and the Gujarat riots in India have led to the proliferation of Muslim terror groups all over the globe, including India. There is no doubt today that the George Bush War against terror has gone horribly wrong. This war is instead breeding fear, frustration and fanaticism throughout the Muslim world. Pakistan, America's once highly trusted ally, which was supposed to lead this war against terror, is itself imploding. The chances of peace in the region have receded drastically after America targeted innocent civilians in tribal Pakhtoon areas in drone attacks.

Pakistan, in fact, is fast turning out to be a failed state. Radical strains in Islam have drawn strength from the acts of inhumanity perpetrated by the West. But the moot point remains: If Pakistan is allowed to fall into the hands of extremist forces, then the fallout for neighbours, such as India, would be calamitous. It is, thus, of critical importance for India to nurture good relations with an emerging section of moderates and realists in that deeply troubled land. Jingoism and hard line policy towards our neighbours may not deliver the desired result and could, in fact, backfire on India. The battle against religious fundamentalism, including militant strains in Islam, cannot be fought in isolation.

In its early years, Islam had started its quest for capturing the mind and soul of the restless tribes of the Arabian deserts and had extended its sway to most corners of the Old World. Its strength lay in the simplicity of its monotheistic faith and urge for selfless enterprise. Somewhere down the line, the world of Islam lost touch with its own roots and failed to keep pace with the Industrial Revolution.

More recently, the Islamic Revolution of Iran triggered events which exacerbated relations between the West and the Islamic world. As a practising Muslim, I certainly cannot absolve my co-religionists of their share of responsibility in this crisis. Wallowing in self-righteous indignation, the followers of Islam have miserably failed to evolve a balanced relationship with the

Western world. Muslims, the world over, are either in a state of denial regarding the real causes of their own woes or are simply in a state of apathy and inertia where they are unable to break out from the shackles which bind them.

I have no compunction in stating that if today a large number of non-Muslims, the world over, share an antipathy towards the Muslims, then a large degree of responsibility rests with my co-religionists. I go even further to state that a section of the followers of Islam have strayed sharply from the teachings of the prophet of Islam, peace be upon him. In fact, any impartial analysis of the history of Islam will confirm that within just a few years of the demise of their Prophet, a politically significant section of followers of Islam chose to abandon his egalitarian, humane and conciliatory approach towards his fellow beings. It is, however, equally true that this deviation was not a permanent feature and for long periods in Islamic history, the followers of Islam did live up to the highest moral principles expounded by their prophet.

India and the War against Terror

Muslims like me, who grew up on a staple of Gandhi–Nehru nationalism, have watched with increasing dismay the fading away of true Indian nationalism. The estrangement of the Muslim community as a whole, especially from the state, should be a subject of grave concern.

The Indian Muslim community's fears, both real and perceived, have led to a situation in which the faith of the community in the state has eroded to dangerously low levels. If corrective measures are not put in place with extreme urgency, we would arrive at a situation wherein every Muslim could be viewed with suspicion. To put it in other words, there would be 200 million terror suspects swarming this country. It is a situation whose consequences are so grave that one finds it nightmarish.

The rising disenchantment of the Muslim community with the justice delivery system in the wake of an alarming rise in the incidence of trials connected to terror cases has been exploited by some *secular parties*. In a bid to gain cheap popularity, some so-called champions of secularism have made clumsy attempts to free some Muslims who are facing trials for crimes, involving incidents related to terror activities. Far from securing the release of innocent Muslims who have wrongly been implicated in such cases, these attempts have given an opportunity to right-wing Hindutva groups to raise the bogey of *appeasement*.

The feeling of alienation becomes more acute against the backdrop of communal riots, as the Muslim minority questions the impartiality of the law enforcement agencies at such times. Note how Wajahat Habibullah, a man of unimpeachable credentials who has occupied some of the most prestigious offices in government, speaks of repeated cases of 'police complicity and collusions' while tackling communal riots. Habibullah, who once headed the National Commission for Minorities, had spoken out about a slew of enquiries conducted by the Commission, which pinpointed the role of the police in targeted killing of Muslims, ironically occurring under governments headed by the so-called secular parties. Habibullah hails from one of the most prominent Muslim families of North India and has, in a recent paper on the trajectory of Nationalism in India, expressed his anguish on the torpedoing of the Communal and Targeted Violence (Prevention Bill) which has been languishing in the Parliament for years.

If political parties had been serious about tackling the twin monsters of organised communal violence and religion-based terrorism in India, then this would certainly have been on the very top of their agenda. The shocking reality, it appears, is that established political parties are more interested in short-term political gain leading from identity politics, rather than addressing the fear, anger and frustration of people in India's Muslim-dominated ghettos. The emerging reality, however, is that an entire generation of Indian Muslims, including a burgeoning population in urban ghettos, is growing up in a climate of suspicion, violence and antipathy. The state watches on with callous indifference even as political parties hungrily grab each opportunity to glutton on political gain.

It cannot be denied that a section of Muslims who stayed behind after partition displayed a certain ambivalence in their rejection of the dream of the idea of a *Muslim homeland*. This dream was finally laid to rest after the break-up of Pakistan in 1971 and the creation of Bangladesh.

Today's Pakistan is certainly no role model for those belonging to the present generation of Indian Muslims who identify with the dreams and aspirations of millions of their own countrymen. It will be a folly to stain them with the past and treat them as the *other*. This can only lead to the ghettoisation of the community such as that took place in Gujarat and more recently in Muzaffarnagar in UP.

By now it should be clear to all that the West is not succeeding in the so-called *war against terror* which had been launched by President George Bush. The fundamental cause of its failure is the premise that it is based on the theory of Clash of Civilisations. It is this erroneous perspective that prevents a more historicised and better grounded approach towards these issues.

It is the failed *war against terror*, which has spawned jihadist groups in Iraq and Syria in the aftermath of the 9/11 terror, strikes in the US. It will be very difficult today for the American establishment to deny the role of Western and Israeli intelligence agencies in propping up the original avatar of the extremist IS in Syria then known as the Free Syrian Army (FSA). This act of folly was no doubt done with certain objectives of achieving regime changes in that troubled area. As mentioned by the noted American journalist Roger Cohen, 'The war on terror, it seems produced only a metastasised variety of terror.' The West will also find it difficult to stand scrutiny for the dubious role played by some of its closest client states in the Middle East for fomenting trouble in that area and playing a double role on the issue of justice or the people of Palestine.

The only viable strategy today for containing and defeating monster groups, such as the IS in Iraq and Syria, is to isolate them from the rest of the Islamic world. Mere military might not be able to destroy such extremist forces. The real battle lies in winning over the minds and hearts of the younger generation of Muslims the world over. Frontline Arab states including Saudi Arabia, who have been promoting American interests in the region with a certain brazen indifference to the broader interests of that region, will now have to swallow a bitter pill. They will have to win over the confidence and join hands with each other, even if in a limited manner, to defeat IS and others like them.

The role of the West in embittering relations between the Shias and Sunnis in the Arab world is quite well documented. In the beginning of the First World War, two British Agents T.E. Lawrence and Gertitude Bell, found it expedient to arm Sunni warlords against the Shiete tribal chiefs. Such divide and rule tactics initially paid off, as a result of which Turkey had to lose its hegemony over the Arabian peninsula. Today, however, the chickens are coming home to roost because of such reckless meddling and intrusion by the West in the affairs of the Middle East.

Under the pretext of *civilising* the heathen peoples of the East, the 18th century Western powers, mainly Great Britain, France, Holland, Spain and Portugal launched one of history's major invasions to subjugate an entire continent. Between 1757 and 1857, the East India Company alone ruled nearly two-thirds of South Asia. From the deserts of Egypt to the palaces of Peking, the West had created a moral justification for ravaging some of the greatest civilisations of the world. The treasures of Egypt, the riches of Mughal India and the fabled wealth of the Chinese emperors were plundered by the colonial powers with impunity in the name of 'civilisation, law and order, and conservation'.

There is no authentic record of the number of people who were killed by different colonial powers in South Asia and the Middle East between 1757 and 1900. The figure is in millions. Here, it must be conceded that barring the massacres by the army of the East India Company in the aftermath of the failed Revolt of 1857 in India, the track record of the British colonialists was generally much better than that of the other colonial powers. For instance, according to the monumental encyclopaedia of Africa, more than two million of Algeria's native population out of its three million people were killed during the first 40 years of French colonial rule. History will bear evidence that the record of the killings during the rules of the colonial powers between 1857 and 1900 would easily overshadow the massacre by the Mongol hordes led by Chengis Khan in the 12th century—the only difference being that the Western colonial powers were killing people under the pretext of *civilising them*. Strangely, the darkest chapters in the history of colonialism, whether in Africa or Asia, unfolded after and despite the civilising influence brought to the world by Industrial Revolution and the Renaissance.

It was earlier in 1757 that the troops of the East India Company led by Robert Clive defeated Nawab Sirajud Daula of Bengal in the Battle of Plassey. This was a turning point in the history of colonialism not just in South East Asia but also in the Middle East. Clive was hailed as a hero in England and can be dubbed as the founding father of colonial rule in India.

The fact remains that despite all attempts of colonial historians to portray Clive as a great conqueror, he will be remembered essentially as a corrupt provincial middle class adventurer who sought legitimacy by looting the vanquished and then acquiring all the trappings of British aristocracy. Clive, perhaps more than anyone else, epitomises the dual moral standards of the West in their perpetual quest for empire. The Battle of Plassey, in many ways, opened the gateways of the Orient to colonial powers. Not just India, but Egypt, Arabia and North Africa fell prey to colonial powers.

The final denouement would come about two centuries later in 1948 when the colonial powers, mainly the US and Great Britain, in a brazen defiance of all international law and modern principles of human rights deprived the legitimate rights of Asian people and handed over a large territory of Palestine to alien people.

The creation of the state of Israel by the West, aided and abetted later by some client Arab states, represents a cataclysmic symbol of Imperialism. By supporting a genocidal government in Israel and persistently stoking internal strife within the Middle East, such as the Shia–Sunni conflict, the West is yet again following a short-term policy of geopolitical gain.

In the 1980s, the US government had opted for a similar path of political expediency by funding radical Muslim seminaries in Pakistan, ostensibly to fight pro-Soviet forces in neighbouring Afghanistan. This approach paid short-term dividends to the West, but it was like playing with fire. The world paid a heavy price for the US government's patronage to the rabidly fundamentalist regime of General Ziaul Haq in Pakistan. Instead of learning its lessons from this fiasco, the US government under President Barack Obama has repeated this disastrous policy in Iraq and Syria.

When President Obama rode to power in the US, there was considerable optimism in Third World countries, including in the Islamic bloc, that the US—which till the middle of the 20th century had occupied a certain moral high ground for its position on issues of rights of the underprivileged in the Third World—would herald a new era in East–West relations. This optimism soon dried off and instead of adopting a more principled approach to the problems in the Middle East, Obama has drifted danger-ously away from public opinion in the Muslim world.

If the US cannot wash its hands off its responsibility for the present catastrophe in Iraq, Syria and of course Gaza, then the Muslim world too cannot but hang its head in shame for the monstrosities which have occurred in Iraq and Syria during this period. Brutal acts of inhumanity committed by rival Shia and Sunni militants cannot be wished away simply by attributing such acts to flawed Western policies. In the ultimate analysis, there has to be collective realisation both in the West and the Islamic world of their own misdeeds. Till then there will be no lasting peace in the world.

As for the followers of Islam, if they fail to understand the message of 'peace, accord and goodwill with their fellow beings, cutting across faiths, beliefs and persuasions' so strongly espoused by their Prophet, they will remain outcastes in today's highly interdependent world. This would not only put them at risk but also their future generations for whose sake this story has mainly been put together.

Postscript

In the past six decades, India as a nation has emerged as a potential super power in South Asia. This, while quite a few other countries in the region suffered due to major internal strife, their plight has often been fuelled by identity politics. Yet, tragically, a sizeable section back home now appears to view secularism not as a source of national energy but as a burdensome symbol of subjugation, appeasement and at best a distant idealism.

There are nagging fears, real or perceived vis-à-vis freedom of expression and possible saffronisation of the state's educa-tional system under the new government. Precious little is being done to allay these fears. The debate over rewriting history, the unseemly controversy over replacing the study of German with Sanskrit in schools run by the Kendriya Vidyalaya Sangathan and the rising prominence of those from the Sangh Parivar in matters pertaining to education and the media are cases in point. For over 2,000 years, India emerged as one of the greatest civilisations because of its capacity to accommodate and assimilate disparate cultures. The next few years will test the tenacity of this ancient civilisation, and its culture and ethos.

Thus, I place this account in the hands of readers to weigh and judge the crosscurrents of times and chart out a vision for the future. A vision based on their wisdom, informed opinion and discretion, I am sure would lead to collective good as has so far been the case with us since Independence.

1

The Empire and 19th-century Jihad

It is the summer of 1862. Three men on horses are moving along the river Kunhar, adjoining the magnificent Kaghan valley, north of Kashmir. Slightly built, the riders keep gazing towards a steep hill not far away. Despite their wheatish complexion, these men do not appear to be locals, a fact which is strikingly clear by their attire. They are in fact Muslim clerics from the district of Dhaka in Bengal, more than 3,000 miles east from this icy landscape. They are on a mysterious pilgrimage to pay homage to their *peer* (spiritual guide), the legendary Saiyid Ahmad Barelvi. His followers believe him to be the *mahdi* or the last Imam of Islam. The three men in search of their peer, like a large number of Muslims all over north India, hold the belief that the Saiyid resides in a remote cave atop the hill on which their eyes are now focused. But here the mystery deepens! Barelvi, the saint whom they seek to meet, had in fact met his end 30 years earlier at Balakot, about 30 km from the town of Manshera in the North West Frontier Province of India. Such is the legend that, years after his death, his ardent followers still believe that Saiyid Ahmad, who died fighting against the forces of Maharaja Ranjit Singh, the Sikh ruler of the state of Punjab, still lives.

Crossing the gurgling streams and rock-strewn perilous mountain paths, the three horsemen finally reach the mouth of the cave in which Saiyid Ahmad and his two associates are said to be living. The three men call out greetings to their peer only to be greeted by a stony silence from inside the cave. With baited breath, they slowly make their way inside the dimly-lit cave. To their great joy, they sight three men wearing capes and turbans sitting with their backs to the mouth of the cave. The

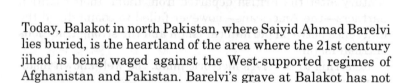

travellers respectfully greet their peer and offer their saalams. There is no response! The travellers cautiously approach the three sitting figures. What awaits them takes their breath away. Instead of their peer, they find three figures stuffed with straw.

The myth of Saiyid Ahmad Barelvi's *resurrection* is about to end, but his legendary exploits will linger on. The question which obviously arises is: What was the mesmeric hold on the fierce Afghan tribesmen exercised by this Muslim cleric from the distant plains of the Indian state of Awadh, that for decades after his demise, the legend of his imperishability lived on?

Today, Balakot in north Pakistan, where Saiyid Ahmad Barelvi lies buried, is the heartland of the area where the 21st century jihad is being waged against the West-supported regimes of Afghanistan and Pakistan. Barelvi's grave at Balakot has not been lost to posterity.

To unravel the legend and reality of Barelvi is critical if we are to penetrate the minds of the 21st century mujahideen (Islamic warriors). Many Western scholars and historians consider Barelvi as the spiritual founder of the present-day jihadi movement in Afghanistan. On the other hand, most historians from the Indian subcontinent have offered a more penetrating analysis regarding the 19th century jihad of Saiyid Ahmad Barelvi.

Saiyid Ahmad Barelvi's religious war against Raja Ranjit Singh's redoubtable army did not ultimately succeed. There are many factors which led to this defeat, after some initial spectacular victories against a foe that was not only better equipped, but also far more formidable.

Saiyid Ahmad Barelvi is also referred to as Saiyid Ahmad *Shaheed* (martyr) by legions of his admirers who consider him to be a martyr in the cause of God. He is widely known for his call for jihad in the NWFP, where Muslim tribesmen were locked in battle of attrition against the mighty Raja Ranjit Singh of Punjab.

There is, however, one critical element in this narrative of 19th-century jihad which deserves a closer look. Barelvi failed in his venture largely because he could not reconcile the tribal Islam followed by the Pathan tribesmen of the NWFP with his own refined puritanical Islam. The large-hearted, but fierce, Pathans were not prepared to jettison their own tribal loyalties and traditions and accept the Islam preached by the literalists. The pre-Islamic traditions followed by most Pathan tribesmen proved too deep-rooted. After the disastrous first Afghan War in 1842, the British were wise enough to follow a policy of minimal interference while dealing with the Pathans. The British colonialists apparently succeeded in dealing with the militant tribesmen of Afghanistan with a minimum of collateral damage because they ultimately came to terms with the Pathan psyche. They did not succumb to the temptation of trying to *reform and civilise* these tribesmen. Today, more than half-a-century after the British departed from India, their coalition partners—the Americans—however failed to comprehend the difference between puritanical Islam and the strong traditions of tribal Islam.

Referring to Barelvi's meteoric jihad, the well-known historian Ayesha Jalal states:

> ...the only real jihad ever fought in the subcontinent to establish the supremacy of the Islamic faith, it ended in dismal failure, owing to the treachery of some of the Pathan tribesmen, who had initially rallied to the cause with alacrity. Instead of pursuing the high ethical ideals for which the jihad had been launched, the movement became embroiled in a series of temporal compromises that led to an internecine war among Muslims.[1]

Saiyid Ahmad Barelvi's call for jihad in the NWFP did not end in triumph for him. Barelvi's call for jihad stemmed not from his hatred towards those with different religious faith, but primarily because he felt compelled to come to the rescue of his co-religionists who he felt were being persecuted by Raja Ranjit Singh. Reports were emanating from Punjab that unwarranted

---

[1] Ayesha Jalal, *Partisans of Allah—Jihad in South Asia* (Lahore: Sang-e-Meel Publications, 2008), p. 1.

sanctions were being imposed on Muslims, and above all restrictions were frequently being imposed on the local populace on practising religious rituals in places of worship.

Barelvi was vanquished largely because of the greed and betrayal by certain Pathan chieftains who flouted his directives for a principled jihad. Barelvi's jihad entailed certain norms of warfare, especially those pertaining to the spoils of war and the policy towards the defeated enemy. Such restrictions were spurned by a section of his own supporters who broke ranks on the issue of plunder and sharing spoils.

Early Years

Saiyid Ahmad Barelvi's father Saiyid Mohammad Irfan was the great-great-grandson of Shah Alamullah, a great Sufi saint and religious scholar during the reign of Mughal Emperor Aurangzeb.

Saiyid Ahmad Barelvi was born in Rae Bareli town near Lucknow in 1786. In those days, education for boys born in families like that of Saiyid Ahmad's began at the tender age of four. The focus was on learning Arabic and Persian. But the young Saiyid did not show much inclination towards the world of letters. His passion was for sports and physical exercise. He became a skilled archer, swimmer and an excellent horse rider. Stories of his physical strength and prowess soon became legendary in the entire area. As he grew older, however, he was drawn to spiritual practices. He would spend hours in prayers and meditation.

Barelvi's idealism may have led to a premature end of his passion for sports but in the decades to follow, his idealism gradually underwent a metamorphosis. The ascetic soon became a passionate votary of anti-colonialism. From the early years of the 19th century, an impression had started to gain strength that the British government was encouraging Christian missionaries in a well-planned move for large-scale conversion of both Hindus and Muslims. The seeds of jihad were truly being sown.

Tryst with Jihad

Today, ironically, most Western thinkers associate jihad with an ideology propounded only by a fringe section of modern-day Islamists. This, however, is a flawed interpretation of jihad in which the jihadi turns into an aggressor. This sharply contradicts the orginal concept of jihad as propounded by the rophet of Islam, who defined jihad as a war of self-defence. (Today, fanatical fringe group of Islamists view jihad merely as a *battle* against the infidels for the purpose of subjugating them.)

Barelvi's idea of jihad was primarily inspired by the Koranic injunction on jihad which states:

> Fight in the way of God against those who fight against you, but do not yourselves be aggressors; for, verily, God does not love aggressors... Fight against them until there is no longer oppression and all men are free to worship God. But if they desist, all hostility shall cease ...[2]

Since the early days of Islam, there are frequent instances in which Muslim rulers have resorted to distorted interpretations of jihad to morally justfy their temporal ambitions. Ayesha Jalal elaborates:

> Few concepts have been subjected to more consistent distortion than the Arabic word jihad—whose literal meaning is 'striving for a worthy and ennobling cause' but which is commonly thought today to mean 'holy war' against non-Muslims. It is paradoxical that Islam, whose very meaning is salam, or peace, has come to be seen as a belligerent religion with fanatical adherents determined to wage perpetual war against unbelievers. This enduring perception stems from an insistence on defining jihad as ideological warfare against non-Muslims, a hopeless distortion of a concept that is the core principle of Islamic faith and ethics.[3]

The result of this ghastly distortion of the term jihad is, thus, playing no small role in spreading ill-will against Islam in the

---

[2] Mohammad Asad, *The Road to Makkah* (Noida: Islamic Book Service, 2000), p. 315.

[3] Ibid., pp. 3–4.

modern world. What is equally undeniable is that a section of Muslims has also fallen prey to this distorted version of jihad.

For centuries after the crusades, Christian critics of Islam succeeded in creating an image of the religion which was at variance with the Islamic values as envisaged by the prophet. In the heat of the emotional conflict, Muslims themselves seem to have forgotten that the word *Islam* from the root *Salam* means *peace*.

> The opening sentence of the Prophet's agreement with the different tribes and religious communities of Medina after the migration (hijrat) from Mecca mentions jahada as striving for the collective well-being of the whole community consisting of believers and nonbelievers. Fighting for God was incumbent upon all Muslims, whereas the defense of Medina was the responsibility of all signatories to the document. Semantically, jahada cannot be interpreted as armed struggle, much less holy war, without twisting its Quranic meaning.
>
> The root word appears forty-one times in eighteen chapters of the Quran—and not always in the sense of sacred war—while prohibitions against warring occur more than seventy times.[4]

What Western historians have been projecting as *the spread of Islam by the sword* is in fact a misplaced notion. They obviously confuse the approach of temporal Muslim rulers, who are only interested in serving their political interests and have scant interest in the letter and spirit of the Islamic concept of jihad.

Saiyid Ahmad Barelvi was, in this sense, the first Muslim modernist reformer of the 19th century who actively sought to redefine jihad in its pristine Islamic framework.

More than a quarter century after his demise, another Muslim reformer, his namesake, Sir Syed Ahmad Khan (founder of the Mohammadan Anglo Oriental College) sought to underline the deeper context behind the injunction of jihad. In "An Account of The Loyal Mohamedans of India," Sir Syed Ahmad Khan wrote:

> Be it known that the object of a Jehad among Mohamedans is not to practice treachery and cruelty and no sane man can with the most distant approach to truth, apply that term to an insurrection characterised by violence crime and bloodshed in defiance of

and utter disregard to the divine commands. These are besides various other conditions of a Jehad not a single one of which is related to violence. Verily is a sad misnomer and a matter of extreme amazement that any person should give the name of Jehad to merciless killings.[5]

Saiyid Ahmad Barelvi was one of the most enigmatic and charismatic characters of north India of the early 19th century. The British rulers had considered him to be the leading exponent of the Wahabi Movement in India. Islamic scholars and most other historians are, however, of the view that while he may have been inspired by the Wahabi Movement of Saudi Arabia, his religious and social philosophy was shaped by his Indian roots and in essence he was a proponent of the Mohamadiya school of thought. In a letter to the Hindu Raja Hindu Rao, Saiyid Ahmad Barelvi had explained his views thus:

It is apparent to you that unfriendly foreigners of a distant land have become masters of the country, that traders have assumed the dignity of 'Sultanat' and destroyed the rule of great rulers and Chieftainship of high placed chiefs by depriving them from respect and honour. Since the rulers and statesmen have sought refuge in privacy, a band of poor and helpless persons has girded up their loins. This weak band does not aspire to any worldly gains. They are inspired by the spirit of service to God without and the arrow reaches its target, the offices and rulers shall remain intact for those who want it, and their dignity and power shall be strengthened. This weak band wants only this much from the great rulers and high dignitaries that while they occupy the 'masnad' of rulership, service to Islam with heart and soul should be done.... The purport of this affectionate letter will truly be explained to you in details by Haji Bahadur Shah who is an old associate of mine.[6]

Barelvi's battlefield exploits, first in Rajasthan against the British and later against Ranjit Singh in the NWFP, assumed legendary proportions. As often happens in such cases, reality often gets distorted and myths are born. But Saiyid Ahmad Barelvi is too critical a historic figure to be turned into a myth.

---

[5] Sir Ahmed Khan, *An Account of The Loyal Mohamedans of India,* Part 2 (Meerut: Mofussilite Press, 1860), p. 96.

[6] Shan Muhammad, *Muslims and India's Freedom Movement* (New Delhi: Institute of Objecive Studies, 2002), pp. 10–11.

His teachings have great relevance today in view of the 20th century Islamic revivalism.

Early Life

At an early age, he left for Delhi to study Islamic scriptures under Shah Abdul Aziz (1746–1824). Shah Aziz was the son of Shah Waliullah, the spiritual founder of the most significant movement of Islamic reform and Islamic revivalism in the 19th century India known as the Tariqa-i-Mohomedia Movement. Shah Aziz initiated Saiyid Ahmad into three different Sufi orders, namely the Naqshbandiyah, Qadiriyah and Chishtiyah orders. But Barelvi's theological and spiritual leanings led him to expend his energies in more temporal affairs. Very soon, he was engulfed by an overwhelming desire to wage battle against the British rulers, primarily because of the issue of religious conversion.

He soon joined hands with Ameer Khan, the ruler of Tonk and around the year 1810 and for several subsequent years proved to be a thorn in the flesh of the British rulers. In 1817, after Ameer Khan had been defeated, Barelvi left the battlefield and was drawn to the Sufi dimensions rooted in Islam's Sufi traditions. Barelvi, in the traditions of Shah Waliullah and Shah Abdul Aziz, was driven by a deep-rooted desire to rid Islam of the malpractices which had crept into Muslim society over the ages. It is necessary here to point out that despite many similarities with the Wahabi Movement, Barelvi's Mohomedia Movement was flexible, egalitarian and included humanitarian principles of waging war based on the traditions of the Prophet.

It is pertinent to point out that while the British dubbed the Mohomedia Movement as a Wahabi-inspired anti-British Revolt, the Sunni Muslims of the early 19th century India, who formed the backbone of this movement, were sharply critical of the Arabian Wahabis for the wanton destruction of a large number of holy shrines in Arabia associated with the life and times of the Prophet.

British historians are, however, quite dismissive regarding Barelvi's projection as a man of noble spirit and religious scholarship.

W.W. Hunter in his landmark *The Indian Muslims* published in 1871 has summed up Western view regarding Barelvi. He wrote:

> The Rebel Camp on the Panjab Frontier owes its origin to Sayyid Ahmad, one of those brave spirits whom our extermination of the Pindari Power scattered over India half a century ago. He began life as a horse soldier in the service of a celebrated freebooter, and for many a year harried the rich opium-growing villages of Malwa. The stern order which the rising powers of the Sikhs under Ranjit Singh imposed on their Musalman neighbours, made the trade of a Muhammadan bandit a perilous and an unprofitable one. At the same time, their strict Hinduism fanned the zeal of the Muhammadans of Northern India into a flame. Saiyid Ahmad wisely suited himself to the times, gave up robbery, and about 1816 went to study the Sacred Law under a doctor of high repute in Delhi [Shah Abdul Aziz]. After a three years' noviciate he started forth as a preacher, and by boldly attacking the abuses which have crept into the Muhammadan faith in India, obtained a zealous and turbulent following. The first scene of his labours lay among the descendents of the Rohillas [in the Jagir of Faizulla Khan, towards Rampur in Rohilkhand], for whose extermination we had venally lent our troops fifty years before, and whose sad history forms one of the ineffaceable blots on Warren Hastings' career. Their posterity have, during the past half century, taken an undying revenge, and still recruit the Rebel Colony on our Frontier with its bravest swordsmen. In the case of the Rohillas, as in many other instances where we have done wrong in India, we have reaped what we sowed.[7]

Western historians have acknowledged that even after his demise, Saiyid Ahmad Barelvi's committed followers put up the stiffest resistance to British rule in north-west India in the days following the Indian uprising of 1857.

Operating mostly from Delhi, the followers of Barelvi largely organised preaching tours. Their main focus was in highlighting the prevailing social ills and campaigning against religious abuses. They largely refrained from raising the issue of religious war, focusing instead on the inner jihad—the struggle for cleansing the spirit.

[7] W.W. Hunter, *The Indian Musalmans*, Introduction by Bimal Prasad (New Delhi: Rupa and Co, 2002), pp. 3–4.

In the year 1821, Barelvi left for Arabia to perform the Haj pilgrimage. His visit to the holy land appeared to have a very strong impact on him. On his return, at Bombay, he announced, 'My purpose now is to drive the Christian unbelievers from the land of the sun.'

Saiyid Ahmad Barelvi returned to Delhi in the year 1823. His mentor Shah Abdul Aziz had passed away during his absence. It was a period of great ferment in the Mohomedia group. They were deeply agitated over reports from Punjab, where Ranjit Singh was leaving no stone unturned in subduing all pockets of resistance from the Muslim tribesmen. Religious sentiments were being stoked and the urge for reasserting the supremacy of the Mughal Empire was growing. The *Mohomedia* group was painfully aware of the fact that despite their growing antagonism towards Christian missionaries, any call for jihad against the British would not carry the seal of religious authority for the simple reason that the British rulers had not directly interfered in the practice of religious rituals of the Muslims. On the other hand, there were reports from Punjab that in many places, the Raja had explicitly forbidden the practice of *azaan* (the call to prayer for the faithful). As the clamour for jihad rose steadily amongst the Muslims of the Gangetic plains, Saiyid Ahmad Barelvi was increasingly drawn to the proposal for migrating to the Punjab and raising the banner of jihad against Ranjit Singh.

In January 1826, Barelvi along with a loyal band of supporters left Rae Bareli for Punjab. They camped at Dalmau Fatehpur before arriving at the princely state of Gwalior ruled by the Maratha warrior Maharaja Daulat Rao Scindia. He was hosted by the maharaja and his brother-in-law Hindu Rao on several occasions. Western historians including Hunter, who cannot resist from describing Barelvi as a mere bigot, find it difficult to rationalise his close friendship with a number of Hindu chieftans of central India. Ironically, the first hurdle before him was to win the support of those Muslim rulers bordering the territories of Raja Ranjit Singh. The two most powerful Muslim rulers of that region, the Nawab of Bahawalpur and the Nawab of Sindh, refused to participate in the call of jihad against Ranjit Singh. Many Pathan tribal chiefs did throw their lot with the *Mohomedia* leaders but on many occasions let down Saiyid Ahmad Barelvi in crucial battles.

At that time, the Peshawar area was held by the two brothers of the influential Barakzai tribe, Yar Mohammad Khan and Sultan Mohammad Khan, vassals of Ranjit Singh. Ranjit Singh enjoyed a close relationship with the British, who considered him to be the only stabilising force in the NWFP. In the British scheme of things, Raja Ranjit Singh was the most important bulwark against the menacing Russian empire which was always seeking an opportunity to get a foothold in that area because of the incessant infighting amongst the warring Afghan tribes.

Both the Barakzai chiefs appeared to welcome Barelvi initially. They saw this as an opportunity to settle scores with their mentor, the Raja. The British were by now, viewing with growing concern, the plans of Barelvi and warned Ranjit Singh of his likely designs.

After spending some time in Peshawar, Barelvi left for Nowshera. Alarmed by this move, Ranjit Singh sent an army under his cousin Budh Singh to tackle him. A fierce battle took place at Akora. Barelvi's small army took a heavy toll of Ranjit Singh's army but was ultimately defeated and retreated to Hund. Khade Khan, the chief of Hund, welcomed him and soon Hund became his headquarters.

In the year 1827, Saiyid Ahmad declared himself to be the Imam or supreme religious leader of north-west India. He started receiving allegiance of individuals who would commit their personal loyalty to him and his cause. Many Pathan tribesmen started referring to him as Saiyid Badshah.

In the year 1830, Saiyid Ahmad had become powerful enough to seize the city of Peshawar, which was till then still under the Barakzais loyal to Ranjit Singh. Saiyid Ahmad's primary objective was the introduction of religious reform and the eradication of those tribal customs which conflicted with Islamic injunctions. This was no easy task but the strength of Barelvi's character and the courage of his conviction continued to bring him success in the battlefields as well as in the hearts and minds of the local populace.

In the year 1831, however, the saga of Saiyid Ahmad Barelvi came to an end in a battle against the Sikh army on the outskirts of Balakot town. He was delivered a crushing defeat. Both Saiyid Ahmad Barelvi and his comrade Mohammad Ismail died in this battle. For a long time, Barelvi's beheaded body could not be identified, giving rise to speculation regarding his ultimate fate. For legions of their supporters, they became martyrs. So much so, that a large number of his followers refused to believe that Barelvi had in fact passed away. The legend grew that Barelvi was in fact unharmed and had taken refuge in the rugged barren hills above Peshawar. A loyal group of his followers would thus continue to wage a battle against Ranjit Singh and later against the British right up to the 1860s.

After the battle of Balakot, the leadership of the Mohomedia Movement came under the control of the Patna group headed by Vilayat Ali and his brother Inayat Ali, both of whom were strong loyalists of Saiyid Ahmad. With the ascendancy of these two leaders, the focus of the Mohomedia Movement or the Ghazis, as they are sometimes referred to, shifted largely to Bengal in place of the NWFP.

Throughout the entire campaign of Saiyid Ahmad Barelvi against Ranjit Singh, the British had maintained a discreet silence on the activities of the *Mohomedia* leaders. In fact, in a perverse way, it suited their political interests that their ally Ranjit Singh should not grow more powerful than necessary and remain in need of British assistance. However, after the death of Ranjit Singh in 1839, a subtle change started taking place in the thinking of the *Mohomedia*. Their main antagonists were now the British, who had started using Christian missionaries for evangelical objectives. Sikh chieftains sought the help of the British for confronting the *Mohomedia Ghazis*. The British Government in fact compelled Vilayat Ali to leave the NWFP and return to Patna. Here, Vilayat Ali was kept under a strict watch by the British. But it was too late. The *Mohomedia* had now started preparing the grounds for waging jihad against the British.

Differences soon arose between Inayat Ali and Vilayat Ali on the critical issue of waging jihad against British rule. In 1852, after the death of Vilayat Ali, the leadership of the Mohomedia Movement was firmly in hands of Inayat Ali. This was a turning point in the history of the Mohomedia Movement. Inayat Ali was a bitter opponent of British rule in India and he now concentrated his full efforts in evolving a pan-India policy for uprooting the British.

It would be a fallacy to suggest that there was homogenity within the Muhammadiyah group regarding the validity of jihad against the British. Saiyid Ahmad Barelvi's assumption of the title of Imam was also questioned by several Muslim tribesmen not only in the NWFP but also in many other parts of the country. A section of the ulema also questioned the authenticity of the Barelvi's jihad against the Sikh rulers of Punjab.

The *Mohomedia* group led by Saiyid Ahmad Barelvi and later by Inayat Ali and Vilayat Ali was certainly not Wahabis—the followers of Mohammad Abdul Wahab—the 18th century Arab puritanical reformer. The Wahabi school of thought was inspired by the Hanbali sect of Sunni Muslims which started in the 18th century and has ever since sprouted radical Muslim groups marked by a rigid and inflexible religious code. The Wahabis can also be considered as the progenitors of the present-day Saudi Salafis.

There has been considerable confusion amongst Western scholars regarding the connection of the Mohomedia Movement with the Wahabis. Islamic scholars emphasise that the Mohomedia Movement was basically a Waliallahi Movement based on the teachings of Shah Waliullah, the pre-eminent Islamic scholar of Delhi who died in 1762. Shah Waliullah, it may be said, drew a limited inspiration from the reformist strains of the Wahabi Movement, but he was certainly not restricted by the dogmatic and rigid approach which characterised the Wahabi school of thought. Shah Waliullah championed the cause of Islamic revivalism, but he was equally aware that a pluralistic society which existed in India during his time would not be compatible with militant strains which marked the Wahabism practised by these 18th century Arab reformers.

The question obviously arises that if the *Mohomedias* were not Wahabis, as dubbed by some Western historians, then who were the real Wahabis in the 19th century India, who raised the hackles of the British rulers resulting in the famous so-called Wahabi trials after the failed Revolt of 1857.

If any 19th century Islamic school can be described as the closest version of Wahabism in India, it was the Faraizi Movement in the mid-19th century Bengal. Its leader was Haji Shariatullah. It is interesting to note that this movement originated not as a religious movement but basically as a peasant uprising in the

Sherpur region in Bengal in 1825. Shariatullah had explicitly declared India under British rule as *Dar-al-Harb* (abode of war). He urged the poorest peasants in Bengal not to pay tax to Hindu zamindars and European indigo planters. His opposition to the tax levied on the peasants was triggered by the Permanent Settlement Act of 1793, imposed by the British in the year. After his death in 1840, his son Dudu Miyan assumed the leadership of the movement. The British finally arrested Dudu Miyan, charging him with treason and he was interned in the Alipur prison where he died in 1862.

Another movement on these lines was led by Titu Mir in East Bengal in the 1820s. Alarmed by Titu Mir's peasant revolt championing the cause of landless labourers and weavers, big Hindu landlords sought the protection of the British administration in crushing this movement. Titu Mir's movement was inspired by Wahabi thought and since most of the peasants and weavers were Muslims, this agrarian revolt acquired a militant communal colour. Titu Mir died in 1831 but his followers seized the opportunity of the 1857 Revolt and spared no effort in venting anti-British fury whenever they got a chance.

The Mohomedia Movement petered out shortly after the failed uprising of 1857 against British rule.

It is however pertinent to understand that the call for jihad given by Saiyid Ahmad Barelvi was radically different from the highly distorted version which thrives today in the land where his exploits took place. For Barelvi, jihad was ennobling. He did not seek to wage war against non-Muslims out of hatred but only to ensure that injustice against the Pathan tribesmen ended.

The word jihad means striving for a just cause. It is time the present-day jihadis have a re-look at the jihad of Saiyid Ahmad Barelvi.

2

The Maulvi of Faizabad and
the Battle for Lucknow

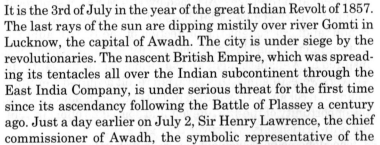

It is the 3rd of July in the year of the great Indian Revolt of 1857. The last rays of the sun are dipping mistily over river Gomti in Lucknow, the capital of Awadh. The city is under siege by the revolutionaries. The nascent British Empire, which was spreading its tentacles all over the Indian subcontinent through the East India Company, is under serious threat for the first time since its ascendancy following the Battle of Plassey a century ago. Just a day earlier on July 2, Sir Henry Lawrence, the chief commissioner of Awadh, the symbolic representative of the British Crown, was killed by a stray musket ball while fighting a formidable battle to save Lucknow from falling into the hands of the rebel forces. At a short distance from the Residency, where Sir Henry had breathed his last, and close to the historic Rumi Gate, an imposing bearded figure addressed a group of rebel soldiers busy building trenches for the final assault on the Residency complex. The rebel soldiers, attired in worn-out faded uniforms, appear to be mesmerised by the words of this bearded man with hypnotic eyes, who is the unchallenged leader of the rebel forces attacking Lucknow.

This imposing individual is Ahmadullah Shah, better known as the Maulvi of Faizabad, the Sufi saint-turned-commander, one of the most charismatic characters of what is often described as India's first war of independence. The common people of Awadh will remember him as Danka Shah (Drummer King).

British historians, often grudgingly, have paid tributes to the valour and leadership of Ahmadullah Shah. Strangely enough, in the history of India's freedom movement, the Maulvi remains a shadowy figure largely relegated to the sidelines. Cleric, Sufi saint, general in the Nizam of Hyderabad's army, visionary leader, jihadi or mere brigand: Who exactly was the real Ahmadullah Shah?

The rise of Ahmadullah Shah as one of the key figures of the 1857 Revolt is too vital an element of the Revolt of 1857 to be ignored by scholars. The arousal of religious passions both amongst Hindus and Muslims following the aggressive proselytising by evangelical Christians is now widely accepted as the most important factor behind the revolt. Confusion, however, still prevails amongst some historians regarding the exact identity of those Muslim religious groups which played the key role in the insurgency. British historians, by and large, including G.B. Malleson and John Kaye, prefer to describe all such elements as jihadis. It is only lately that new age historians, such as William Dalrymple, have gone deeper to probe the finer nuances of the different Muslim religious and social groups that were active participants in the revolt. The terms *jihadi, ghazi* and *mujahideen* have been used loosely by British historians and later by most Indian historians too. British historians, however, tend to dub such assorted groups as *brigands and vagrants*. Another blanket term for describing such elements is to refer to them as Wahabis. Jihad it certainly was, for the likes of Ahmadullah Shah, but what was it that prompted this call for a holy war? Was it a clash between Christianity and Islam? Were these Mujahids consumed by a pathological haterd for the Christians? Or was this an uprising against a ruler who fosterted coercion to challenge the ancient religious faiths of his subjects.

Had the role of Ahmadullah Shah in the 1857 Revolt received due acknowledgement and deeper study by post-independence Indian historians, it could have perhaps thrown more light on helping distinguish between the so-called Wahabis and the other *mujahideen* groups involved in the 1857 Revolt.

P.J.O. Taylor, who has extensively chronicled the events of *The Great Mutiny*, has described Ahmadullah Shah as 'one of the ablest leaders of the insurrection'. Other British historians also, often grudgingly, do acknowledge his humane qualities—a tribute which they largely ignore while describing the attributes of many other leaders of the revolt.

Despite receiving such scholarly acknowledgement for his exploits in the uprising from most British historians, Ahmadullah Shah largely remains a shadowy character shrouded in mystery, unwept and unsung by his own people in his own land. He hardly finds a place in history textbooks.

Awadh was the epicentre of the Revolt of 1857, and Ahmadullah Shah had largely dominated the exploits which took place in and around Lucknow, the capital of the province during those tumultuous times.

Rift between the Ulema and the British: The Genesis

Before we examine the role of Ahmadullah Shah in the Revolt of 1857, we need to understand the roots of the simmering hostility between the British rulers and the Muslim clergy in India which ultimately reached its climax in the middle of the 19th century.

The end of the 18th century was a period of deep churning and turmoil in Hindu and Muslim middle-class society. Amongst the Muslims, the inspiration for waging jihad against the British rule had of course been initially raised, as mentioned earlier, by Shah Abdul Aziz, son of the religious reformer Shah Waliullah (1703–1762).

Born in the year 1703, Shah Waliullah was a mystic, religious scholar and social reformer rolled into one. It is his school of thought that is often referred to as the Walliullahi Movement, which is regarded as the seminal 18th century movement for reform amongst Indian Muslims. It is the seed from which germinated almost all schools of reform including the Mohomedia Movement in the 19th century in north India, the Faraizi Movement for agrarian and socio-religious reforms in Bengal, the Saiyid Ahmad Barelvi Movement for jihad (not to be confused with the later-day Barelvi Movement of Sunni Muslims) and finally the Deoband Movement in the mid-19th century.

Shah Waliullah stood for discarding those social practices in Islam imbibed through indigenous and Persian influences which, in his view, conflicted with the fundamentals of Islam. He averred that that Hindu and Shia influences had diluted the purity of Islam, following the decline of the Mughal rule in Delhi.

He was the first Indian Islamic scholar who advocated the need of a rational approach in interpreting Islam in the light of science. He opposed certain practices of Indian Sufis which he considered as *bidat* (unacceptable innovations). He stood for the synthesis of Sufism with *ijtihad* (independent judgement and innovation based on the spirit of *Hadith*—teachings emanating from traditions followed by the prophet). To sum up, he stood for an Arabised form of Islam, the main pillar of which was monotheism.

Shah Waliullah's son Shah Abdul Aziz (1746–1824) was his spiritual successor. In the year 1803, he issued a fatwa (religious decree) which is considered a landmark pronouncement giving religious sanction to Indian Muslims to consider British rule as *Dar-al-Harb* (a land ruled by an enemy of Islam). The major factor leading to this call for jihad had been the persistent manner in which Christian missionaries—aided and abetted by the official machinery of the British East India Company—launched a systematic movement for religious conversions. Both Hindus and Muslims were getting increasingly restless over the manner in which their religious beliefs were denigrated and trampled upon by the rulers in all those areas where the East India Company was the sovereign ruler (It may be noted that no member of the Muslim clergy had dubbed any Indian state ruled by a Hindu king as Dar-al-Harb.).

The fatwa, as mentioned earlier, by Shah Aziz was as follows:

In this city (Delhi) the Imam-ul-Muslimin wields no authority. The real power rests with Christian officers. There is no check on them; and the promulgation of the Commands of Kufr means that in administration and justice, matter of law and order, in the domain of trade, finance and collection of revenue—everywhere the Kuffar (infidels) are in power. Yes, there are certain Islamic rituals, e.g. Friday and Id prayers, adhan and cow slaughter, with which they brook no interference; but the very root of these rituals is of no value to them. They demolish mosques without the least hesitation and no Muslim or any dhimmi can enter into the city or its suburbs but with their permission. It is in their own interests if they do not object to the travellers and traders to visit the city. On the other hand, distinguished persons like Shuja-ul-Mulk and Vilayati Begum cannot dare visit the city without their permission. From here (Delhi) to Calcutta the Christians are in complete control. There is no doubt that in principalities like Hyderabad, Rampur, Lucknow etc. they have left the administration in the hands of the local authorities but it is because they have accepted their lordship and have submitted to their authority.[1]

The above fatwa did not evoke any immediate response, but triggered a simmering discontent amongst Muslims against British rule. Nearly half-a-century later, this fatwa was the basis on which the *mujahideen* waged war against the British when the Revolt of 1857 broke out. It is one of the most critical pieces of evidence for those who seek to unravel the roots of the jihad by sizeable sections of Indian Muslims against the British in the 19th century India!

History behind the 1857 Seige of Lucknow

In the year 1775, Prince Asaf-ud-Daula ascended the throne of Awadh, succeeding his father, the redoubtable Shuja-ud-Daula. Shortly after ascending the throne, Asaf-ud-Daula shifted his capital from Faizabad to Lucknow. Thus was born the modern city of Lucknow.

Little did the refined, artistic-minded, generous but weak ruler of Awadh know that his quarter-century rule over the richest surviving kingdom of north India would be marked in history for the most contradictory reasons. On one side, he laid the foundation of making Lucknow a centre par excellence for art, culture and architecture not just of north India, but arguably of the entire Orient during the last quarter of the 18th century.

---

[1] Syed Masroor Ali Akhtar Hashmi, *Muslim Response to Western Education* (New Delhi: Commonwealth Publishers, 1987), p. 21; Tariq Hasan, *The Aligarh Movement and the Making of the Indian Muslim Mind (1857–2002)*, (New Delhi: Rupa and Co., 2006), pp.xxv–xxvi.

Prized works of art, literature and architecture thrived in the city of silver and gold which was then the city of the Nawabs.

Adventurous carpetbaggers, the European travellers thronged the lanes of this city of luxury and indulgence. The Nawab was, however, weighed down by a life of indulgence and debauchery.

Taking full advantage of this situation, the East India Company, flushed with its recent success in Bengal, hatched one of the most devious plans to annex the Indian heartland through a web of deceit, arm twisting and intrigue.

Shortly after Asaf-ud-Daula ascended the throne, the British—realising that his fighting capabilities were limited—threatened and cajoled him to sign a humiliating treaty which compelled him to cede nearly half of his kingdom to the East India Company; thus drastically reducing his revenues. The British had gained a stranglehold on a major territory of north India without firing a single shot. The rulers of the small principalities and landed gentry under the rule of the Nawab of Awadh were seething with rage at this act of subterfuge of the East India Company. But there was little they could do.

The manipulative manner in which the British in south India finally defeated Tipu Sultan, the Tiger of Mysore, bore heavily on their minds. This defeat of Tipu Sultan in May 1799, by means of treachery, rather than by the valour of the forces of the Company, had defined the invulnerable formula of success for the British—divide and defeat.

After the demise of Asaf-ud-Daula in 1797, the British supported the claim to the throne of his putative son Wazir Ali. However, a few months later, they felt that he was not really serving their interests in the manner in which they would have liked. They promptly decided to replace him with his uncle Sadat Ali Khan, who they felt would be more of a puppet ruler. This move further rubbed salt in the wounds of the native chieftains of Awadh. This proxy rule of the British was even more humiliating for them than the prospect of being ruled directly by the *firangi* (foreigner). But shortly after Sadat Ali Khan ascended the throne, he was forced to sign yet another humiliating treaty with the Company. The powers of the Nawab were further depleted. The East India Company was determined to show the utter contempt they felt towards the native princes.

During this entire rule by the successive Nawabs of Awadh, the hallmark of the dynasty was the overwhelming permeation of a remarkable syncretic culture in which Hindus and Muslims lived in complete peace and harmony. It was at this stage that the British struck upon the stratagem of exploiting the Ram Janambhoomi–Babri Masjid issue between Hindus and Muslims. It was half-a-century later that the British would reap the harvest of this defining characteristic of this potent strategy.

The process of humiliation of the people of Awadh continued right up to 1856, when the Company finally decided that this pretence was no longer needed. They thus decided to completely do away with the then Nawab, Wajid Ali Shah. The Company declared that 'Awadh was under direct rule of the Company'. Nawab Wajid Ali Shah was sent to exile in Calcutta.

Awadh was seething with discontent at this ultimate humiliation.

Ahmadullah Shah and the Battle of Lucknow

Urdu and Persian journals published in that era provide a graphic account of the events of that period. *Tilism*, an Urdu newspaper published from Lucknow, provides original accounts of the situation in Awadh during the build-up of the Revolt. In the early part of the 19th century, Lucknow was a city with a much larger population than Delhi (With a population of around six lakh in the 1850s, Lucknow was the largest city of India at that time.). It was a city of gardens and palaces compared to which Delhi was a pale shadow of decadence and decay.

The impact of the annexation of Awadh by the East India Company in the year 1856, however, led to a steep decline in the fortunes of the city of Lucknow. It was in this atmosphere of dissent, distress and disarray that Ahmadullah Shah entered the stage.

The first act of this brief but stormy period in the history of Awadh took place significantly enough in the city of Faizabad on 23 February 1857. The daily *Sadiqul Akhbar* has recorded that event for posterity. It so happened that some ladies belonging to a well-placed Hindu family were involved in an altercation with police constables in the city of Faizabad. The women involved in this incident were arrested. This led to a riot against the police leading to large-scale violence in that town. Ahmadullah Shah, at that time, happened to be interned in the district jail of Faizabad for his seditious activities in the state of Awadh. According to an account carried in *East India Company Aur Baghi Ulema* by Mufti Intezamullah Shahabi, Ahmadullah Shah had been arrested in Faizabad after he felled a British police officer Lieutenant Thomas in a sword fight. According to this account, Shah was poised to kill the police officer but ultimately refrained from doing so as his foe was lying unarmed on the ground. A strong police force overpowered Shah and he was put in shackles. As we will read ahead, it was this small incident which provided the spark leading to the Battle of Lucknow.

A few months earlier, shortly after the annexation of Lucknow, Ahmadullah Shah had stationed himself in the capital of Awadh, which was then seething with discontent. The newspaper *Tilism* has recorded the events as follows:

> These days a person called Ahmadullah Shah in the disguise of a faqir but having all paraphernalia of royalty has arrived in the town and stayed in the sarai of Mutamad-ud Daulah now has shifted to Ghasiyarimandi...People of the town visit him in a large number on Mondays and Thursdays to take part in the mystic gatherings (majalis-i-hal-o-qal). A number of feats are performed in midst of these gatherings...such display takes place every morning and evening for the viewing of the masses.[2]

Again on 30 January 1857, the paper reports:

> Ahmadullah Shah in Ghasiyarimandi is very fearless in saying whatever he wishes to say and a large crowd is always there, often Maulavi Amiruddin Ali is remembered. Although he is unable to do anything, orally he always pleads for jehad.[3]

Within a few months of his stay in Lucknow, Ahmadullah Shah had attracted a large number of *mureed* (followers). Each evening a large number would assemble at his house for

---

[2]Shireen Moosvi (Ed.), *Facets of the Great Revolt – 1857* (New Delhi: Tulika Books, 2008), p. 41.

[3] Ibid., p. 41.

spiritual, religious and social regeneration. These gatherings or *mehfils* as they were referred to were a strange mixture of the spiritual and temporal worlds. The proceedings of the evenings would usually commence with sessions of *qawwali* (a style of Sufi devotional music in which several singers are accompanied by music) followed by sessions of meditation (*habs-i-dum*). As the evenings would extend to the late hours of the night, the conversation would gradually drift towards the cause of jihad and the urgent need to overthrow British rule.

The *kotwal* (police) of the city of Lucknow started receiving reports from his informers that in the very heart of the capital of the state, there was a man who was openly raising the banner of revolt. His call for jihad was too serious to be ignored by the police of the city.

What exactly was this Sufi-turned-revolutionary preaching? Was he a religious bigot clamouring for the restoration of Muslim rule in India? What were his views on Hindus? The answers to these questions have great relevance today as they had a century and a half ago.

Noted historian Farhat Hasan, in his paper titled *Religion in the History of 1857*, has analysed Ahmadullah Shah's ideology as follows:

> Ahmadullah Shah, for example, who was the leader of the ghazis and the jihadis at Lucknow was not a Wahabi, but a Sufi saint of the Qadiri. The Qadiri saints were averse to all forms of intolerance, and were firm believers in religious eclecticism; Wahabi puritanism was repugnant to them. S.Z.H. Jafri, in his study of the Shah, argues that a Wahabi identity did not preclude other identities, and that Ahmadullah Shah was both a Wahabi and a Qadri Sufi, and included both identities in his religious and political mission.[4]

British historians, such as P.J.O. Taylor, are on the other hand dismissive about Ahmadullah Shah's claim for greatness. Taylor describes Shah as follows:

> Ambitious and devious, he was a Moslem religious leader with pretensions to kingship. He managed to ingratiate himself with

---

[4] Ibid., p. 140.

the Delhi sepoys who saw in him a leader who, because of the divine support he persuaded them he had, could not fail. He certainly displayed more military genius than the Begum's generals.[5]

Taylor also suggests that Ahmadullah Shah's relations with Hindus in the city of Faizabad were not cordial. However, he does not substantiate this charge by producing any evidence in support of his claim.

Taylor and most other British historians usually refer to Ahmadullah Shah as 'the Maulvi of Faizabad'.

Colonel G.B. Malleson of the Bengal Infantry has provided some of the most authentic first-hand accounts of the 1857 Revolt from the British point of view. His works became public during the 1857 war itself. He has written over half-a-dozen books in several volumes describing in detail all events connected to the Revolt.

In his seminal work *The Indian Mutiny of 1857*, Malleson has provided a vivid and authentic account of the exploits of Ahmadullah Shah:

Who all the active conspirators were may probably never be known. One of them, there can be no question, was he who, during the progress of the Mutiny, was known as the Maulavi. The Maulavi was a very remarkable man. His name was Ahmad-ullah, and his native place was Faizabad in Oudh. In person he was tall, lean, and muscular, with large deep set eyes, beetle brows, a high aquiline nose, and lantern jaws. Sir Thomas Seaton, who enjoyed, during the suppression of the revolt, the best means of judging him, described him 'as a man of great abilities, of undaunted courage, of stern determination, and by far the best soldier among the rebels'. Such was the man selected by the discontented in Oudh to sow throughout India the seeds which, on a given signal, should spring to active growth. Of the ascertained facts respecting his action this at least has been proved, that very soon after the annexation of Oudh he travelled over the North-west Provinces on a mission which was a mystery to the European authorities; that he stayed some time at Agra; that he visited Delhi, Mirath, Patna, and Calcutta; that, in April 1857, shortly after his return, he circulated seditious papers throughout Oudh; that the police

[5] P.J.O. Taylor, *A Star Shall Fall* (New Delhi: HarperCollins India, 1995), p. 219.

did not arrest him; that the executive at Lakhnao, alarmed at his progress, despatched a body of troops to seize him; that, taken prisoner, he was tried and condemned to death; that before the sentence could be executed, the Mutiny broke out; that, escaping, he became the confidential friend of the Begum of Lakhnao, the trusted leader of the rebels.

That this man was the brain and the hand of the conspiracy there can, I think, be little doubt. During his travels he devised the scheme known as the chapati scheme. Chapatis are cakes of unleavened bread, the circulation of which from hand to hand is easy, and causes no suspicion. The great hope of the Maulavi was to work upon the minds, already prone to discontent, of the sipahis. When the means of influencing the armed men in the service of the British Government should have been so matured that, on a given signal, they would be prepared to rise simultane-ously, the circulation of chapattis amongst the rural population of the North-west Provinces would notify to them that a great rising would take place on the first favourable opportunity.

It is probable that, whilst he was at Calcutta, the Maulavi, constantly in communication with the sipahis stationed in the vicinity of that city, discovered the instrument which should act with certain effect on their already excited natures. It happened that, shortly before, the Government of India had authorised the introduction in the ranks of the native army of a new cartridge, the exterior of which was smeared with fat. These cartridges were prepared in the Government factory at Dam-Dam, one of the suburbs of Calcutta. The practice with the old paper cartridges, used with the old musket, the 'Brown Bess', already referred to had been to bite off the paper at one end previous to ramming it down the barrel. When the conspirators suddenly lighted upon the new cartridge, not only smeared, but smeared with the fat of the hog or the cow, the one hateful to the Muhammadans, the other the sacred animal of the Hindus, they recognised that they had found a weapon potent enough to rouse to action the armed men of the races which professed those religions. What could be easier than to persuade the sipahis that the greasing of the new cartridges was a well-thought-out scheme to deprive the Hindu of his caste, to degrade the Muhammadan.[6]

On 8 June 1857, the atmosphere in the city of Faizabad was surcharged. News had been trickling in for several weeks

---

[6] G.B. Mallesan, *The Indian Mutiny of 1857* (New Delhi: Rupa & Co., 2006), pp. 11–13.

regarding the rising anger amongst the common people against the British rulers. By late afternoon on that fateful day, a riotous mob started moving towards the Faizabad Jail where Ahmadullah Shah had been lodged. Such was the fury of the mob that within hours, the gates and barricades of the jail had been broken. The frenzied mob was searching for Ahmadullah Shah, who was found with shackles on his feet. The Maulvi was carried on the rebels' shoulders to a nearby house. The city elders rushed to pay homage to him and gave their solemn pledge to stand by him in his call for a holy war against the British.

The next few days at Faizabad were a very testing period for Ahmadullah Shah. Wajid Ali Shah, the Nawab of Awadh had, a few years earlier, issued orders for the construction of some temples at Hanuman Garhi at the site of a *destroyed mosque*. Ahmadullah Shah wanted to reconstruct the mosque. The rebel forces included a large number of Hindus and they were strongly averse to this move. In his research paper on *A Profile on Ahmadullah Shah*, Syed Zaheer Jafri mentions:

> The Mahants of Hanuman Garhi are reported to have offered the British assistance and 'exerted themselves to keep the troops steady'. It was natural for the Hindus to feel alienated, therefore they thought of withdrawing their support to him as, 'just now he is planning for the destruction of Garhi, nothing can be predicted for the future'. The difference of opinion among the officers of the sepoys over the question of leadership was also made known to Shah.[7]

Realising that discretion was the need of the hour Ahmadullah Shah decided to leave Faizabad and took the road to Lucknow.

Subsequently, he was unanimously chosen as the leader of the rebel forces for the battle to capture Lucknow. The rebel troops comprised both Hindus and Muslims, including those from Faizabad. Just before sunrise, on 30 June 1857, the British forces launched a surprise attack on the rebel forces stationed at Chinhat, a few kilometres from the city of Lucknow. A week earlier, Sir Henry Lawrence had made arrangements for all women and children belonging to British families to shift inside the Residency compound. In a bid to embitter relations between

[7] Shireen Moosvi, *Facets of the Great Revolt 1857* (New Delhi: Tulika Books, 2008), p. 42.

Hindus and Muslims, he called for an assembly of loyal Hindu and Muslim troops.

Mallesan recorded the scene as follows:

> The Darbar was held on the evening of the 12th of May. Sir Henry seized the occasion to make to the assembled natives, in their own language, an address which, if it had then been possible for words to affect the question, could scarcely have failed to produce great results. He began by alluding to the fears which had been expressed by the Hindus for their religion. Turning to them, he pointed out how, under the Muhammadan rule prior to Akbar, that religion had never been respected; how the third prince in succession to Akbar had reverted to a similar system. Turning then to the Muhammadans, he reminded them how the great sovereign who had founded the Sikh kingdom would never tolerate the exercise of the faith of Islam at Lahor.[8]

Malleson's revelations clearly established that the foundation of the empire rests on divide and rule. Sir Henry warned the troops that under Muslim kings, Hindus had been forcibly converted and cruelly persecuted. Addressing Muslim sentiments, he said that the Sikhs would never allow the followers of Islam to practice their own religion. He claimed that the British had no such bias and treated all religions as the same.

The days which followed would indicate that the words of Sir Lawrence had fallen on ears, which were not ready to listen to his impassioned appeals.

The display of unity amongst Hindus and Muslims in Awadh in the next few months was exemplary and could be considered to be as the laying of the foundation of the modern secular state of India.

As dawn was breaking on the morning of 30 June 1857, Sir Henry Lawrence decided to move his troops towards Chinhat. In all, there were about 700 troops and 11 artillery guns including an eight-inch Howitzer drawn by an elephant. In a short while, the British troops arrived at the bridge over the Kukrail river. Sir Henry Lawrence was on horseback, leading his men. Disturbed by the fact that he could still not sight the rebel forces, Sir Henry stopped his horse and scanned the horizon to trace any sign of

[8] G.B. Malleson, The Indian Mutiny of 1857, (New Delhi: Rupa & Co, 2001), p. 90.

movement. There was an uneasy and eerie silence all around. Sir Henry decided to retreat. Suddenly there was hectic movement all around. Hidden behind some clumps of trees and hillocks, the rebel forces led by Ahmadullah Shah launched a blistering attack. For more than an hour, there was a heavy exchange of cannon and within two hours, nearly half of the British force had been felled. Sir Henry decided to retreat. This too was not an easy proposition unless the British force could reach the Kukrail Bridge, before the rebels took control of it. Sir Henry, however, managed to take control of the bridge where he planted his artillery. This move prevented the total rout of the British force. The surviving members of Sir Henry's troops somehow managed to scramble back to the sanctuary of the Residency building. This, indeed, was a major victory for Ahmadullah Shah, the commander of the rebels. It was a conclusive show of might which bestowed upon Ahmadullah Shah a certain mystique of invincibility. The siege of Lucknow had begun.

On the evening of 1 July 1857, the residents of the entire city of Lucknow heard a huge explosion. Rumours started floating that the Residency had been blown up by rebel fire. As the dust and the din started settling down and darkness descended on the city, it slowly came to light that what had actually transpired was that Sir Henry had ordered the garrison at Machchi Bhawan to be blown up lest it fell into the hands of the rebels. Essential arms and ammunition were relocated to the main Residency building. Sir Henry was preparing himself for a last-ditch battle even as Ahmadullah Shah was giving the last-minute touches to what he thought would be the final battle against the British forces in the state of Awadh.

Sir Henry Lawrence was restless throughout the night of 1 July 1857. He was hoping against hope that he would be receiving reinforcements from Allahabad and perhaps Delhi before it was too late. The morning of the next day was spent in clearing the rubble at Machchi Bhawan. He had just about 774 troops left with him to defend the Residency. Sensing victory, Ahmadullah Shah ordered his men to maintain the pressure. Ahmadullah Shah was the people's commander and was always on the frontline, extolling his men to live and die for honour.

In later years, British historians would be left wondering as to how a Muslim cleric was able to inspire his men, both Hindus and Muslims, to perform deeds of valour and undertake unusual hardships. The answer is clear for those who wish to see it—the mettle of character. The concept of secular leadership such that exists in today's modern society had yet not taken birth. What was in place then, was the need of a special attribute necessary for a leader—a stout heart and the commitment of justice to all his men irrespective of religion or creed.

Sir Henry was in the practice of occupying a particular room in the Residency from which he could observe the movements of the rebel troops on both sides. On 2 July 1857, he was sitting on his bed conferring with Adjutant General Captain Wilson. His nephew George Lawrence was also in the room at that time. There was a sudden explosion inside the room after a shell from the rebel forces exploded. The room was plunged in darkness and as attendants rushed in to investigate, they found George Lawrence and Captain Wilson lying in a state of shock but with just minor injuries. On his own bed lay Sir Henry Lawrence, gravely wounded and gasping for breath. He passed away two days later. The post of chief commissioner of Lucknow was then assumed by Major Banks. He too did not last long and fell prey to another major assault by the rebel troops who kept firing day and night. The British forces were in complete disarray for the next few days. The post of chief commissioner was vacant. What kept their hopes alive was the hope that British troops led by General Havelock were moving towards Lucknow and would be there in three weeks.

On the evening of 3 July, Ahmadullah Shah issued a proclamation on behalf of the rebel forces. This document is a striking illustration of Ahmadullah Shah's vision for his native land. The proclamation read:

> The Hindus and Muslims passed their days in peace and tranquillity since the days of their predecessors. For some time, the Quam Angrez became ruler after occupying these territories. Now since they were desirous of taking away the beliefs of these two groups by grandeur, it appeared proper to expel them (not only) from these territories (but also) from this consideration or keeping it in view (even) from the territories of Hind. Therefore, it is incumbent upon the Raisan and the inhabitants of the territories of Awadh that they should reside in their houses with composure and join the army with men and money so as to be of

good name and of exalted rank both in this and that world and those men who have remained to be a thorn in the flesh of the people at large in their capacity of 'Barqandas', it is incumbent upon them that they should surrender their weapons and be the employees of the Army.[9]

At this stage, the events in and around Lucknow and Delhi had led to complete chaos in Calcutta, the capital from where the British were operating. The success of the rebel forces not just at Lucknow but at Kanpur, Jhansi and large areas of Bihar, had deeply unsettled the British rulers. Conflicting orders to General Havelock added to the confusion and gave enough time to Ahmadullah Shah to consolidate his hold over the surrounding areas of Lucknow right up to Unnao.

On 6 August 1857, there were celebrations amongst the rebel troops parked on the other side of the Gomti River when news was received that Bahadur Shah had been crowned as the Emperor of India. The rebel army had been desperate to find a legitimate leader for the people of Awadh. Since Wajid Ali Shah was a prisoner of the British at Calcutta, the field was open. A large section of the populace and the rebel troops were keen to appoint Ahmadullah Shah as the Nawab of Awadh. However, he had other plans.

It is doubtful whether he aspired to the throne of Lucknow, for according to the legend on his seal, he styled himself as Khalifat- ullah or vicegerent of God. He was an office which combined temporal and spiritual authority, and his claims could not be reconciled with allegiance to any earthly power. Barkat Ahmad and the cavalry were said to favour the claims of Suleiman Qadr, a prince of the royal house of Oudh. This probably explains his supersession in favour of the members of the dominant party. The booming of the cannon that raised false hopes in the entrenchment of approaching succour celebrated the formal installation of Birjis Qadr. The coronation must have improved the sepoy morale and inspired them with fresh confidence.[10]

---

[9] Ishrat Husain Ansari and Hamid Afaq Qureshi, *1857 Urdu Sources*, Translations (Lucknow: New Royal Book Company, 2008), pp. 125–126.

[10] Surendra Nath Sen, *Eighteen Fifty-Seven* (Calcutta: The Publications Division Ministry of Information and Broadcasting Government of India, 1958), p. 210.

On 11 August 1857, the rebels mounted a savage artillery attack on the Residency in which a portion of the Residency building collapsed, and over a dozen people were buried under the debris.

The siege carried on for weeks. It was in September that the commander-in-chief of the British army in India Sir Colin Campbell decided to personally lead the attack to confront the rebel forces at Lucknow. The commander-in-chief ordered the British forces to move towards Lucknow. By 23 September 1857, the British forces had succeeded in capturing villages about 25 kilometres from Lucknow on the Lucknow–Kanpur road.

A furious battle took place near Sikandar Bagh on 25 September 1857, in which the British forces lost more than 207 officers. However, a decisive victory for any of the two parties was still elusive. The British forces were fast running out of provisions.

In the first week of November, it was announced that the commander-in-chief of the British forces would himself move towards Lucknow.

> The fall of Delhi had enabled Brigadier Wilson to send out two columns, one of which under the command of Colonel Greathed proceeded to Agra via Bulandshahar and Aligarh. At Agra Greathed routed the Indore rebels who tried to surprise the city, and the column proceeded on its way to Kanpur. At Firuzabad Colonel Hope Grant assumed command and the column reached Kanpur in the last week of October. Hope Grant then marched for Alambagh and fought an action with the rebel force at Bantera. He arranged for the transport of the sick and wounded from Alambagh to Kanpur, and halted at Bantera according to the orders of the Commander-in-Chief, who joined him there after a forced march of thirty-five miles. Sir Colin Campbell was pressed for time. He wanted to return to Kanpur before the rebel force, then at Kalpi, came against it.[11]

By this time, the tide had started turning. The fall of Bahadur Shah Zafar at Delhi and the rout of Nanaji at Kanpur had cast a gloom on the rebel forces entrenched in the other side of

[11] Ibid., p. 226.

the river Gomti at Lucknow. Fierce fighting continued in and around Lucknow. By the last week of November, the British forces had succeeded in defeating the rebels and the siege of Lucknow had ended. Ahmadullah Shah left Lucknow, defeated but still not vanquished.

Early Years

Till recently, the early life of Ahmadullah Shah had escaped serious notice, primarily because, his exploits had remained limited to first-hand accounts of the revolt in Persian and Urdu texts. These accounts, which include *Ahsan-ut-Tawarikh, Tarikh-i-Shahjahanpur, Naqsh-i-Sulaiman,* and *East India Company Aur Baghi Ulema* are now available in English, thanks to the efforts of researchers, such as Dr H.A. Qureshi and Professor I.H. Ansari.

Ahmadullah Shah, whose original name was Ahmad Ali, was in fact the Prince of the Chinapattan state near today's Chennai in south India. He was the second son of Nawab Mohammad Ali Khan and carried the title of Dilavar Jung. His grandfather was Jalauddin Adil who hailed from Kabul. His exact date of birth is not recorded but, according to estimates, he was born around the year 1810. His education was mainly focused on Islamic studies and he acquired a proficiency in Arabic and Persian. His exceptional learning abilities included a phenomenal memory coupled by other qualities of head and heart. He soon drew the attention of the Nizam of Hyderabad. He was then barely 16 years old. For a few years, he served in the Nizam's army and then in the court of the Nizam of Hyderabad in different capacities. His rapid rise in the estimates of the Nizam also earned him many enemies. An attempt was made on his life by his detractors but he had a miraculous escape. These events only added to his mystique.

His stint with the Nizam of Hyderabad had tested his inner mettle and also whetted his appetite for further exploits. During his stay in Hyderabad, he took lessons in English and soon acquired a reasonable proficiency in this language. He persuaded his father to permit him to visit England, where he was exposed to the lifestyle and mindset of the British nobility. According to one version which finds its place in the 19th century account by Moinuddin Hasan, he travelled all over Europe for nearly 20 years in the garb of a mendicant. He could speak in seven languages. His return journey to India via Arabia, where he performed Haj, completely changed the course of his life.

It is believed that some mystical experience at Mecca and Madina had a very deep impact on his mind. His attention now shifted to the affairs of the mind and the spirit, away from the world of statecraft. His spiritual search led him to the doorsteps of a great Sufi of the Qadri order, Saiyid Qurban Ali Shah, in a remote corner of Bikaner in Rajasthan. His *peer* and patron bestowed upon him the title of Ahmadullah Shah. It was on the advice of his *peer* that he now shifted to the city of Gwalior. Here, Mehrab Shah Qadri, another Sufi of the same order, formerly accepted him as his disciple. This was the most critical phase in the brief life of Ahmadullah Shah.

This was a period when the British launched a major offensive of racial and cultural domination. The authorities with the help of Christian missionaries started treating Indians, both Hindu and Muslim as worthless heathens. The East India Company was leaving no stone unturned for *saving the souls of the corrupt and wild heathens* who in their considered opinion had to be *civilised*.

Ahmadullah Shah also visited Delhi and came in contact with some well-known Sufis and religious scholars, such as Khwaja Mohammad Nasir and Sadruddin Azurdah.

Azurdah gave him a letter of introduction to Mufti Inamullah of Agra in whose house he stayed for a long period. It was here that his fame as a Sufi mystic grew. His large group of *mureed* (disciples) included many Hindus like Babu Beni Prasasd Ilahabadi.

The persistent attempts by Christian missionaries to attack Islam and Hinduism led to great animosity and resentment amongst the local populace, especially those belonging to the elite and scholarly sections.

The missionaries had established two printing presses, including one at Agra. The other press was at Mirzapur where they published a newspaper called *Khair Khwae Hind* (Well Wishers of India). The contents of the published material were largely very offensive towards Hinduism and Islam.

A transformation was taking place in the personality of Ahmadullah Shah. The Sufi mystic—who often would go into trances—was turning into a revolutionary. He soon started taking out processions in which he would ride a horse or an elephant. The processions would be accompanied by the beatings of huge drums. These strange processions earned him the nickname—Danka Shah.

Ahmadullah Shah had to soon contend with bitter opposition from a section of the local ulema. These individuals became his bitter enemies because of his growing popularity amongst the masses. They instigated the British authorities to take action against him on the charge of treason. Ahmadullah Shah managed to wriggle out from this situation by leaving Agra.

The sequence of events following Shah's departure from Agra provides striking evidence of his cordial relations with people of different religious faiths.

From Agra, Ahmaduullah went to Aligarh and stayed as a guest of the Hindu Raja of Mursan, who treated him with great deference. He was given gifts by the Raja, including a prized stallion. He then left for Gwalior and avoided visiting Agra where rumours were afloat that he would be arrested on charges of treason if he visited the city.

It was at this period that a communal clash between Hindus and Muslims took place at Hanumangarhi in Ayodhya. Maulvi Amir Ali, a well-known Muslim cleric, was assassinated in this clash. The Shah decided that it was time that he shifted to Lucknow which was becoming the centre of all revolutionary activity. He also felt safer in Lucknow where his *jihadi activities* were still not in the knowledge of the local authorities.

It was here that he came in contact with Azimullah Khan, the adviser to the Maratha Chief Nanaji Rao. Azimullah was one of the plotters behind the Revolt. His meeting with Ahmadullah Shah was to be the ultimate turning point in the events which followed.

The Sufi saint had become a revolutionary. This transition had not been sudden. It was the accumulated hostility between the ulema and the British which had been brewing since the time of Shah Abdul Aziz since the early part of the century.

The End

Ahmadullah Shah decided to withdraw from Lucknow and with a loyal band of supporters shifted to Bari near Sitapur. It was here that he was joined by the forces of Begum Hazrat Mahal, who was leading the troops loyal to erstwhile Nawab Wajid Ali Shah. She was the mother of Birjis Qadr, who had earlier been anointed as a successor of Wajid Ali Shah. It is said that initially Ahmadullah Shah was reluctant to join hands with Begum Hazrat Mahal. Ultimately, however, Birjis Qadr persuaded him to agree to the proposal and buttressed this arrangement by becoming his *mureed* (spiritual disciple).

At this juncture, it may be said that Ahmadullah Shah had become the de facto ruler of Awadh. It was at this stage that the British persuaded the Gorkha army of the Nepal sovereign to join hands with them against the rebels. Hemmed in from both sides, Ahmadullah Shah and his loyal mujahideen distinguished themselves in different skirmishes by daring acts of valour. He was, however, let down by some officers owing allegiance to Prince Birjis Qadr, who were tempted to indulge in plunder, rather than consolidating the territory under their control. These officers betrayed him at the last minute and withdrew from the crucial battle of Bari. Following this defeat, Ahmadullah Shah withdrew from Mohammadi near Shahjahanpur. He started consolidating his hold on the area, based on the unstinted support of the mujahideen. On 15 March 1858, a formal coronation of Ahmadullah Shah was held at Mohammadi where he was declared the official ruler of Awadh. Coins were issued in his name. He forged an alliance with the Rohillas of the Bareilly region led by Nawab Bahadur Khan and rebel leader Azeemullah Khan.

For a short while, it appeared that Ahmadullah Shah would succeed in changing the course of history by reversing the tide and forcing the British to withdraw from Awadh. However, destiny had another course charted for him. Once again he was betrayed by his own countrymen. This time it was the Raja of Pawayan (a small principality in the neighbouring area). The Raja tricked him by inviting him over: a trap laid for him at the behest of the British.

Ahamadullah Shah died fighting against all odds. For this act of treachery, the British gifted the Raja a sum of ₹50,000.

The saga of Ahmadullah Shah reveals many facets of the anti colonial uprising in India. He was a religious scholar, a Sufi and ultimately a real *jihadi*. To explore Shah's *jihad* against the British with the help of hitherto untapped historical documents is of vital importance.

Religious sentiments no doubt played a major role in the uprising and *the letter and spirit of jihad* was freely invoked by the rebel leaders to arouse religious fervour amongst the Muslims. But it was not a clash between Christianity, on one hand, and Hindus and Muslims, on the other. It was a battle to protect one's own territory from an alien ruler who was flagrantly using the weapon of religious conversions for entrenching their hold upon conquered people.

3

The Deoband Connection: Revolt and Revivalism

The district of Saharanpur on the extreme west of what is today the state of Uttar Pradesh (UP) is famous for the Islamic seminary of Deoband, a non-descript town about 20 kilometres from the district headquarters. In the year 1858, when the embers of the revolt against the British were dying down, the twin townships of Thanabhawan and Shamli, 70 kilometres from Saharanpur on the road to Delhi were still simmering with discontent. What took place in these two towns during that turbulent period left its mark not just on the history of the uprising, but also laid the foundation for the establishment of the Darul Uloom Theological School at Deoband, a short distance from these two towns.

Many Western scholars today erroneously blame the Deoband School for being the ideological fountainhead of modern-day militant Islamic Wahabism. This specious approach falsely links the Deoband seminary with those Wahabi-inspired madarsas dotting the landscape of Pakistan, which have been the breeding grounds of militancy since the 1980s. This is a fallacy that does not bear the scrutiny of history. Both Wahabiism and the Deobandis seek the pristine pure form of Islam such as what existed during the first five decades of its existence. Both of them are reformist movements. Yet there are fundamental differences between the two. The Wahabis are fanatically opposed to any form of saint worship and for them even the tomb of the Prophet of Islam carries little significance. Their hallmark is self-righteousness and an obsession for the literalist interpretations of the Holy Scriptures. They have scant respect for the spiritual content of religious faith so prominent in the Deobandi school of thought.

The Deoband School in stark contrast to the Wahabi stood for the utmost respect for the spiritual guide known as the *peer*. It was directly linked to the Sufi schools belonging to the Qadiri and Naqqshbandi orders.

For this reason alone, it is imperative to unravel the truth about the birth and the growth of this famous Islamic seminary. Western scholars have referred to the Deoband school as 'the most important and respected theological seminary of the Muslim world next to Al Azhar of Cairo'.

During the early days of the 1857 Revolt, an uneasy calm had prevailed in the town of Thanabhawan. The neighbouring towns of Meerut, Bijnore and of course Delhi had witnessed bloodshed and felt the horror of a full-scale war. The residents of Thanabhawan were gradually realising that it was only a matter of time before things would change in this sleepy town. Amongst the residents was a certain Haji Imdadullah, who was related to the Delhi-based Walliulah family of Islamic scholars. Apart from his connection with Shah Waliullah's family, Imdadullah had also earned the reputation of being a devout Sufi saint.

One day, a dispute arose between a Hindu moneylender and a person belonging to a prominent family of Muslim clerics. The town at that time was under the administrative control of the British. Instead of expeditiously resolving the dispute between the Hindu moneylender and the Muslim cleric, the British official-in-charge thought it expedient to give a communal colour to this incident. He chose to fan the fire to spread ill-will between the local populace of Hindus and Muslims.

According to one account, the young cleric in question had purchased an elephant from a Hindu trader. He had planned to join the rebel forces. This information somehow leaked out and the District Collector summarily ordered that the cleric, a certain Hafiz Mohammad Zamin, should be hanged. The execution of Zamin without recourse to due legal process triggered off mass protests in the entire region. The local populace was up in arms and two intrepid young men took the lead in the mass upheaval that ensued. These two were Maulana Rashid Ahmad Gangohi and Maulana Qasim Nanautawi. Haji Imdadullah, their spiritual guide, was declared as the formal Imam or chief of the jihadi revolutionaries.

The ulema of Shamli issued a decree sanctioning jihad against the British rulers of India. Unlike other kinds of jihad, this was a call for religious war against what the ulema considered a regime wrongfully persecuting the followers of Islam. This call for jihad against the British had its ramifications in most parts of north India. Ultimately, the impact of this decree did get diluted, but at a deeper level, as we will see, it left a lasting effect on the psyche of the ulema of north India. The rag-tag forces led by the ulema of Shamli had the spirit to fight, but were hardly in any position to match the well-equipped British forces. The resistance was smashed within a matter of a few weeks and those who died were officially declared *shaheed* (martyrs) by the clerics. A large number of the ulema who escaped death in the battle-field were either sentenced to death or imprisoned for life in the Andaman Islands jail, then referred to as Kala Paani. The leader, Haji Imdadullah, who inspired this Revolt in this tiny township of north India, managed to sneak away to the adjoining state of Punjab. From there, with the help of some secret supporters of the jihadis, he undertook the arduous land journey to the holy city of Mecca in Arabia. In Mecca, which was then a part of the Ottoman Empire, he was given refuge and was held in great esteem by the local populace, who referred to him as Mohajir Macci which means *the refugee of Mecca*. He remained in Mecca till his death away from his beloved homeland.

This and many other incidents involving Muslim clerics in north India led to the famous *Patna trials* against the so-called Wahabi mujahideen. Most of these so-called Wahabis were based in Patna and in some districts of what is today western UP, mainly Saharanpur and Badaun districts. The most severe charges were against Maulvi Abdul Rahim, Maulvi Yahya Ali and Maulvi Ahmadullah. They were all sentenced to death but later their sentence was commuted to life imprisonment. They were sent to the Andamans jail where they spent the last years of their lives far from their homeland. All three belonged to prominent families of religious scholars of Patna.

This was just the story of one city. The Andaman jail was host to a large number of such prominent Muslim scholars who had participated in the anti-British stir on the premise that they were fighting a holy war to save their homeland and religious faith.

Nearly eight decades after these incidents, the well-known freedom fighter and scholar Tufail Ahmad Manglori wrote a detailed account of the role of Muslim ulema in the Revolt of

1857 in his Urdu book *Musalmanon Ka Rashan Mustaqbil*. An abridged version of this work was later translated and titled *Towards a Common Destiny: A Nationalistic Manifesto* (Manglori was one of the illustrious protégées of Sir Syed Ahmad Khan, the founder of the MAO College at Aligarh).

> In the penal settlement in the Andamans a galaxy of ulema had assembled including Maulavi Fazl-i-Huq Khairadi, Maulavi Mazhar Kareem and others. Their presence turned the island into a centre of learning. Books were written and compiled. The work was done from memory but the books written were most remarkable...The penal settlement in the Andamans was founded for those prosecuted in the 1857 disturbances, and the first to grace the camp with their presence were the Ulema of India.[1]

The period immediately following the failed uprising of 1857 was a very testing period for the ulema of Saharanpur. They were finding it exceedingly difficult to reconcile themselves to the inevitability of British rule. It was gradually dawning upon them that the sun was not setting on the British Empire, not only in India but in the greater part of the old world as well. It took a few years for them to accept the fact that their European masters were not just superior to them in the battlefield, but also heralded a new revolution founded on the principles of science, technology and commerce.

The buffeted ulema of Saharanpur gradually came to terms with their defeat. They decided to lay down their swords and begin a different type of jihad—the battle to conquer their own selves and the heart and mind of their own people. The seeds of the Deoband seminary were being sowed in the minds of these vanquished clerics. They got together and in the year 1867, Maulana Qasim Nanautawi (1832–1880), founded the Deoband madarsa. The objectives for establishing this madarsa were twofold—to teach a puritanical Islam as upheld by Shah Waliullah and Shah Abdul Aziz and also simultaneously to revive in the students a sense of national identity which they felt was under threat because of foreign rule.

---

[1] Tufail Ahmad Manglori, *Towards a Common Destiny: A Nationalist Manifesto* (New Delhi: People's Publishing House, 1994), p. 83.

After the revolt in Delhi had been crushed by the British, the city had been devastated. The main target of the rampaging victors had been places of worship.

> The entire population of the city was expelled for a time. The mosques of the city were occupied: the Jami Masjid for five years, the Fatehpuri Masjid for twenty. The Zinatu'l-Masjid in Darya Ganj was used as a kitchen until it was restored almost half-a-century later by Lord Curzon. In 1860 it was decided to clear a large area around the Red Fort, and though financial compensation was given, there was no recompense for losing a building like the Akbari Masjid, built by a Begum of Shah Jahan, and long a major center of the reformist effort. Madrasahs, including the Daru'l-Baqa, restored by Mufti Sadru's-Sudur Azurdah, were razed, as well. In the Kuchah Chelan mahallah, where Shah Abdul Aziz had preached and the great religious and intellectual families had long resided, the British shot perhaps fourteen hundred people.[2]

This had resulted in a major exodus of ulema from Delhi to neighbouring towns where British influence was muted. Deoband had become one of the favoured destinations of Muslim clerics along with Kandla and Bareilly.

Rashid Ahmad and his associate had spent their early years as special pupils of Maulana Mamluk Ali, one of the founding fathers of the most significant madarsas of the Waliullahi school of thought at Delhi. This madarsa had been established at Delhi in 1841 by Maulana Mohammad Ishaq, a grandson of Shah Abdul Aziz.

The origins of the Deoband School can be traced directly to Shah Abdul Aziz and his father Shah Waliullah. The Walihullahi school of thought, as earlier mentioned, is rooted deeply in the Sufi traditions of India, while simultaneously seeking to re-establish the Islamic precepts based on Quranic directives. Like Wahabism, it sought to rid Islam of certain superstitious practices based on alien influences. Unlike Wahabism, however, it was not obsessed with the idea of negating interpersonal relations between followers of different religious beliefs and

---

[2] Barbara Daly Metcalf, *India's Muslims—An Omnibus—Islamic Revival in British India–Deoband, 1860–1900* (New Delhi: Oxford University Press, 2007), pp. 84–85.

appropriating to itself the right of propagating the concept of a direct connection with the divine. Wahabism was dogmatic, but the Walihullahi school was based on moderation without compromise on basic belief.

Dr Tarachand, one of India's greatest historians of the 20th century, has described the events leading to the establishment of the Deoband madarsa in his masterpiece *History of Freedom Movement* thus:

> Shamli and Deoband are, as a matter of fact, the two sides of one and the same picture. The difference lies only in weapons. Now the sword and the spear were replaced by the pen and the tongue. There at Shamli in order to secure political independence, freedom for religion and culture, resort was made to violence, here at Deoband the start was made to achieve the same goal through peaceful means. The roads though diverging from each other, led towards the same destination. It was undoubtedly a great achievement and remarkable was the vitality and enthusiasm of the Muslims who within a short span of time after the fateful days of 1857 and under the most discouraging circumstances were able to start afresh to devise ways and means for the safeguarding of their religion and culture, which they felt was threatened by the British official educational system.[3]

Dr Tarachand's authoritative analysis of the spirit of the Deoband Movement is also reflected in Santimoy Ray's *Freedom Movement and Indian Muslims*.

The Deoband seminary was primarily inspired by the Hanafi school of thought. Unlike the Wahabis, the Deoband ulema were proponents of a strong Sufi doctrine.

Barbara Metcalf explains:

> The ulama of the madrasahs represented a Sufi leadership separate from the most characteristic institution of later Sufism, the guardianship of the tombs of the medieval saints. Indeed, Deobandi opposition to certain Sufi customs, notably that of urs and pilgrimage, directly challenged the centrality of the tombs and the networks of support for them. The Deobandis offered an alternate spiritual leadership, geared to individual instruction rather than to mediation, stripped of what they deemed to be deviant custom.

[3] Santimoy Ray, *Freedom Movement and Muslims* (New Delhi: National Book Trust, 2011), p. 26.

They were among the leading Sufis of the day. At the school the post of sarparast in particular was staffed by revered and influential Sufis: Muhammad Qasim, Rashid Ahmad, Mahmud Hasan, and Ashraf Ali Thanawi, the last of whom has been widely considered the preeminent Sufi of modern India.[4]

Today, many Western analysts find it expedient to dub the Deoband Movement as part of the Wahabi movement. This confusion may have been accidental as probably was the case with WW Hunter. The trials of the Deobandi freedom fighters and the revolutionaries of the *Mohomedia Tariqa* were all categorised as the trials of the Wahabis. This pernicious trend of distorting history continues till this day. Western analysts and many Indian historians find it convenient to dub both the Wahabis and the Mohomedias in the same category. But militant Wahabism w̶ ̶ ̶ d̶i̶f̶ ̶ e̶i̶ ̶ om the anti-colonial thrust of the *Mohomedia* he wor l is today paying a heavy price because of these perceptions.

In the year 1857, Hafiz Saiyid Abid Hussain, Maulana Mehtab Ali and Shaikh Nihal Ahmad had established a madarsa in the Jama Masjid of Deoband. This Arabi *maktab* (school) operating at the level of a basic school was transferred to a new building in the year 1867 and raised to the level of a religious seminary. This was the birth of the Darul Uloom Deoband. The founding fathers of the seminary Maulana Qasim Nanautawi and Maulana Rashid Ahmad Gangohi were both, as earlier mentioned, associated with the armed rebellion at Shamli 13 years back. They were imbued with a rebellious spirit. Rashid Ahmad Gangohi had spent six months in prison for his active participation in the rebellion. Two directives of the Prophet were the guiding principles of the spirit of Deoband. The first principle was *Afzalul jihad* (highest form of jihad is to utter a word of truth to an oppressive ruler). The second guiding principle derived from the teachings of the Prophet was as follows: *Hubbul watan-e-minal imaan* (the love of one's country is an element of Islamic faith).

Once the above two principles and the role they played in India's freedom movement are understood, we can arrive at a certain clarity of vision regarding the true spirit of the Deoband

---

[4] Barbara Daly Metcalf, *India's Muslims-Islamic Revival in British India: Deoband, 1860–1900* (New Delhi: Oxford University Press, 2007), p. 157.

Movement. The spirit of Deoband, if understood in letter and spirit can help in a better understanding of true jihad and the East's struggle against colonialism. This holds true both for neo-colonialists as well as those Islamists who stand for a senseless virulent form of jihad.

The system of education at Darul Uloom Deoband was based on a method of religious education referred to as the *Dars-i-Nizamia*. The founder of this system was the 18th century scholar of Lucknow, Mullah Nizamuddin. The building where he stayed and conducted his studies was known as Firangi Mahal in Lucknow.

The Deoband School adopted the *Dars-i-Nizamia* and provided a six-year course in the study of *Tafsir, Hadith, Fiqh, Usul-i-fiqh* and *Faraid* (these are the Islamic disciplines based on the Quran and the *Sunnah* (traditions of the Prophet).

It is very clear that the founding fathers of the Deoband seminary did not favour the inclusion of modern sciences in the curriculum of the institution. On different occasions, they affirmed that though they were not opposed to the study of modern sciences, they thought it unwise to include them in the six-year course offered by the school.

This shortcoming in the curriculum of the Deoband School would have a lasting impact on the minds of its products in the generations to come. Unlike the Aligarh School founded by Sir Syed Ahmad Khan in the same period, the Deoband School was handicapped by the fact that its products would often be confronted by problems which they would find difficult to overcome in the absence of knowledge of English and modern sciences. The failure to equip their students in acquiring English language skills would, in the decades to come, hinder the Deoband School from confronting the challenges which they would face in the 20th century India.

The first teacher at the Deoband School was Mullah Mahmud and the first pupil was Mahmud-ul- Hasan, who was later to become an important figure in India's freedom movement and the founding father of the Jamia Millia Islamia, New Delhi.

The Deoband school was predominantly inspired by the spiritual legacy of the Chishtia school of Sufi thought. After the passing away of Maulana Qasim Nanautawi, Maulana Rashid Gangohi became the head of the school.

In 1873, Maulana Mahmud-ul-Hasan joined the teaching staff. Very soon his fame as an Islamic scholar spread beyond the boundaries of India. He was regarded as an authority on the subject of *Hadith* (sayings of the Prophet). Students from Afghanistan and all over the Middle East were drawn to him and revered him as a master. Amongst his most devoted pupils was a certain Hussain Ahmad Madani. He was another personality who was destined to play a central role in India's freedom movement. These were two of the greatest Islamic scholars of India in the 19th century. Their words and thoughts had become legion throughout the Islamic world. In the pages ahead, we will see that their role in India's freedom movement was almost unparalleled.

Recalling his early years at Deoband, Maulana Hussain Ahmad Madani wrote:

> I was then in my twelfth year but I was very small. And because a boy so small from such a distance was so unusual, I was treated with great kindness. I would go to my teachers' houses to help with writing and accounts and receive great kindness from the wife of Mahmud Hasan in particular.[5]

The atmosphere at the Deoband School was based on the classic Eastern model of religious schools marked by a very close relationship between the teacher and the student.

The late 19th century witnessed the birth of two other religious schools of thought in north India. The *Ahl-i-Hadees*, a Sunni sub-sect, was in a very limited sense similar to the Deoband School. Unlike the Deobandis, they were opposed to the system of Islamic law as propounded by the different Islamic schools of thought. They propagated a line similar to the Deobandis in as much as they sought a return to the basic sources of Islamic thought, that is, the Quran and the *Hadith*. They too wanted a purge of certain practices which had crept into the lives of Muslims in India, such as worshipping at tombs of saints. But unlike the Deobandis, they were not enamoured by the idea of anti-colonial overtures. The third group to emerge during this period was the Barelvi School. It propagated a continuation of

---

[5] Husain Ahmad Madni, The Jihad for Islam and India's Freedom, edited by Barbara Metcalf (Oxford, England: Oneworld Publications, 2009), p. 59.

the customary approach towards tombs of saints and *peers*. The Barelvi School did not stand for individual's responsibility but for an enlarged role of the ulema and the individual Sheikh in the day-to-day life of an average Muslim. In other words, the Barelvi believed in the idea of intercessors or religious guides. The *Ahl-i-Hadees* and the Deobandis were both opposed to the excessive importance given to Sufi shrines. The Deoband School however stood for a limited reform in the system practised at the tombs of Sufi saints, but they gave full respect to the Sufi masters by offering *fatiha* (blessings) at the tombs of Sufi saints. The *Ahl-i-Hadees* was close to the Wahabis because they too propagated a complete break with the customs prevailing at the tombs and *dargahs* (Sufi Islamic shrines) of Muslim saints. With the passage of time, the *Ahl-i-Hadees* would become more and more radical under the influence of Saudi Salafism. This radicalisation would be accompanied by a singular lack of tolerance and obsessive self-righteousness.

It is however clear that because of its anti-colonial thrust, the Deoband Movement soon became a major votary of India's freedom movement. In 1878, a pioneering step in India's freedom movement took place when Maulana Mahmud-ul-Hasan established the *Samar-al-Tabariya*. This can arguably be called the first association which explicitly advocated ridding India of the foreign yoke. In 1885, when the Indian National Congress was established, the *Samar-al-Tabariya* was amongst the first few groups to announce its support for the Congress.

The *Samar-al-Tabariya* can be considered amongst the very first organisations of its type seeking the independence of India. Shortly after the Indian National Congress was founded, a very historic fatwa was issued under the signature of 200 Muslim theologians of north India in the year 1888. This historic document, later titled *Nusrat-al-Abrar*, was issued under the signature of one of the leading Muslim theologians of that period, Maulana Abdul Qadir Ludhianwi. This fatwa decreed that Muslims had full religious sanction to join hands with their Hindu brethren for the struggle of liberating their country from foreign rule. The leading lights behind this historic document were of course the leaders of the Deoband Movement led by Maulana Rashid Ahmad Gangohi and Maulana Mahmud-ul-Hasan.

The news of this fatwa set alarm bells ringing in ruling circles of India. The Government feared that this fatwa could strike at the very roots of British rule in India. Orders were immediately issued to seize all copies of *Nurat-al-Abrar* and destroy them. As the 19th century drew to a close, theologians of the Deoband school were busy setting the agenda for a full-scale involvement in the country's freedom movement.

The Deoband School, inspired by Shah Waliullah, had sought to purify and rationalise Islamic thought to a great extent. But it failed to take its cue from the parallel Aligarh Movement which was gathering steam barely 200 kilometres away in the city of Aligarh. Sir Syed Ahmad Khan, the founding father of the Aligarh Movement, was seeking a synthesis of modern scientific education. His stress was on *truth and scientific inquiry*. If the Deoband Movement had drawn greater inspiration from the Aligarh School, Deoband would undoubtedly have become the greatest Islamic seminary in the world.

4

Deoband and the Roots of
the Khilafat Movement

The *Deoband Movement*, as it is now understood, has been
viewed by a large number of leading Western scholars, including
the renowned Francis Robinson as the 'most constructive and
most important Islamic movement of the nineteenth century'.[1]
If one does accept this thesis then how do we explain the recur-
rent insinuations linking this school of thought, to modern-day
fringe Islamic groups which preach terror? The answer to this
question is both complex and yet simple. For the devout Muslim,
the word of the Quran is final and divinely inspired. But there
is a catch in this—the Holy book is written in Arabic and this
language in all its richness and grandeur is complex and frequently confusing for the non-Arab readers. This has, from very
early times led to sharp differences amongst scholars regarding
interpretation of key texts. The Deoband School, sought to steer
clear from political issues in its formative years but very soon it
started gravitating towards social and political issues.

The dominant section of the Deoband ulema gave their whole
hearted support to the Indian National Congress (INC) which
was spearheading India's freedom struggle. They did so because
they saw no contradiction in the essence of their religious beliefs
and the spirit of nationalism.

This could take place because the Deoband School of thought
is primarily an apolitical ideology. In different parts of the
Indian subcontinent, its political content has varied according
to local realities.

The Deobandi pattern of not organising politically, but allying with parties that seemed likely to secure Muslim interests
and well-being, would continue after independence. Those
Deobandis who, in the years before Partition, supported the
Muslim League demand for a separate Muslim state organised

---

[1] Francis Robinson, *Islam and Muslim History in South Asia* (New Delhi:
Oxford University Press, 2009), p. 255.

as the Jamiat Ulema-i-Islam (JUI), which would become a political party in Pakistan after independence.[2]

This explains how today the Afghan Taliban is also linked to the Deoband school of thought following their association with the madarsas run by the Jamiat Ulema-e-Islam, a breakaway group of the original India-based Jamiat Ulema-e-Hind, known for its liberal political views. The radicalisation of these madarsas took place only in the 1980s following the US funded jihad against Soviet backed regime which held power in Afghanistan during that period.

The early years of the 20th century witnessed the rise of sharp anti-British sentiments at the Deoband School. These sentiments intensified with the advent of the Turkish War in 1911. The ulema feared that the Western countries would not be content just by dismantling the Ottoman Empire—they would have little compunction in targeting and controlling the holiest shrines of Islam—the cities of Mecca and Medina. This was something which they would rather die than accept.

It was at this period that a group of ulema from Lucknow and some polital activists from other parts of the country decided to establish the Anjuman-e-Kaba society. It had the tacit support of different thelogical schools including the Firangi Mahal at Lucknow and the Deoband School. The Aligarh group led by the Ali Brothers was at the fore- front. Maulana Abdul Bari of the Firangi Mahal was the founder president and Mushir Ahmad Qidwai, a leading Muslim politician and landlord from Lucknow was the general secretaty. The confrontation between the British rulers and the Muslim ulema in India was now being formalised.

But the full story was unfolding out at Deoband.

The Deoband Saga

Maulana Rashid Ahmad Gangohi, one of the founding fathers of the school, died in the year 1905. The mantle of the leadership of the Deoband School then fell on the shoulders of Maulana

---

[2] Barbara Daly Metcalf, *India's Muslims–An Omnibus: Islamic Revival in British India–Deoband, 1860–1900* (New Delhi: Oxford University Press, 2007), p.viii.

Mahmud-ul-Hasan. The freedom movement of India was then about to enter a watershed period. Maulana Mahmud-ul-Hasan was destined to play a very critical role in the years that followed. The British intelligence agencies were keeping a close eye on Deoband. The government was determined to prevent the Deoband School from becoming politically active. The district authorities mounted pressure on the school management to abstain from political activities. Differences cropped up between Maulana Mahmud-ul-Hasan and Maulana Hafiz Mohammad Ahmad over the issue of participation in national politics.

Maulana Mahmud-ul-Hasan possessed all the qualities of an able leader. Gentleness, humility, endurance, political acumen and scholarship marked his personality. His profound scholarship attracted students not only from different parts of India, but also from other neighbouring countries.

During his term as principal, the number of students at the school rose from 200 to 860. Among his students, the most popular were Syed Anwer Shah Kashmiri, Maulana Masoom Ansari, Maulana Hussain Ahmad Madani, Maulana Shabbir Ahmad Usmani, Kifayatullah, Maulana Mohammad Aezaz Ali Amrohi and Maulana Syed Manazir Ahsan Gilani.[3]

The school was visited by prominent nationalists, both Hindus and Muslims. Despite the prying eyes of the intelligence agencies, the school started becoming an ideological hub of anti-British resistance.

One of Maulana Mahmud's favourite pupils at Deoband was Obaidullah Sindhi, a charismatic figure who had converted to Islam from Sikhism. Sindhi was destined to play a larger than life role in India's freedom struggle.

Obaidullah Sindhi was born in a Sikh family in what is today the state of Sind, Pakistan. He embraced Islam in his youth and joined the Deoband School for higher education in theology. His devotion to Islam and scholarship brought him close to his revered teacher Maulana Mahmud-ul-Hasan, who trained him in theology and infused in him a revolutionary spirit.

By the close of the 19th century, Maulana Mahmud-ul-Hasan's name had already become a household name in India. By virtue

---

[3] Shan Muhammad, *Muslims and India's Freedom Movement* (New Delhi: Institute of Objective Studies, 2002), p. 94.

of his strong character, he exercised tremendous influence over his pupils. On passing out from the Deoband School, Obaidullah Sindhi established a madarsa at Irshad Peer in Ghanda district in Hyderabad Sind in 1901 and soon established another one in a neighbouring district in 1912. Soon there was a chain of madarsas all over India which had only one objective—to oust the British.

Maulana Mahmud-ul-Hasan also wanted better relations between Aligarh and the Deoband School. The Mohammaden Anglo Oriental College, Aligarh had been founded by Sir Syed Ahmad Khan in 1877 for primarily imparting modern education to the upper class and the middle class Muslims. The Darul Uloom Theological School Deoband, on the other hand was focussed entirely on the teaching of Islamic Theology. It sought to cater to all classes of Muslim society and its emphasis was on reform of traditional curriculum.

There was little interaction between these two schools—in fact a palpable disconnect prevailed! Maulana Mahmud-ul-Hasan therefore introduced an exchange program between the two schools. Special arrangements were made for the teaching of theology to the Aligarh students. Deoband students on the other hand were given lessons in English language and some introductory courses in science and maths. This step can be considered as a pioneering move for a synthesis between modern education and traditional madarsa *education* in India.

The Deoband School was however destined to play a much larger role in the scheme of affairs than what could be expected by a mere theological school. The exercise of tracing the trajectory of the Deoband School's role in the freedom struggle can be carried simply by following the story of one of its most illustrious pruducts—Maulana Obaidullah Sindhi. Obaidullah Sindhi was a man full of vitality. Warm and fearless, he was imbued by a revolutionary spirit. He became the first victim of the British government's strong-arm methods at the Deoband School. In 1913, he was expelled from Deoband after he was charged by the administrator for breach of school discipline by openly participating in anti-British politics.

The reason for this extreme step was the activities of the Jamiat-ul-Ansar, an organisation founded by Maulana Mahmud-ul-Hasan in the year 1906. The objective of this ambitious project was to create a bridge among religious affairs, social issues and politics. It was the foundation stone of a new edifice that would pave the way for the ulema to play a proactive role in the political affairs of the country.

Obaidullah Sindhi, later known as Maulana Obaidullah Sindhi, was the key man behind the concept of the Jamiat-ul-Ansar. The members of this organisation were all alumni of the Deoband School. The inner circle of Obaidullah Sindhi included Anis Ahmad, Khwaja Abdul Hai and Qazi Ziauddin.

The Jamiat-ul-Ansar was the seminal organisation for later-day movements, including the Silk Conspiracy Movement and ultimately the Khilafat Movement.

> The Jamiat had an inner circle also which was a secret organisation and its aim and objectives were not known. But this much was obvious that it was working against the British interests. The Jamiat also collected funds for printing and distributing revolutionary and anti-British literature within and outside India. Maulana Obaidullah Sindhi worked as its Nazim for four years.[4]

The outbreak of the Balkan war in 1911 deeply impacted Muslim public opinion in India. It further embittered the relations between Muslims and the British, especially in politically aware countries, such as India. The Muslim worlds viewed the Balkan war as a blatant attempt by the Western countries to corner and subdue Muslim Turkey. It was at this stage that the Deoband seminary turned into a hub of anti-colonialism and served as a nodal point not only for raising funds but also for organising active support, including medical assistance to war-hit Turkey.

Obaidullah Sindhi set up a revolutionary cell in the city of Lahore at the Sufi Masjid. His exploits earned him the nickname 'Colonel'.

The intelligence agencies were keeping a strict vigil on the activities at Deoband. The management of the Deoband seminary was sharply divided on this issue. The majority sentiment was of course behind Maulana Mahmud-ul-Hasan since he had

[4] NaimUllah Khan, 'Political Ideas and Role of Maulana Obaidullah Sindhi,' Thesis work for PhD in Political Science, Department of Political Science, Aligarh Muslim University, Aligarh, 1981.

emerged as a towering figure amongst the Muslim ulema in the country. The section led by the secretary of the managing committee of the seminary Maulana Hafiz Mohammad Ahmad was of the opinion that the existence of the seminary should not be sacrificed at the altar of anti-British politics. In pursuance of this policy, Maulana Obaidullah Sindhi, Maulvi Anees Ahmad and some others were expelled from the seminary. The expulsion provided a valid excuse to Maulana Sindhi to shift his base from Deoband and consolidate his organisation in Punjab and the NWFP.

Maulana Muhammad Mian, an alumnus of the Deoband seminary, was one the prominent alumni of the Deoband School who placed their services in the hands of Maulana Mahmud-ul-Hasan. Some of the others actively involved in this entire drama were Maulvi Murtaza of Bijnore, Maulana Ahmadullah of Panipat and Maulvi Zahoor Mohammad of Saharanpur.

By the year 1913, the city of Delhi was turning into a major hub for revolutionary activities of the Deoband alumni. The centre which was coordinating these activities was none other than the *Nazaratul Muarif*, an organisation founded by Maulana Sindhi.

On the surface, this organisation was established to promote Islamic thought. Two books published by the *Nazaratul Muarif* during this period propounded the objectives of this organisation. These two books, *Taleem-ul-Quran* and the *Kuliad-e-Quran* provide a rich insight into the ideology of the revolutionary ulema of that period. Maulana Sindhi was in fact advocating the cause of jihad against the British in collaboration with some like-minded Hindus.

It was a period of great churning of ideas not only in India, but also all over the world. The national movement in India was moving to a different plane.

The two newly established organisations, the *Nazaratul Muarif* and the *Darul Irshad* of Calcutta were serving as the seminal organisations for the ulema-led anti-West socio- political movement in eastern India.

It was during this period that a youthful Islamic scholar who later became a leading light of India's freedom movement, Maulana Abul Kalam Azad, established another organisation in Calcutta, with the similar objectives. It was called the *Hisballah.*

Maulana Azad had already succumbed to the charisma of the Deoband stalwarts, Maulana Mahmud-ul-Hasan and Maulana Hussain Ahmad Madani.

Within a short span of time, the *Hisballah* had secretly recruited 1,700 young men from all over India. They were responding to the stirring call for launching what they were told was a jihad against British rule in India. The *Hisballah* was actively coordinating its activities with other nationalist organisations, including the group known as the Ghadar Party led by the enigmatic Lala Hardayal.

On the night of 16 October 1914, the Chowki Man Railway Station near Ferozpur in the state of Punjab was attacked by a group of armed revolutionaries. The objective behind this abortive attack was to loot a large number of arms and ammunitions from a consignment of arms that was to be delivered to a nearby army depot. The original plan of the revolutionaries was to carry out simultaneous attacks at army depots at Lahore, Rawalpindi and Ferozpur. The British intelligence agencies got a scent of this plot and managed to foil it at the eleventh hour.

The British government was carefully observing the activities of the *Hisballah*. Maulana Azad therefore decided to mislead the government by slowing down the activities of the *Hisballah* and started another organisation. This was a period of great ferment in the entire Muslim world. The anti-colonial movement in the Muslim world was gathering momentum. Pan-Islamic and nationalist movements were gathering strength in Turkey in the West right up to Indonesia in the Far East. Nationalist and pan-Islamic sentiments were being fuelled by the growing realisation that for more than a century, the colonial masters from the West had used all their powers of deceit, deception and brutal force to ravage and plunder the entire East, a greater part of which had till then been dominated by the followers of Islam. Anti-colonial sentiment was spreading like wild fire throughout the length and breadth of Asia. From Japan, China, Philippines, Indonesia, India, Afghanistan, Persia, Arabia and Turkey, a new era was emerging. In each of these countries, the sentiments were the same. For nearly 150 years, the colonial masters led by Great Britain, Spain, Portugal, France and Holland had used every sinister weapon to dehumanise, subjugate and rule over the East. Many of these colonial powers positioned themselves as champions of modernity, science, technology and the Christian values of humility, forgiveness and justice. But the people of the East had seen through this facade and were trembling with silent rage against the colonial masters.

The anti-colonial movements in China and Japan were also gathering momentum. In the Islamic world and in countries like India, where the followers of Islam were in sizeable numbers, a remarkable synthesis of anti-colonialism, pan-Islamism and Indian nationalism was evolving. The history of the anti-colonial movement in the Muslim world, which forms the crux of this work, is a very complex story with myriad hues manifesting themselves in different areas of what is described as the Islamic world.

Any attempt to unfold the story of that tempestuous era will be incomplete without the saga of one of the most colourful and charismatic leaders of the pan-Islamic movement in the East during that era—the scholar, activist and revolutionary who is known today as Jamaladdin Al-Afghani. This enigmatic person visited India several times towards the end of the 19th century and what is more he served as a role model to an entire generation of Indian Muslims who were drawn towards anti-colonialism. The story of Al-Afghani opens during the last quarter of the 19th century and ends in the early 20th century.

Jamaluddin Al-Afghani, Pan-Islamism and the Struggle against Colonialism

Born in the year 1838 in Asadabad, a tiny village in Persia, Jamaluddin Al-Afghani received his early education in the seminaries of Tehran. He is also reported to have visited some madarsas in North India in search of higher learning in the field of Islamic philosophy. In his early years, Jamaluddin became an unalloyed champion of reform in Muslim society. Very soon, his attention was drawn to the brazenness with which the European nations were imposing their tyrannical agenda upon their hapless colonial subjects. Like many others under the colonial yoke, he was consumed by an overriding passion for ridding the East from the clutches of the imperialistic powers, but unlike other revolutionaries, he evolved a global strategy for overthrowing the colonial powers. Perhaps this is because his wanderings took him from Kabul to Istanbul, and then on to Cairo and Moscow. He first moved to Afghanistan, where the colonial intelligence apparatus became aware of his fierce anti-British sentiments. At some time in the 1860s, he revisited India to apprise himself of the aftermath of the failed uprising of 1857.

During his stay in Kabul, Al-Afghani had come close to the Ameer of Afghanistan. The British government believed that Al-Afghani was trying to persuade the Ameer to hatch a conspiracy with the rulers of Russia for uprooting the British from India. It was in the 1860s that a master plan was being prepared in Kabul for triggering off an armed revolt against the British government in India. It was Al-Afghani's dream to draw the fierce Pathans inhabiting the mountainous terrains of Afghanistan for spearheading into the battle against British imperialists. His way of thought was to first light the flames of revolt in India and then spread spirit of freedom all over the Middle East. Great Britain was then expanding its domains in Egypt, the Arabian peninsula, Persia and above all in the territories of the Ottoman Empire.

In 1868, Al-Afghani faced a setback when his mentor, the Ameer of Afghanistan, was defeated by his half-brother Sher Ali, who was propped up by the British. Al-Afghani tried to flee from Afghanistan but was captured and imprisoned in Kabul. Fortune smiled again on him when Ameer Sher Ali revolted against his British benefactors. Soon after his release, Al-Afghani made a fervent call to the people of Asia, writing, 'O sons of the East, don't you know that the power of the Westerners and their domination over you came about through their advance in learning and education and your decline in these domains.'[5]

Al-Afghani's call was primarily directed towards the people of India, who he felt were being terrorised and exploited by their colonial masters. Afghani's call for modernising education and introducing reforms in Islam may not have initially appeared to be very different from a similar call made by another prominent Muslim reformer and educationist from India, Sir Syed Ahmad Khan. But due to their differing worldviews, it did not take long

[5] Pankaj Mishra, *From the Ruins of the Empire* (UK: Penguin Books, 2012), p. 59.

for Sir Syed Ahmad Khan and Al-Afghani to confront each other. They soon turned into bitter opponents.

Al-Afghani was of the staunch opinion that whereas the Muslim world was decaying from within, its biggest external foes were the Western countries. In his scheme of things, there was no question of any compromise with the colonial masters. On the other hand, Sir Syed Ahmad Khan, pioneer of the Aligarh Movement, was of the opinion that since Indians were not yet in a position to defeat their British masters on the battlefield, they should adopt a policy of adjustment and compromise for the sake of equipping themselves with Western education, science and technology.

In 1869, Al-Afghani went to Turkey with the objective of operating his movement from Istanbul. In the decades before his arrival in Istanbul, the country had witnessed a major influx of Europeans in Turkey. In fact, Westernisation dominated entire society in Turkey. Business and trade were fast slipping out from the hands of the locals. The Muslim ulema were unable to comprehend the speed with which the social scenario was changing. The irony of the situation was not lost on Al-Afghani. He was seeking refuge in the capital of the Ottoman Empire, the seat of the spiritual and temporal power of the Islamic world. To his dismay, he realised that Istanbul, the home of the Caliph of Islam from where the entire Islamic world sought inspiration was, ironically enough, moving towards unalloyed Westernisation. Al-Afghani realised that the entire economy of the Ottoman Empire had gradually been usurped by European bankers. Like the Mughal rulers of Delhi in the last stages of their empire, the Caliph of the Ottoman Empire had been reduced to a mere figurehead. Turkey was being ruled from behind the scenes by countries such as Britain, Russia and France. It was a period of great turmoil for Turkish nationalists, who were watching helplessly as Turkey was loosing the battle from within. The last edifice of Islam was crumbling.

The challenge faced by Al-Afghani and the Turkish patriots was to somehow ensure that Turkey marched ahead with its drive for modernisation, while simultaneously preserving the essence of Islamic values and traditions.

In a speech at Istanbul in 1870, Al-Afghani made a clarion call to the entire Muslim world saying:

Are we not going to take an example from the civilised nations? Let us cast a glance at the achievements of others. By effort they have achieved the final degree of knowledge and the peak of elevation. For us too all the means are ready, and there remains no obstacle to our progress. Only laziness, stupidity, and ignorance are obstacles to (our) advance.[6]

Al-Afghani, in fact, was asking the Muslim world to 'reform or perish'. In this, he was risking the possibility of a direct clash with the tradition-bound ulema.

At this stage, he decided to shift his base to Egypt, where he continued his movement for reform. His radical approach for reform invited the wrath of the theologians at the Al Azhar University. He however managed to play a pivotal role in guiding the destiny of Egypt's most influential newspaper *Al Ahram*. While supporting reform in the Muslim world, Al-Afghani continued to target the British government for its policies in India.

Pankaj Mishra in his epic *From the Ruins of the Empire* writes:

In an essay published in early 1879 called 'The True Reason for Man's Happiness', al-Afghani denounced British claims to have civilised India by introducing such benefits of modernity as railways, canals and schools. In his defence of India, al-Afghani was ecumenical, praising Hindus as well as Muslims.[7]

Al-Afghani called upon the Indian Muslims to refrain from religious fanaticism while simultaneously giving a clarion call for launching jihad against the British. He wrote:

With a thousand regrets I say that the Muslims of India have carried their orthodoxy, nay, their fanaticism to such an evil extreme that they turn away with distaste and disgust from sciences and arts and industries.[8]

Al-Afghani kept travelling for the next few years, relentlessly pursuing his objective of ridding the Islamic world and in fact

---

[6] Pankaj Mishra, *From the Ruins of Empire—The Revolt Against the West and the Remaking of Asia* (London: Allen Lane, 2012), p. 70.

[7] Ibid., p. 83.

[8] Ibid., p. 92.

all Asian countries from the yoke of colonial rule. At the turn of the century, he paid a visit to Moscow. The government of India was keeping a careful watch over his activities because of his close links with some revolutionary groups active in Afghanistan and India. It was during his visit to Russia that he came close to Dalip Singh, the son of late Maharaja Ranjit Singh who had sought refuge in Moscow while nursing grievances against Great Britain. Al-Afghani and Dalip Singh hatched a plot which would lead to a war between Russia and Great Britain. The objective of this plan was to secure the freedom of India with the help of the Russian army, some Afghan tribal chieftains and a group of Indian revolutionaries. He did his best to persuade the Czar of Russia to join hands in this desperate venture. In fact, he went one step ahead and invited the Czar to accept Islam. The plan did not work, but the seed had been sown for another international plot in which the governments of Germany, Turkey, Persia and Afghanistan would be lured with the offer of launching a military strike against the British rulers of India. Al-Afghani then visited Persia and made a bid to persuade the Shah of Persia to join hands in his grandiose plans for evicting the British first from India and then from all over the Middle East.

Anyone who wishes to understand the growth of pan-Islamism in the 20th century cannot afford to ignore the trajectory of Al-Afghani's journey from strident anti-colonialism to Arab nationalism, from reform to revolt. Al-Afghani was a strong votary of a more liberal, rejuvenated Islam. He strongly opposed religious fanaticism. Ironically enough, his fierce opposition to the Christian West ultimately turned him into an icon for the likes of Egypt's Syed Qutub, the founder of the Muslim Brotherhood Movement who, in turn, served as an iconic figure for the likes of Osama Bin Ladin nearly a century later.

Jamaluddin al-Afghani was in no way a protagonist of terror or religious hatred. He was an ardent champion of religious reform, modern education and scientific thought. As his days were coming to an end, he intensified his efforts for promoting the cause of pan-Islamism for ridding the people of the East from their colonial masters once and for all. He did not live to see his dreams turn into reality. Others, lesser men sought inspiration from him after he was no more. He remains today a role model for anti-colonialism. It remains a moot question whether the Islamic world today would have been in some ways different had the Muslim rulers and the colonial masters of his time responded in a positive manner to the issues raised by Al-Afghani. He died at Istanbul, Turkey in the year 1897.

Al-Afghani was undoubtedly the century's foremost proponent of Islamic universalism and anti-colonialism. In India, the Deoband ulema led by Sheikh-ul-Hind Maulana Mamud-ul-Hasan and Maulana Hussain Ahmad Madani drew inspiration from him. It was Maulana Azad who can be considered as the chief proponent and interpreter of Al-Afghani's political thinking based on certain significant interpretations of puritanical jihad. Maulana Azad's concept of jihad based on Al-Afghani's philosophy has to be probed for a deeper understanding of the Muslim world's broader conflict today with the West.

As year 1914 was drawing to a close, there was a flurry of activity amongst different revolutionary groups based not just in India, but also in countries such as Afghanistan, Canada and the US. The jihadi elements associated with the Deoband seminary were connecting with other revolutionary outfits, such as the Ghadar Party led by the exiled Hindu leader from Punjab Lala Hardayal. There were also a number of similar groups mostly involving Sikh migrants in Canada, the US, Hong Kong and Singapore. This motley crowd represented disparate ideologies, but shared a common objective for achieving complete independence for India.

Like Al-Afghani, Maulana Azad shared a deep disdain for the tradition-bound Muslim clergy. He strongly felt that Islam had grown fossilised primarily because, over the centuries, the ulema had resisted all attempts to practice *ijtehad* (reform) which had earlier played a role in Islamic renaissance and had a sanction which was enshrined in its fundamental principles. Maulana Azad was also influenced in his thinking by certain nationalist Bengali groups which had struck roots and were drawing strength from rising anti-British sentiments in the eastern part of India. In the year 1908, Azad travelled extensively all over the Middle East. He too was deeply impressed by the rise of nationalism and anti-colonial sentiments in countries such as Egypt. Activists like Mustafa Kamil of Egypt greatly impressed him.

In the year 1912, Azad launched an Urdu weekly *Al Hilal* from Calcutta. This weekly, raised the banner of jihad against British rule.

In 1911, when Italy attacked Libya, the trail of destruction and the reckless behaviour of the invading forces further embittered relations between the Muslim world and the colonial powers of the West. In India, nationalist Muslims including men like Maulana Azad were now completely convinced that the only answer to the intransigence of the West was to reply back in the same coin.

The proverbial last straw as far as the Indian Muslims were concerned was the killing of Muslims in police firing in Kanpur when they were protesting against the demolition of a roadside mosque. The police firing led to a large number of casualties. The demolition of the mosque had been ordered by the state government for the purpose of widening a road. It was after this incident that Maulana Azad wrote, 'The more our freedom is curbed, the more shall we feel inspired to assert it.'9

It was at this stage in his life that Maulana Azad extensively explored the concept of jihad in his writings.

Through his newspaper *Al Hilal*, Azad fearlessly espoused the cause of jihad. He emphasised that the essence of Islam was peace and the highest form of jihad was the inner struggle by an individual 'against the baser instincts'. But his writings are also replete with the other form of jihad—armed struggle in self-defence when it becomes a question of survival.

Noted historian V.N. Datta has summed up Azad's idea of jihad thus:

According to Azad, Islam stands for peace but it also sanctions the use of force as a defensive measure in any armed conflict. Azad used the word Jihad in terms of its religious as well as political connotations. Jihad means in common parlance a struggle for the faith, either a struggle against the enemies of the faith (holy war) or the struggle against one's baser instincts. For Azad Jihad is of three types: (1) Jihad of property, the giving of goods; (2) Jihad of the voice; and (3) Jihad of life which justifies war. Azad was a peace-loving man who promoted goodwill and amity

---

9 V.N. Datta, *Maulana Azad* (New Delhi: Ramesh Jain Manohar Publications, 1990), p. 70.

among people but for the political liberation of a country from foreign rule, he thought it a religious duty to use force wherever necessary. Azad praises in al-hilal the gallantry of Muslim soldiers during the Tripolitan war which he described as a glorious example of Jihad. He also pleads for the boycott of British goods and the use of Swadeshi in India as a justifiable act against the British rule in India.[10]

This was the time when the Government of India was coming down heavily on those newspapers and journals which were pitching for an overthrow of the foreign rule in India. It so happened that in May 1913, there was a closure of an Urdu weekly *Urdu-e-Moola*, published by the noted scholar turned activist Maulana Hasrat Mohani from Aligarh. Maulana Mohani's stirring call for an armed revolt was too much for the British to digest.

Azad immediately jumped in defence of Mohani. He wrote, 'The more our freedom is curbed, the more we shall feel inspired to assert it.'

The government finally cracked down on Azad, and his paper was forced to shut down sometime in December 1914. He was asked to leave Bengal in two days.

The government also targeted a number of other Urdu newspapers and amongst those who suffered closure were *Taihid, Comrade* and *Muslim Gazette*.

But Maulana Azad was made of sterner stuff. Barely a year after *Al Hilal* was closed down, he launched another paper—*Al Balagh* (The Message). He continued to air his revolutionary views, but this time his language was guarded. Meanwhile, the activities of the revolutionaries were hotting up.

The Christmas Day Plot

As the winter of 1915 was setting in, one of the most dramatic plots aimed at the overthrow of the British Empire was being planned in India. It was a well-orchestrated move taking shape in smoke-filled restaurants and seedy bar joints in different

[10] Ibid., p. 66.

parts of the world. In London, Berlin, Los Angeles, Hong Kong, Singapore, Kabul and Tehran, the plotters who belonged to different nationalities subscribing to different ideologies were joining hands to strike out at the common enemy, the minions of the British Empire.

It was the unfolding of yet another episode in the chronicles of The Great Game—at that time old rivalries within the European powers were manifesting themselves.This time however the lead role was being played by the colonial subjects. The key players in this clandestine game were some Sikh migrants in Europe and America operating under the aegis of the Ghadar Party led by the ultra-nationalist Lala Hardayal. Ironically enough, their main collaborators in this plot were the Muslim jihadi groups spread all over north India, Afghanistan, Persia and many parts of Europe.

America had till then not entered the fray of World War I. The American arms industry was busy catering to the sudden rush in demand for all sorts of armaments. Indian revolutionaries made full use of this opportunity and were buying arms available in the open market. The revolutionaries had a long shopping list in preparation for what was dubbed as *The Christmas Day Plot*. It was to take place on the eve of Christmas day at Calcutta. The idea behind this ambitious plot was to overrun the British army outpost stationed at Calcutta, breakdown all communication lines between Calcutta and the country and then move towards Delhi. This attack was to coincide with another attack from the North West Frontier where nearly 2,000 British troops of Pathan origin were to revolt and launch an attack.

All the pieces on the chessboard were in place, or so the revolutionaries thought. Expectations in the revolutionary camp were running high. The cadres of the Ghadar Party in the US and Canada were working round the clock, tying up all the loose ends. The key point in this entire operation was to arrange for shipping the arms and ammunition safely and swiftly from the Western coast of the US to Calcutta. German secret agents were actively conniving with the Indian revolutionaries in the US for working out all the details of the *The Christmas Day Plot*. They helped the revolutionaries in securing two ships for this purpose and in fact provided most of the funds for this operation. The two ships *Annie Larson* and *The Maverick* were acquired in a very surreptitious manner by the German agents, avoiding the prying eyes of the British intelligence services.

The role of *Annie Larson* was to carry the cache of arms from San Diego port in California to a remote island off the Mexican coast. From there, this secret consignment was to be reloaded on *The Maverick*, which had been selected to carry it across the Pacific Ocean to a secret destination at Java in South-East Asia. From Java, this huge consignment of arms would be transported through a land route crossing through all the countries of South East Asia and finally through Burma into Calcutta. In Calcutta, the Ghadar Party had set up a fictitious import–export firm Harry and Sons, which would serve as a cover for securing the entry of this consignment.

Everything was working to clockwork precision. The revolutionaries had however underestimated the British secret services, whose suspicions were aroused by the mysterious activities of the *Annie Larson*. They sought the help of the American Coast Guard and before the *Annie Larson* could keep up its rendezvous with *The Maverick*, it was seized by the American Coast Guard. The crew of *The Maverick* kept waiting for several days and then finally decided to leave for Java. On board were a number of Ghadar Party volunteers who were to participate in the armed revolt. But the capture of the arms consignment had already dealt a death blow to the ambitious *Christmas Day Plot*.

The seizure of the arms consignment had fully alerted the entire British secret service. From Kabul to Calcutta, British secret agents were shadowing all Ghadar Party activists and also the jihadi groups. For all practical purposes, the master plan for destroying the British Empire has been foiled at the eleventh hour. If the arms consignment had not been confiscated by the American Coast Guard and if the *Christmas Day Plot* had been even a partial success, the history of India's freedom struggle would have taken a different turn. *The Christmas Day Plot* had been planned and was being executed by organisations owing allegiance to Hindu nationalist groups, Sikh revolutionaries and Muslim organisations, inspired by the call for jihad.

Till this point of time, all the major communities of India were sharing equally the responsibility for freeing India from the yoke of foreign domination.

There was no Muslim League or Hindu Mahasabha or Tablighi Jamat and the seed of Pakistan had not been sowed till then.

The Christmas Day Plot and the Silk Conspiracy Case were two sides of the same coin. The planning of both these plots took place in the same period and the master plan of both these plots rested on the premise that when the Ghadar Party volunteers moved to West from Calcutta, the jihadis led by Maulana Mahmud-ul-Hasan along with a number of Pathan deserters from the British Indian Army would move eastwards from Kabul.

Both these armed bids to overthrow British rule from India ultimately failed. There is however an illuminating connection between the two. Broadly speaking, the two form a pivotal part of the narrative of the 20th century Asian renaissance. The Silk Conspiracy Case is arguably amongst the significant landmarks in the history of India's freedom struggle. What is equally intriguing is the manner in which this story has faded away from the national discourse.

The events connected with the Silk Conspiracy Case may be considered as the precursor to the Khilafat Movement.

For Indian Muslims, right from the pre-Mughal times, it was an article faith that the Sultan of Turkey was regarded as the Khalifa or spiritual head of Islam. It was also an article of faith that keys of the holy places in the Arabian Peninsula should remain in Muslim hands. In 1911, when the Balkan War intensified and Christian countries invaded Turkey, Indian Muslims were harbouring hopes that England would come to the rescue of Turkey because 'England had an alliance with Muhammadan powers'. This did not happen and the estrangement of England not only with the Indian Muslims but the entire Muslim world in the 20th century had begun. Fear had set in amongst the Muslims that with the fall of the Ottomans, the key holy places of Islam would fall into the hands of the Christians. There is a strong thread which begins with the 18th century Mohomedia Movement launched by Shah Waliuulah and moves down to Syed Ahmad Barelvi's jihad in the first half of the 18th century. It then connects to the opening of the Deoband School in the second half of the 19th century. It then heralds the advent of Maulana Mahmud-ul-Hasan and his protégé Obaidullah Sindhi, who followed a hardline form of the Mohomedia Movement.

The core of this ideology was the need of a deeper relationship between the ulema and the socio-political life of the community. It would ultimately lead to the birth of the Khilafat Movement.

The other seminary which would ultimately play an important role in the Khilafat Movement was the Lucknow-based Firangi Mahal. The main contribution of this school to the future Khilafat Movement was its emphasis on bringing the Western-educated Muslim elite into the forefront of the movement.

The Khilafat Movement took roots when the relations between Hindus and Muslims in India were going through a rough patch following the communal riots in several parts of India in 1918. The Khilafat Movement served as a balm which would provide a short-term relief to the damage caused by these disturbances.

When Gandhi held a meeting with Muslim leaders at Dr Mukhtar Ahmad's house in Delhi in December 1918, he fully realised that the time was opportune for building bridges between Hindus and Muslims. He knew well that the Indian Muslims were deeply upset by the fact that though they had supported British in their war efforts, this had not been reciprocated by the colonial masterts. The support of the Indian Muslims had come despite the fact that the allied armies were waging war against the Ottoman Empire which claimed to be fighting on behalf of the Islamic world. The Indian Muslims however felt betrayed by the behaviour of the British not only towards them after the war had been won but also towards their other Muslim allies—the Arabs. But this story comes later.

As we will learn in the pages ahead, there was a deep fault-line running across the very foundation of a Hindu–Muslim detente resting on a radical religious sentiment like the issue of the Islamic Khilafat. Muslim leaders like Maulana Abdul Bari of the Firangi Mahal School had reluctantly agreed to Gandhi's non-violent *satyagraha*, but deep down they were sceptical because their objectives did not coincide. This anomaly was a critical one: the Khilafat Movement was in essence a religious movement of the Indian Muslims—it had been converted into a national issue on grounds of sheer political expediency.

In a multi-religious country with deep internal fissures, mixing of politics with religion can be a dangerous game. As future events would later show, even a genius like Gandhi was destined to lose out in this gamble!

5

The Silk Conspiracy Case, 1914–1916

The summer of 1916 is drawing to a close. The air is thick with the smoke of war. Europe and the Middle East are burning.

East of the river Tigress on the rockstrewn road from Baghdad to Isfahan, two men riding a horse-driven carriage look around anxiously to check whether they are being followed. Beyond their vision on the east lie the lofty austere Zagros Mountains—stark and devoid of any vegetation. Above all, the minor peaks and ridges stand the snow-capped Mount Sabalan like a silent sentinel. On the west, the eroded mountainous terrain descends onto the plains of Mesopotamia.

The rugged terrain through which the road travels is frighteningly desolate. It takes a heavy toll on the old, creaky carriage which comes to a crashing halt as the wheels give way. The two men jump down and somehow coax the driver to abandon the carriage and prepare the horses for carrying them across to the town of Kirmanshah where they have an appointment to keep.

The two men are strikingly dissimilar in appearance. The older of the two is tall and thickset, of European stock. Dr Von Hentig is a German diplomat occupying the rank of a legation secretary. The other man is of medium build and is unmistakeably of north Indian descent. He is Raja Mahendra Pratap, the ruler of a minor state of Mursan, a few miles from the city of Aligarh in the United Provinces.

They are on a secret mission to Kabul. Their objective is to persuade the Ameer (king) of Afghanistan to help in an armed overthrow of the British regime in India. In this daring mission, they have also secured the patronage of the Caliph of Turkey who believes that an armed attack on India led by Indian freedom fighters backed by Afghanistan could lead to a swift end

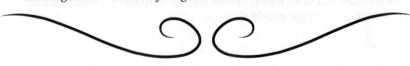

of British rule in India. This in turn would ultimately result in the dismemberment of the British empire. The axis powers, Germany and Turkey, have been surrounded by the allied forces and the prospects of imminent defeat loom large. The key to this desperate venture by the axis powers lies in the hands of the Ameer of Afghanistan, His Majesty Ameer Habibullah Khan. Time is however running out fast for Turkey as the British government has got wind of this sinister move. British spies in Kabul are swarming all over Kabul. This city has become the hub for armed Indian revolutionaries comprising a number of disparate groups under the umbrella of the Ghadar Party. It is becoming increasingly clear that if the ruler of Afghanistan agrees to cooperate, the hard-pressed British army would find it difficult to suppress any armed rebellion in the North West Frontier Province of India.

The two lonely figures continue their ascent towards the outskirts of Kirmanshah where a small group of fierce-looking fighters led by the legendary Rauf Bey anxiously await them.

The high drama which was reaching its climax has been recorded by the British Home Department as the Silk Conspiracy Case and in the annals of India's freedom movement as the *Reshmi Rumaal Tehreek*.

The Conspiracy

Even as the stormclouds of war were gathering on the horizons of Europe in the year 1914, a conspiracy was being hatched by disparate groups in India for an armed revolt against British Raj. In content and drama, it was quite similar to the revolutionary move which was to be led nearly two decades later by Netaji Subhash Chandra Bose.

From the seedy bars of San Francisco to the sands of the Arabian desert, from the Kaiser's palace in Germany to the palace of the Ameer of Afghanistan in Kabul, from the coffee bars of Turkey to the ramshackle nondescript buildings of the Deoband Theological School of India—the web of the conspiracy was spread over three continents. Involved in this intrigue were different groups of Indian freedom fighters who had joined hands to garner the support of the governments of Germany, Turkey, Persia and Afghanistan. It was a daring masterplan for uprooting the British not only from India but from all its other footholds in the Asian continent. There were also many bit actors in this sensational plot.

The Sedition Committee report of the year 1918 prepared by the British government in India has documented in great detail this entire case. The entire plot was conceived, planned and executed by *Junood Allah* (the Army of God) on one hand, and the Ghadar Party on the other. The latter was founded in America in the year 1913, primarily by Sikh migrants from Punjab and a group of Hindu revolutionaries led by Lala Hardayal.

The Sedition Committee report of 1918, one of the most critical historic documents prepared by the British Government in that era, has recorded this drama in the following words:

> In 1916, the plot known to the government as 'Silk Letter Case' was discovered. This was a project hatched in India with the object of destroying the British rule by means of an attack on the North West Frontier, supplemented by the Mohammadan rising in this country. For the purpose of instigating and executing this plan a certain Maulana Obaidullah crossed the North-West Frontier early in August 1915 with three companions, Abdullah, Fateh Mohammad and Mohammad Ali....
>
> The Provisional Government also proposed to form an alliance with the Turkish Government and in order to accomplish this object, Obaidullah addressed a letter to his old friend Maulana Mahmood Hasan. This together with another letter dated the 8th Ramadhan (9th July, 1916) written by Mohammad Mian Ansari, he forwarded under a covering note, addressed to Sheikh Abdur Rahim of Hyderabad Sindhi, a person who has since been absconded. Sheikh Abdur Rahim was requested in the note to send all the enclosures by hand of some reliable Haji (pilgrim) to Mahmood Hasan at Mecca, or even to convey them himself if no trustworthy messengers were obtainable. We have

ourselves seen the letters to Mahmood Hasan which comes into British hands. They are neatly and clearly written on yellow silk. Mohammad Mian's letter mentioned the previous arrival of Turkish and German missions, the return of the Germans, the staying on of the Turks but without work, the runaway students, the circulation of Ghalibnama, the Provisional Government and the projected formation of an 'Army of God'.[1]

The story begins in the year 1914. The Balkan War which preceded the First World War had considerably weakened the tottering Ottoman Empire. Muslims the world over, especially in India, were deeply upset by the role played by the Western powers in this limited war. When the world war finally broke out, the beleaguered Ottoman rulers took recourse to religious sentiments to shore up their support in confronting the increasingly aggressive Western block. Subsequently, the Ottoman ruler issued a call for jihad in the month of November against the governments of Great Britain, Russia and France. The call for jihad was given to all Muslims living in Asia and Africa under colonial rule. Essentially, it was a struggle to hold power in the strategically important Eastern Europe. It was however given a religious angle.

Maulana Azad took the cue from this call and under the guidance of his spiritual mentor Maulana Mahmud-ul Hasan, worked out a secret plan. The central role in the field was to be played by Maulana Mahmud-ul Hasan's favourite pupil Maulana Obaidullah Sindhi.

Few turn-of-the-century anticolonial nationalists in India matched Obaidullah Sindhi in his penchant for high political adventure. A devotee of Shah Waliullah educated in the finest traditions of Deoband, Sindhi espoused a revolutionary nationalist ideology that bordered on romantic idealism.[2]

Sindhi left for Kabul in August 1915 to persuade Afghan tribal chiefs and Ameer Habibullah to join hands in this secret

---

[1] Naim Ullah Khan, 'Political Ideas and Role of Maulana Obaidullah Sindhi,' Thesis for PhD in Political Science, Faculty of Social Sciences, Department of Political Science, Aligarh Muslim University, Aligarh, 1981, pp. 158–159.

[2] Ayesha Jalal and Niaz Ahmad, *Partisans of Allah, Jihad in South Asia* (Lahore: Sang-e-Meel Publications, 2008), p. 203.

plan for jihad. Maulana Azad proceeded to the foothills of the Hindukush and held a clandestine meeting with Maulana Saif-ur-Rehman who was to coordinate with the legendary fighter Haji Turang Zai. In September 1915, Mahmud-ul Hasan left India for Arabia. The Indian government's Criminal Investigation Department (CID) was however maintaining a close watch on him. He knew that one false move and he would be behind bars and the plot would be foiled. Maulana announced that he was going on the Hajj pilgrimage and the authorities swallowed his story.

On his arrival in Arabia, he immediately conferred with the Turkish Commander-in-Chief Ghalib Pasha, who promptly agreed to the proposal for arranging to issue yet another fatwa, by leading ulema in Arabia in support of the call for jihad against British rule in India. This religious decree also called upon the people of Arabia to fully support this war to be launched by Indian freedom fighters against the Government of Great Britain. This document was described as the *Ghalibnama*. An Islamic Bank was set up in Arabia for financing this jihad.

In Kabul, Mahmud-ul Hasan's trusted pupil Maulana Sindhi was making hectic efforts to win over Ameer Habibullah, who initially appeared to be quite enthusiastic but then started having second thoughts. The British authorities had become suspicious, sensing that something was amiss. They started tightening the screws on the ameer. Sensing trouble Maulana Sindhi realised that it was now or never. He had some very vital information which he wished to convey to Maulana Mahmud-ul Hasan and Maulana Hussain Ahmad Madani, who were stationed in the holy city of Mecca. It was a top-secret message and the only way to send it from Kabul to Mecca was through a circuitous route. Three letters which were written on silken handkerchiefs were sent by a bearer to India and from there they were to be carried by another bearer who would travel to Arabia by ship.

The person who was deputed to carry these letters from Kabul was Sheikh Abdul Haque. For reasons which are still not clear, instead of reaching Sheikh Abdul Rahim (the messenger who was to carry them to Arabia), the handkerchiefs fell into the hands of Rab Nawaz Khan, a police officer who was posted in Multan in Punjab. Rab Nawaz initially did not fully comprehend the explosive contents in the handkerchiefs. It was only a few days later, to be precise on 13 August 1916, that the contents of the letters were translated and placed before the commissioner of police of Multan.

The Silk Conspiracy had been exposed at the last minute! In the months that followed, dozens of followers of Maulana Mahmud-ul Hasan in different parts of the world including Arabia were to be arrested along with him and his protégée Maulana Hussain Ahmad Madani. Of those arrested, 59 were finally convicted for their involvement in this case. A major factor which led to the collapse of this ambitious conspiracy was the revolt of the Sheriff of Mecca, who broke away from the Ottoman Empire on the instigation by British agents like T.E. Lawrence, popularly known as 'Lawrence of Arabia', and his close associate from his Oxford University days, a lady secret agent by the name of Gertitude Bell. The Ameer of Afghanistan, who was also pushed and cajoled, finally, succumbed to the pressure of the British.

Raja Mahendra Pratap: The Backdrop

As a young man, Raja Mahendra Pratap, who was a student of the Mohemmadan Anglo Oriental College (MAO), was known for his humanitarian qualities, valour and patriotic zeal. His father's family was very close to Sir Syed Ahmad Khan, the well-known educationist, Muslim social reformer and founder of the MAO College in the north Indian town of Aligarh. Mahendra Pratap, whose Muslim friends considered him to be some sort of a Sufi, flung himself into the activities of the INC immediately after he passed out from college. But he was an unusual man inspired by humanitarian values and fired by the imagination of freeing his country from the shackles of British rule. As soon as he assumed charge of his huge family estate, which included several properties in Aligarh and Dehradun districts, he, with an open heart, started pouring his resources into different charitable ventures. But destiny had other plans for him. In the years to come, he was to travel all over the globe like a modern-day Marco Polo. By sea, by land and by air, this unusual man criss-crossed Europe, Asia and America inspired by a dream. For more than three decades, he remained in exile living the life of a gypsy, meeting kings, rulers and revolutionaries and could return to his homeland only after India became free in 1947.

Early Years

It was on 20 December 1914 that Mahendra Pratap, then a young man of 28, left Aligarh one day in the early hours of the morning leaving behind his young wife Balbeer Kaur and two small children. Mahendra Pratap was a man who passionately believed in the *religion of love*. His transparent humane values had brought him close to a number of Muslim revolutionaries whose activities were centred around the Deoband Theological School, located not very far from his home district Aligarh.

At that time Maulana Mahmud-ul Hasan was the rector of the Deoband Theological School. He was no ordinary scholar and his writ covered almost the whole of India not only because of his scholastic status, but also primarily because of his stature as a spiritual leader of the Sunni Muslims in India. His fame and respect had by then spread all over the Islamic world.

In the world of Islam, the Maulana was referred to as *Sheikhul Hind* (spiritual leader of the Indian Muslims). But the Maulana's persona extended beyond the realms of lslamic theology and spiritual wisdom. He was a man of great political vision and foresight.

Maulana Mahmud-ul Hasan, the Muslim theologian and Raja Mahendra Pratap, the Hindu prince-turned-freedom fighter, soon came close to each other! The two became comrades and later co-conspirators in one of the most exciting adventures in the freedom movement of India.

On 10 February 1915, Raja Mahendra Pratap, under the assumed name of Mohammad Peer, arrived in Berlin. His journey from India to Berlin was full of twists and turns. The British government had been tipped off regarding his plans to visit Germany. The story of his journey had all the ingredients of a spy thriller. He somehow managed to reach Switzerland after eluding British agents all along the sea route. In Geneva, he took shelter in the house of Virendra Chattopadhya, elder brother of Indian freedom fighter Sarojini Naidu, also known as the *Nightingale of India.*

Chattopadhya, sensing that Raja Mahendra Pratap was a bit nervous, decided to accompany his guest to Berlin. Raja Mahendra Pratap was deeply impressed by his host's sincerity and commitment and decided to share his secret plans with him. He let Chattopadhya know that his present mission was to convince the ruler of Germany Kaiser William II to support an armed rebellion against British rule in India. To arrange a meeting between the ruler of Germany at a time when the World War was on was not an easy task, especially in view of the fact that Raja Mahendra Pratap did not carry any formal credentials. Chattopadhya, with the help of Lala Hardayal, another Indian who was actively involved in the movement however managed to arrange a meeting with the Kaiser.

> I found Kaiser standing alone in the hall. I recognised him imme-diately, having seen his photos so often. He advanced a few steps as I approached. I saluted him in the Indian fashion. He gave me his hand and we shook hands. He spoke English with an accent. I learned later that he did it sometimes to show that he was speak-ing a foreign language. But his English was of course perfect.
>
> We talked for about twenty minutes. For ten minutes at least I was expecting that the Kaiser would take seat and ask me to sit down too, however we remained standing all the time, facing each other. Mr. Zimmerman was standing to my left at some distance.
>
> Kaiser began to speak of some prophecy that the English rule must come to an end in India during these years. I was prepared for such a turn in our talk. I immediately put forth, however, 'Yes your Majesty, they in India often say that the English rule must come to an end after their one hundred years reign, it is already time for them to go.' I must say that I do not assert that I uttered these very words but these words express best what I said at the moment.
>
> Kaiser was well prepared for the interview in spite of his very heavy duties of ruler and Commander-in-Chief he had found time to remember something about my relation with the Phulkian States of Punjab. He spoke of Jind, Patiala and Nabha, and of their strategic position in case of a military move from the side of Afghanistan.[3]

[3] Raja Mahendra Pratap, *My Life Story 1886–1979*, Vol. 1: 1886–1941, edited by Dr Vir Singh (Delhi: Originals, 2004), p. 41.

On a chilly, dark night on 10 April 1915, a heavily clad
Mahendra Pratap accompanied by Dr Von Hentig, who represented the Kaiser, reached the Berlin railway station to board
the train bound for Vienna. In Vienna, they were joined by
another Indian revolutionary Maulana Barkatullah of Bhopal.
Their next stop was Istanbul, the capital of Turkey, where
they had sought an audience with his Majesty Sultan Rishad,
the ruler of the Ottoman Empire and the Caliph of the entire
Islamic world.

Raja Mahendra Pratap was aware that if the Sultan agreed
to bless their mission and conveyed his acceptance of this plan
to the Ameer of Afghanistan, the path to an armed revolution in
India against the British regime would become possible.

Maulana Barkatullah's role in this delicate and highly secre-
tive mission was crucial because he was well versed in Arabic
and it was up to him to persuade the ruler of Turkey regarding
the critical importance of ending British rule in India.

The historic meeting is recorded by Raja Mahendra Pratap
thus:

> Here we were shown into a room. There was the old Sultan. He
> shook hands and then he sat down and asked us to take seats
> opposite to him. The conversation went in a very round about
> way. Sultan spoke Turkish, Chamberlain translated it into French
> and then Dr Von Hentig translated it for me into English. The
> Sultan was very anxious about our safety in our long hazardous
> journey. But he wished us well and hoped that we would succeed
> in reaching our destination. When we were leaving, Sultan rose,
> took a few steps towards the door, and bade us good-bye.[4]

The next day as promised, the Sultan sent a senior official
to the hotel where the Indian group was staying and handed
over several letters of introduction for helping them in their
dangerous mission, including one personal letter by the Sultan
addressed to Ameer Habibullah of Afghanistan. The Indians
were overjoyed as they had not expected such swift results.

From Turkey, they boarded another train and then went by
boat on the river Euphrates to Baghdad in Iraq. For the next
few days, Raja Mahendra Pratap and his colleagues embarked

[4] Ibid., p. 43.

upon a journey reminiscent of the famous travellers of yore. By foot, on horseback and on horse-driven carriages, they made their way through blistering deserts and mountain passes, where strong winds blinded their vision and left their throats parched. From dawn to dusk they travelled, while icy winds would beat mercilessly upon them. They could not rest for more than a few hours each night for fear of the contingents of the enemy force who were constantly hovering in the vicinity and keeping strict vigil on all the roads.

At Kirmanshah, they had a very fruitful meeting with Rauf Bey, who promised to help them in their secret mission. Weeks later, exhausted by the torturous journey, they heaved a sigh of relief as they entered Afghan territory.

They were given a warm welcome by their compatriot and fellow conspirator Maulana Barkatullah of Bhopal who had been waiting for them anxiously for several weeks. Maulana Barkatullah was accompanied by a group of fierce-looking Afridi tribesmen.

As their journey was coming to an end, Raja Mahendra Pratap reminisced on the past few months which now seemed like a dream. Inspired men they were, but when they left the shores of their respective countries, little must they have known of the strange lands they would visit and the remarkable people they would meet. It is said that those who dream are those who dare, and those who dare are those who win. In the next few weeks, Mahendra Pratap and his comrades would succeed in establishing India's first provisional government in exile. It was a remarkable milestone in India's quest for attaining freedom but for strange reasons, this epic achievement has been left as a footnote in the history of India's freedom movement.

The Kabul Protocol

Crossing the snow-capped Hazara Mountains along narrow treacherous paths, Raja Mahendra Pratap and his comrades covered the journey between Herat and Kabul in a month. Riding horses purchased at Herat, they crossed rivers of icy water to reach Kabul on 2 October 1915.

As news of the arrival of the freedom fighters from India spread in the city, a large group of locals collected on the out-skirts to accord them a warm welcome. The government had already received prior information about these visitors and a detachment of Afghan soldiers under a local commander were sent to escort the visiting party.

With a big fanfare, the visitors were taken to a guest house near the famous *Bagh-e-Babar* gardens. After months of arduous travelling, the scents of blooming flowers and wafts of cool breeze from the fountains had a fairytale quality for these weather-beaten travellers. The government of Afghanistan treated them as state guests, rolling out the red carpet.

Raja Mahendra Pratap later recollected:

> For a few days we lived in a kind of uncertainty. Food was plenty. View was fine. We could see and enjoy green valley below and high mountains in the distance. It was a beautiful nature's picture constantly hanging in front of our rooms. But we were not allowed to go out of the four walls of our garden. There was sufficient space to walk and run, but we were State prisoners, this thought began to prey upon us. Now and then there was a bit of heated talk with the government agent who looked after us.[5]

But behind the air of festivities and the red-carpet hospitality, there was a veil of uncertainty regarding the response of the Ameer of Afghanistan. The Ameer was not inclined to antagonise the British government and was keeping his cards close to his chest. Some tribal Afghan chieftains close to Obaidullah Sindhi warned the Indian group not to be careless in their movements. There were reports that British spies could hire some Afghan mercenaries to eliminate Raja Mahendra Pratap. This grim pos-sibility could lead to grave consequences—not only would it deal a major blow to India's freedom struggle but if the assassins were Muslims, it would have serious repercussions for Hindu–Muslim unity in India. It may be noted that this was the period when Hindus and Muslims were moving closer to each other and the Muslim League and Congress were about to arrive at a formal understanding under the Lucknow Pact.

[5] Ibid., p. 48.

The Indian Mission held numerous meetings with top-ranking Afghan officials. To give credibility to their protracted negotiations with the Afghan Government, it was decided to establish an *Indian government in exile*. This move may appear rather farfetched today, but it is sufficient to surmise that at that time it marked a decisive move to consolidate anti-colonial forces in the war-torn world.

Raja Mahendra Pratap would recall:

> Provisional Government of India: It was founded as early as the 1st of December 1915. It was my birthday, too. Only a few friends gathered in my room that night and we formally formed the Provisional Government of India. I became its 'life president' or the president so long as a regular government was established by us in India, it was to be of course by our Indian National Congress. Maulana Barkatullah was appointed Prime Minister, and Maulana Obaidullah was entrusted with the portfolio of the home ministry. Later we had several secretaries from the Indian brethren whom we had helped to gain their freedom. Two of them today hold important jobs. Mr Mohammad Ali who was with us, got an important post in the Third International. I believe, he is still at Moscow. Another secretary Mr. Allah Nawaz is Afghanistan's Minister AT Berlin. With the help of such devoted coworkers we could do some service of India. When the story of the freedom of our country will be written some day, this chapter of our Provisional Government of India will receive due consideration.[6]

Several weeks drifted away thus. One bright and sunny day Raja Mahendra Pratap and Obaidullah Sindhi were sitting on the balcony sipping tea when their Turkish friend Dr Munir Bey excitedly barged in saying that Munir Bey excitedly barged in and informed them that King Habibullah had given them an appointment. They immediately rushed to his palace.

Accompanied by Maulana Barkatullah and Captain Kazim Bey of Turkey, Raja Mahendra Pratap was ushered to the King's ornately furnished private chamber. The Indians proudly presented the letters of the Kaiser of Germany and the Sultan of Turkey, inviting the ruler of Afghanistan to forge a common front against Britain. The meeting lasted till late afternoon when the

[6] Ibid., p. 51.

King retired for afternoon prayers which was followed by a lavish luncheon. Keeping the religious sentiments of Raja Mahendra Pratap in mind, the King had arranged for Hindu cooks for serving exquisite vegetarian meals, especially for him. The chief guest however politely declined to dine at a separate table and preferred to partake the lavish spread at the royal table where delicious Afghan dishes were being served.

The meeting, however, proved inconclusive and it was decided to continue the talks. The next day the Indian party led by Raja Mahendra Pratap and Maulana Barkatullah were invited once again. The Afghan King also held separate parlays with the German delegation and then with representatives of the Sultan of Turkey led by Captain Kazim Bey.

The first request which the Indian delegation made was that of a large number of Indian freedom fighters languishing in Afghan jails following cases of treason by the British should be released unconditionally.

In a gesture of goodwill, the King ordered the immediate release of all Indians including Maulana Obaidullah Sindhi who had earlier arrived in Kabul for preparing the ground for Raja Mahendra Pratap and his group. After his release from jail, much to the joy of his comrades, Maulana Sindhi was made a royal guest. The mood in the Indian camp was turning festive. The governments of Germany and Turkey were keeping a careful watch on the turn of events. The stage was now being set for an armed uprising against the British rule in India starting from the NWFP.

There was, however, still a major obstacle: while King Habibullah was sympathetic to the proposal, he was not prepared to rush into any reckless move which would bring him in a direct confrontation with the British. He sought certain assurances from the Indian mission. He wanted a watertight assurance that if the Afghans launched an armed attack on British India with the help of Turko-German forces, then the Indian rulers of different princely states should openly participate in the uprising. This assurance was clearly beyond the mandate of the Indian mission. Raja Mahendra Pratap and his associates were painfully aware of the enormity of this demand.

Obaidullah Sindhi, who had been trying to organise some sort of rebellion with the help of different Islamic Mujahideen groups in the North West for several months, was however not prepared to back out. He, under the guidance of Maulana Mahmud-ul Hasan, had established a well-knit network in this region before his detention by the Afghanistan authorities. His main success was in Lahore where he had established a cell of radical Muslim youth; even more important, he had won over some Hindu and Sikh youth for joining hands in this audacious venture.

Similarly, in the Yaghistan area of Aghanistan, Haji Turang Zai, another emissary of Maulana Mahmud-ul Hasan had been organising an underground anti-British movement amongst the tribals. The objective was to build pressure on the Afghan ruler to end his neutral policy and openly participate in an armed rebellion. The driving force behind this movement was a spirit of pan-Islamism. The attempts of the British to dismantle the Caliphate and to dismember the Ottoman Empire had embittered Muslim sentiments all over the world, and the tribal chiefs of Afghanistan were searching for an opportunity to settle scores with the British. Sindhi found fertile ground for sowing the seeds of revolt.

The Government of India had fully prepared itself for a decisive battle in the North West Frontier and Afghanistan. Kabul was teeming with spies of His Majesty's Government and emissaries of the British were also in constant touch with the Afghan authorities.

Combined forces of a group of Afghan tribes led by Haji Turang inflicted heavy defeats on the British forces. But the King preferred to maintain a distance from these *jihadi elements'*. He told these tribals that while he fully shared their sentiments, the time was not ripe for an open confrontation with the British.

To win over the tribal chieftains, he distributed a huge largesse amongst them. The British government then roped in some pliable members of the Muslim ulema and managed to persuade them to issue a fatwa which forbade the tribal chiefs to participate in a jihad against the British without obtaining the blessings of their King Ameer Habibullah.

This move was a masterstroke of British diplomacy. It was also a striking pointer to the fact that the British in particular and the West as a whole has never hesitated in exploiting religious sentiments whenever they found it expedient.

King Habibullah was enticed and lured by expensive gifts
and above all he was promised that his son, the prince, would
be anointed his successor bypassing the claims of his brother.
Habibullah succumbed to the British advances, but he did not
have the courage to completely capitulate before the British.
But what was quite clear that he kept the Government of India
fully posted about the moves made by Raja Mahendra Pratap
and Obaidullah Sindhi.

The King announced that he would decide later on the issue
of joining the jihad against the British. He was sure that the
tribal chiefs who were being patronised by the British would
support his pro-British leanings. The meeting was held, but
much to his dismay the only person to support his viewpoint in
the Council of tribal chieftains was his son Prince Inayatullah.
Furious at this turn of events, the King announced that despite
the chieftains' unanimous decision, he would not participate in
the war against the British. In the months ahead, he would pay a
heavy price for this decision but that of course would come later.

The King of Afghanistan also urged the British to attack Iraq
so that the Turko-German forces could not reach Afghanistan.
The British readily accepted this suggestion and thus, succeeded
in preventing a major setback in the North West Frontier of
India. Had the King of Afghanistan not supported the British,
the course of the war could well have been altered because the
end of the British Empire in India would have dealt with a major
blow to the prestige of the Empire.

It was during these fateful days that Ghalib Pasha, the
Turkish Governor of Hejaz in Arabia, handed over a letter to
Maulana Mahmud-ul Hasan at Madina addressed to the tribals
of the Indian North West Frontier. The letter was accompanied
by a fatwa by some leading members of the ulema of Turkey
urging the tribal leaders to join hands in the holy war against
the British. Copies of this letter were to be distributed all
over India. The original letter was written on a piece of silken
cloth and hence this episode was referred to by the British
Government as the *Silk Conspiracy Case*. The message is also
referred to as the *Ghalibnama* as it carried the signature of
Ghalib Pasha.

The Rowlatt Committee which investigated the case in India
later submitted a secret report which included some extracts

from the above letter. Many historians however dispute the authenticity of these extracts and are of the opinion that the British deliberately distorted the contents of this letter for fabricating evidence against Maulana Mahmud-ul Hasan and his colleagues.

The Rowlatt Committee report, however, included the following extracts from the above letter:

> The Muslims of Asia, Africa and Europe, equipped with all sorts of weapons, have started a 'jihad' in the path of God. Thanks to Him Who is Omnipotent and Eternal, the Turkish armies and 'mujahidin' have succeeded in subduing the enemies of Islam. Therefore, 0 Muslims attack the tyrannical Christian regime which has kept you enslaved for years.
>
> Devote all your efforts with determination to kill the enemy, expressing your hatred and enmity towards him.
>
> You should know and Mawlawi Mahmud Effendi, formerly a teacher at Deoband (India), came here and consulted us. We have supported his programme and issued necessary instructions. Have full confidence in him when he comes to you and help him with men and money and whatever he asks for.[7]

The Retreat from Kabul

Even as negotiations between leaders of the Provisional Government and Ameer Habibibullah were faltering, Maulana Sindhi as Home Minister of this government wrote an impassioned letter addressed to the heads of different princely states of India. The letter was carried by a special envoy of the Provisional Government, a certain Kala Singh. This letter was accompanied by 47 letters addressed by the German Chancellor and seven letters by the Sultan of Turkey. All these letters were addressed separately to almost all leading princes of different Indian states. Some princes loyal to the British Government got wind of these letters and Kala Singh was arrested while he was in the process of delivering these letters.

---

[7] Ziya-ul-Hasan Faruqi, *The Deoband School and the Demand for Pakistan* (Calcutta: Asia Publishing House, 1963), p. 61.

Back in Kabul, it was gradually dawning upon the Indian revolutionaries that the winds of change were blowing but alas not in their favour.

By this time wild accounts of what the Indians and Germans were up to in the Afghan capital were beginning to filter through the passes to a jittery Delhi. 'Extraordinary stories have reached us from Kabul,' the Viceroy advised London. However, he considered many of them to be greatly exaggerated, and remained confident that the Emir, despite the pressures on him, would not join the Holy War. On November 5, ten days after the Emir's first meeting with the mission, he went further. According to the Viceroy's sources, the Emir had flatly turned down their invitation to join the Holy War, telling them firmly 'that he could not break his alliance with the British Government'. This, as we know, was simply not true, although the Viceroy was happy to believe it. Nonetheless, he warned London that powerful individuals among the Emir's entourage were trying hard to force him to join the Holy War, 'but so far without success'.[8]

Yet another chapter in the great game was drawing to an end.

But then, early in December 1915, when the German mission had been in Kabul for two months, the Emir suddenly summoned to his palace the British Indian government's official Muslim agent in the capital. Leading him into his private office, he locked the door behind them so that they could not be disturbed. The Emir then told him that he had an important secret message for the Viceroy which could not be put in writing lest it fall into the wrong hands. It must be delivered by the agent in person. 'I am not a double dealer,' he was to assure the Viceroy. 'I intend to stand by the British if I possibly can.' The British must not judge him by any individual actions which the pressure of public opinion and of those around him might force him to take. Nor should the Viceroy believe any wild rumours or bazaar gossip which might reach Delhi. Although he intended to remain faithful to his word, he could not risk showing, openly, any partiality for the British lest he be accused by his subjects of betraying the faith.[9]

---

[8] Peter Hopkirk, *On Secret Service East of Constantinople—The Plot to Bring Down the British Empire* (London: John Murray, 2006 edition), p. 163.
[9] Ibid., p. 164.

Winter was finally settling down in Kabul, sometime in early December 1915 when the Ameer summoned the Agent of the Government of India to his private office. The Ameer told the Agent that he had a very secret message for the Viceroy. He emphasised that the contents of this top secret should not be shared with any one and it was imperative that the message should be conveyed in person to the Viceroy by the Agent. The content of the message was direct and precise: 'Come what may I will stand by your Government but this message is meant for your ears only. Public opinion in my country is against your Government and I cannot afford to let my people know of this solemn pledge to you.'

This top secret was delivered to the Viceroy in New Delhi.

No one in Kabul was aware of this clandestine move but Raja Mahendra Pratap and his friends were aware that the tide was not favouring them. It was imperative that the German Minister at the Shah of Iran's Court in Tehran was apprised of the turn of events. The plan was that since the Ameer was not ready to oblige, a band of about 1,000 Turkish fighters should be dispatched urgently to Kabul to instigate a revolt within the Afghan army. These Turks would raise the banner of jihad to persuade their Afghan brethren to join them. This mission also failed because the secret messenger double crossed the Germans. Instead of going to Iran, he rode away to the Russian frontier and delivered the message to the Agents of the Russian government. The Russians immediately alerted the viceroy and the ameer was immediately sounded of this threat.

The mood in the Indian camp was somber. With the timely assistance of the Afghan Prime Minister Nasrullah Khan, Raja Mahendra Pratap and Maulana Sindhi somehow managed to secure the release of their student supporters who had been kept in detention at Yaghistan.

It was at this stage that another group of ulema from Deoband arrived at Kabul. The group included Maulvi Mansur Ansari and Maulvi Saifur Rehman. But despite all the pressures that the ulema could apply, the strategy was not working. The grand strategy masterminded by the Germans and the Ottomans was about to collapse.

A brief coded report on the situation in Kabul was now prepared by Hentig and his colleagues. This was entrusted to a secret courier, a Persian, with orders to ride forthwith to Tehran, where he was to deliver it into the hands of Prince Henry, who was anxiously awaiting news of the mission's progress. But the courier, unknown to the Germans, had formerly been in Russian service. Instead, therefore, of riding straight for Tehran, he made for Meshed and handed over the message to Russian officials he knew there. Unable to read it, they passed it to St. Petersburg, where it was eventually deciphered. Realising its significance, the Russians alerted the British ambassador, Sir George Buchanan, to its contents, which were then passed via the Foreign Office to the Viceroy.[10]

The Indian mission and the two Germans Niedermayer and Hentig realized that their plan was not taking off. Finally on 21 May 1916, the two Germans left Kabul. The Indians lingered on, but soon they too gave up. Raja Mahendra Pratap, however, kept his links with Kabul. In the days ahead, he played a crucial role in strengthening the strategic links between the Indian revolutionaries and the Afghans.

But the plot had fallen apart! For the next 25 odd years, Raja Mahendra Pratap continued his efforts for building up international support for India's freedom. He was a wanted man in India but he kept his mission alive, travelling all over Asia and Europe, building bridges with different anti-colonial groups. He returned to India only after India gained Independence in 1947.

Drama in the Arabian Desert

Even as the clandestine activities (as mentioned earlier) were unfolding in Kabul, a parallel sequence of events was reaching tragic climax in the holylands of Mecca and Madina.

Eighty kilometres east from the shores of the Red Sea on the peninsula of Arabia, lies the ancient city of Mecca, the holiest place in the world of Islam. At a short distance from the holy city are the granite hillocks of Jabalkora. The fierce rays of the sun pour down molten fire on the barren valleys and sunbaked

[10] Ibid., p. 165.

torrent beds. West of the holy city, the Hejaz. Mountains rise sharply above the barren landscape where nothing survives in the burning silver sands.

A few hours by a camel ride, southeast of Mecca is the city of Taif where in sharp contrast the landscape, abruptly rises opening onto a green tract covered with shady trees laden with fruit of pomegranates, apples and peaches swaying in the fragrance of the cool mountain breeze.

May 4, 1916: Ghalib Pasha, the Turkish Governor of the province of Hijaz, in which this area lies, is holding a secret meeting with the highly revered figure from India Sheikh-ul-Hind Maulana Mahmud-ul Hasan, whose face is calm and carries no trace of the troubling urgency of his mission. The Maulana plans to leave Taif the same day for Istanbul where the ruler of the Ottoman Empire and the Caliph of Islam awaits him. Maulana, is accompanied by his most trusted disciple and advisor, the noted scholar Maulana Hussain Ahmad Madani... As the talks proceed Maulana Madani enters the room and, whispers something into the ears of his mentor. Earlier that morning Maulana Mahmud-ul Hasan had a premonition – that they may not make it to Turkey.

It is becoming clear that Shareef Shah Hussain, the Sheriff of Mecca, the keeper of the Holy shrine of the Kaba, is about to raise the banner of revolt of the Arab people of the Hijaz against Turkish rule. It is one of the most masterful moves planned and executed by the British Government in the Middle East during the First World War. The forces of Shareef Hussain started encircling the city of Taif even as the holy men from India are planning to get away under the cover of darkness. However, a last-minute hitch upsets the carefully laid down plan by Sheikh-ul-Hind. The camel which was to carry Sheikh-ul-Hind has not arrived. Hussian Ahmad Madani persuades his peer to abandon his journey and go into hiding before they are captured by the forces of the Sheriff of Mecca, whose entire strategy is being masterminded by the British Colonel T.E. Lawrence also known as 'Lawrence of Arabia'.

Maulana Hussain Ahmad Madani recorded:

We could not understand why Shaikhul Hind was so insistent on leaving Taif. However, it became clear to us only after enemy forces surrounded Taif. It seems that Shaikhul Hind had an intuition of the impending danger that eluded our vision. Since he had great fortitude and forbearance and also stood firm in his belief of destiny, he stopped asking for sawari (means of transportation) after inquiring about it twice or thrice.[11]

A few days later, on the 22nd of the Islamic month of Safar, as the sun sets over the holy city of Mecca, Shareef Hussain, a direct descendent of the Prophet of Islam, now rules over a greater part of the Arabian peninsula. It is on this day that the Sheriff of the holy city of Mecca issues an ominous proclamation:

If Maulana Mahmud-ul Hasan who is underground 'does not surrender before Isha (night) prayers then two of his close associates, who have already been arrested, Maulana Aziz Gul and Maulana Nusrat Hussain, would be flogged to death.'

If this does not work, then a similar fate awaits Maulana Hussain Ahmad Madani, who has been arrested earlier the same day and steadfastly refuses to disclose the whereabouts of his Sheikh and spiritual leader and the details of his secret mission to Turkey.

It is only a matter of time before the spies of the British trace Maulana Mahmud-ul Hasan. He is arrested and lodged at a secret location.

The irony of this high drama cannot escape the history of that tumultuous period. In a masterly stroke of international entry and backdoor diplomacy, the British government succeeded in tearing down the carefully preserved unity of the Islamic world and virtually dealing a death blow to the centuries-old tradition of Khilafat (spiritual leadership) which bound together the world of Islam since its very inception.

In the guise of restoring freedom to the people of Arabia, the colonial powers had made the Sheriff of Mecca the biggest pawn in the great game of the 20th century. If the Sheriff had not swallowed the bait, the entire history of the Middle East might have taken a different turn and perhaps it would have been a different world today. The defeat of the Turks in Arabia was the prelude to the notorious secret pact between the colonial powers to divide the entire Middle East amongst themselves

[11] Maulana Syed Mohammad Miann, *The Prisoners of Malta* (Asira'n-e-Malta), translated by Mohammad Anwer Hussain and Hasan Imam (Delhi: Jamiat Ulama-i-Hind in association with Manak Publications, 2005 edition), p. 45.

like a pack of wolves who select portions for themselves over the carcass of a prey.

For Indians, then in the throes of a grim battle to rid themselves of British rule, the above developments in West Asia were of deep significance. Muslim religious leaders, especially those belonging to the Deoband seminary, were then moving to the centrestage of the freedom movement in India. There is no doubt that a section of these ulema was also motivated by the ideals of pan-Islamism. These men, no doubt, viewed British imperialism as the biggest threat to their vision of the 20th century Islam.

It would however be simplistic to be dismissive of these Muslim ulema as many Western historians are simply dubbing them as *revivalists*. As our story unfolds, it becomes increasingly clear that while a section of the Muslim clergy were clearly obsessed with the idea of confronting Western imperialism, it is equally true that they were fully aware of the need for working out an amicable relationship with their Hindu fellow countrymen. In fact, a major thrust of the Deoband Theological School was to prepare the ground for working out an honourable place for Islam in India's pluralistic society. It is mainly for this reason that the Muslim League could never achieve a breakthrough at the Deoband School—which it should have if one accepts the simplistic reasoning of Western analysts. After all, Muslim separatism and Islamic revivalism should have been mutually complementary. But the fact is that this chemistry never succeeded. Why it did not do so is something which deserved a deeper study than what it has received.

For several days, Maulana Hussain Ahmad was unaware of the whereabouts of his *peer* and mentor. Finally, the government decided that since Maulana Mahmud-ul Hasan was in frail health, it would be prudent that his disciple and confidante Maulana Hussain Ahmad Madani should give him company in his internment. Hussain Ahmad was overjoyed by this opportunity of serving his *peer*.

On 12 January 1917, Maulana Mahmud-ul Hasan and three others were taken to Egypt, where they spent a few weeks in a harsh prison. During this period, they were interrogated several times by senior British officials who had arrived from India for this purpose. Both the clerics showed no signs of any fear during the course of protracted interrogations.

A few days later, the prisoners learnt that they were being shifted to a high security prison of Malta where they would be spending the next few years.

Maulana Mahmud-ul Hasan's official biographer and Islamic scholar Maulana Syed Mohammad Mian in his seminal account *Asira'n- e Malta (The Prisoners of Malta)* records:

> The prison of Malta was considered to be a virtual concentration camp where ranking army officers or hardcore and dangerous political prisoners refusing to divulge secrets were kept. When the Muslim prisoners reached Malta on February 21, 1917, they were specially disembarked in the evening hour so that the Christian populace of the Malta City could see them and become happy.[12]

There were about 3,000 prisoners of war at Malta at that time. Of them a large number were Egyptians, Turks and other Arabs.

Initially, for a few weeks, the five are kept in tents which are bare and uncomfortable. Then, they are shifted to a huge hall with curtain partitions.

Maulana Mahmud-ul and Maulana Hussain Ahmad Madani spent a lot of time in meditation. Maulana Mahmud-ul Hasan, because of his exalted spiritual status, is given the privileged status of an army captain as is given to some other persons of high ranks in their respective countries. Other Muslim prisoners soon learnt of the piety of Maulana Mahmud-ul Hasan and often visited him to seek succour and blessings.

About a year after they had been interned at Malta, all the five clerics were summoned for a special interrogation by a high-ranking British official Sir Richard Burns. Maulana Mahmud-ul Hasan and Maulana Hussain Ahmad Madani were questioned in great detail about their views regarding whether they thought India was *Dar-al-Harb* (land of war ruled by enemies of Islam) or *Dar-al-Islam* (abode of peace) and whether they thought that jihad was mandatory for Indian Muslims in the present circumstances. They were presented with a written questionnaire and were asked to give written replies. Both the clerics were smart enough to provide truthful

---

[12] Ibid., p. 55.

but nuanced replies. Sir Burns, despite persistent questioning, was not able to pin down the two clerics.

There is a detailed account of this interrogation in *Asira'n-e-Malta* which reveals the policy and beliefs of the two leading Islamic theologians of their era:

> Question: The paper we have here says that you are trying to unite the Sultan of Turkey with Iran and Afghanistan in order to make a united attack on the Indian government to overthrow British rule in India and establish an Islamic government.
>
> Answer: I am really surprised at your naivete. You have been ruling the country for a long period now. Do you think that the plea of an ordinary person like me can reach the ears of kings? Do you think a person like me can remove the animosity of years between them? Supposing this is achieved, do they have enough soldiers that they would spare them to go to India and fight a war? And even if they spare and make contingents of soldiers to reach India, do they have enough strength to challenge the British might?[13]

Sir Burns was no minor official but was himself quite a scholar on Islam and spared no efforts to understand the minds of these learned prisoners who were spending their days in the company of some of the most hardened prisoners of war.

> According to Maulana Husain Ahmad, Uzair Gul [one of the detainees] just brushed off such questions: 'Do you think I am a Muslim? Doesn't a Muslim believe in the Qur'an? Then why are you asking me about jihad?'(Asir-i Malta:186). Burn had been forewarned by the director of central intelligence in India that 'Uzair Gul detainee was 'a really dangerous fanatic' but he found him not even looking like an 'ordinary Pathan' with his fair skin, brownish beard, and ready smile. 'Uzair Gul denied any knowledge of any political activity in his native frontier. Throughout, Burn wrote, 'the strongest note was one of personal devotion to the Maulana,' summed up by the young Wahid Ahmad's comment that he wanted to be wherever the Maulana was, 'the holiest man in the world'.[14]

[13] Ibid., p. 54.

[14] Barbara D. Metcalf, *Makers of the Muslim World: Husain Ahmad Madani—The Jihad for Islam and India's Freedom* Oxford: Oneworld Publications, 2012 edition), pp. 38–39.

Hussain Ahmad Madani's views on colonialism and British imperialism were also recorded by Sir Burns. Recalling his interview with Sir Burns a few years later, Hussain Ahmad Madani would write:

....the poor Turks were Asian, not Europeans; Muslim, not Christian; weak, not strong. So their good deeds became bad; their kindness, oppression...what I heard with my own ears made my hairs stand on end...When I think of it, I am astonished at God's forbearance and fail to understand why the earth does not open and the sky break...how long ...will the blood of God's creation be the victim of their sharp and harsh fangs? O Allah, be the Helper and Friend of your weak servants. Oh Provider, protect your true religion. Oh Lord, correct us. Erase from the earth our enemies as you did Pharaoh, Haman, Qarun, Namrud, Shaddad.[15]

His biographer Maulana Syed Mohammad Mian records:

Europe's habit, he wrote, in a judgment that many others would also make in the decades that followed, is to enforce the law on the weak but to dress the law in new meanings according to their whim when they themselves act.[16]

The travails of the five Indian prisoners were further deepened when one of them, Hakim Nusrat Hussain, passed away after a brief illness far away from his homeland unwept, unsung, a forgotten martyr in foreign land. He had left behind his aged father, young wife and two small children. It would be weeks, possibly months before the hapless family would learn that the only breadwinner of the family had been laid to rest in a distant land.

The unexpected demise of this spirited young man had cast a dark shadow over the group who, by then, had become more like a close-knit family.

Isolation and the very thought that one's close ones are thousands of miles away can be the harshest of punishments. Unlike their other compatriots in India who had the relative comfort

---

[15] Asir-i Malta, pp. 184–185, cited in Ibid., pp. 39–40.
[16] Ibid.

that though incarcerated, their loved ones are not far away, the prisoners of Malta had nothing but their memories to comfort them. But that little comfort too was not for long.

One day a letter arrived from home for Maulana Hussain Ahmad. His nephew Wahid Ahmad who was also interned with him noticed his uncle grow pale on opening the letter.

Maulana Husain Ahmad in his memoir never spoke of his own losses, but in a letter to one of his elders he noted the tragedies that befell his family in the course of the war. His biographer Muhammad Miyan compared this reticence to the silences of the Companions of the Prophet about the suffering they endured in the Meccan period.[17] The Turks in Medina facing the Sharif's revolt arrested Hussain Ahmad's father and his two brothers, Sayyid Ahmad and Mahmud Ahmad as British subjects, and transported them to Turkey along with other Indians and Arab supporters of the British. Habibullah, Husain Ahmad's father died in Adrianople. This blow was the greater since Habibullah's cherished hope in emigrating to Medina had been to be buried in the Prophet Muhammad's own city. The women and children left behind in Medina were not only bereft of male support but suffered the deprivations caused by the British blockade. Husain Ahmad's stepmother, his wife, his 18-month-old son Ashfaq Ahmad, and Syed Ahmad's wife and daughter all died.[18] Left in Medina were only his own 10-year-old daughter Zohra and Mahmud Ahmad's wife, who after great difficulties, reached Adrianople. On the return journey to Medina, while travelling through Syria, little Zohra would die as well.[19]

In the annals of India's freedom struggle, it is difficult to find many who suffered personal losses as huge as this stalwart.

Hussain Ahmad recognised, as many would do after this war, the terrible impact of war on those who fought it and those who were caught up in it. He witnessed many suicides on Malta, many others lost to various forms of what he called 'madness'.

[17] (M. Miyan 2005:101)

[18] Husain Ahmad Madani, *The Jihad for Islam and India's Freedom* (edited by Barbara D. Metcalf, Oxford, England: Oneworld Publications, 2009), p. 41.

[19] Asir-i Malta, pp. 184–185, cited in Barbara D. Metcalf, *Makers of the Muslim World: Husain Ahmad Madani—The Jihad for Islam and India's Freedom* Oxford: Oneworld Publications, 2012 edition), pp. 41–42.

Mr. Sidar, the poor Bengali, who shared no language with his fellow Indians except a bit of English with the Hakim, was one of those whose sanity was lost. Nothing against him had ever been proven (Asir-i Malta:137).[20]

Homecoming

Following the declaration of the Armistice on 11 November 1918, hopes soared amongst the Malta prisoners regarding their early release. One by one they were being set free, including some accused of grave war crimes, but not so lucky were these four clerics from India.

The fear in London was that the 'undesirable Indians,' as they were initially called at the time of deportation—now 'the dangerous Muhammadan malcontents' or 'Indian Moslem agitators'— were likely to inflame public opinion, already negative, against the terms of the peace settlement with Turkey at a time when post-war discontent in India was simmering. The four surviving prisoners, insisting there was no case against them, petitioned the Secretary of State for India in May 1919 for release to 'their own country' and the Khilafat Delegation in the following April took a complaint about the continued detention to London itself. Since the beginning of 1918, the Government of India had in fact secretly urged their release, arguing that detention was far more harmful than release, and pointing out, ironically, in relation to Maulana Mahmudul Hasan, their chief suspect throughout, that 'hitherto he ha(d) not been a publicist or a political agitator' at all.
Finally, with the closure of the camp, arrangements were made for the four to leave. Husain Ahmad left Malta a different person than he had arrived. But what he took from his time on Malta, and the use he put it to thereafter, depended critically on his earlier experience that had made him the disciplined and focused Islamic scholar that he had by then become.[21]

On Friday 12 March 1920, the four ulema revolutionaries were finally released from internment.

---

[20] Ibid., p. 42.
[21] Ibid., pp. 48–49.

Shaikhul Hind Maulana Mahmood Hasan and his companions were taken out from the prison at Malta and escorted to India. On his way back to India, he was kept for eighteen days in 'Saidi Bashar' and quarter to two months in 'Suez' under complete government surveillance and escort. Only when he reached Bombay on 20th of Ramazanul Mubarak 1338 H, corresponding to June 8, 1920, he came to know that he was set free.[22]

Years of hardship in a foreign jail had not snuffed out the burning desire in Maulana Mahmud-ul Hasan to strive for the freedom of his homeland. Maulana Husain Ahmad writes:

After bearing hardships of the prison and exile when Hazrat Shaikhul Hind Rahmatullah Alaih returned to India, we found no change in his spirit to fight the colonial regime and his hatred against the British. The imposition of martial law in the country, the implementation of the Rowlatt Act and the Jalianawala Bagh massacre within the country, and the act of dismemberment of the Ottoman Empire, and the inhuman behaviour with the Turks outside India upset him. The moment he set his foot in Bombay, he met Maulana Shaukat Ali and other members of the Khilafat Committee. Maulana Abdul Bari from Firangi Mahal, Lucknow, and Mahatma Gandhi from Ahmedabad came to receive Shaikhul Hind Maulana Mahmood Hasan in Bombay. Having talked to them and other leaders of the Khilafat Committee in open and seclusion, Shaikhul Hind too approved the launching of 'Non-Violence Movement' to liberate India. He endorsed the decisions of the Khilafat Committee and the Indian National Congress put before him.[23]

Drama in the Desert: Historical Background

To analyse the role of the Muslim ulema in the history of India's freedom movement and their persecution by the Sherrif of Mecca, when they had sought refuge in Arabia, it is imperative that the

[22] Maulana Syed Mohammad Mian, Maulana Syed Mohammad Mian, edited by Maulana Syed Mohammad Mian Translated by Mohammad Anwer Hussain and Hasan Imam (New Delhi: Jamiat Ulama-i-Hind in association with Manak Publications Pvt Ltd, 2005), p.56.

[23] Ibid., pp. 56–57.

chain of events preceding the capitulation of the Sheriff of Mecca before the British government is fully understood.

In the year 1517, Egypt was conquered by the Turks, who had just two years earlier achieved a similar victory in Persia. Salim-I of Turkey had thus become the master of Arabia, Iraq, Syria, Persia and Egypt. It was during this period that the then Sheriff of Mecca volunteered to hand over the keys of the holy city of Mecca to the ruler of Turkey. The ruler of Turkey, thus, became not only the emperor of the Ottoman Empire, but also the protector of the Holy Kaba and thereafter the Caliph of the entire Islamic world.

In the year 1703, a certain Mohammad Ibne Abdul Wahab was born in the town of Ayaina, in Arabia. He was educated in Basra and Madina. He started a movement of religious reform in Arabia. The idea behind this movement, which was later referred to as Wahabism, was to end certain practices which according to Abdul Wahab were taking Muslims to some sort of idolatry. In other words, Abdul Wahab sought to restore Islam's former *purity*, while simultaneously attacking the growing acceptance of superstitions, mainly worshipping at tombs of saints and religious persons. Wahabism was given patronage by the House of Saud which ruled central and eastern Arabia. By the year 1799, Abdul Aziz Ibne Saud succeeded in capturing the holy cities of Mecca and Madina but their hold over this region ended in1818, when the Sultan of Turkey regained this area.

The brief period of freedom from Turkish rule had however inspired the latent dream of an independent Arab Empire. Secret societies started mushrooming all over Hijaz, Syria, Iraq and Najd for such a united Arab Kingdom. In the decades to come this dream fuelled by a trans-Arab awakening would play a pivotal role in preventing an early disintegration of the British Empire and changing the course of the World War I. In the year 1898; Wilhelm II visited Turkey on the invitation of the Sultan. In a strategic move, Wilhelm II reached an agreement with the Sultan for constructing a railway line connecting Turkey to Baghdad and Basra and ultimately Mecca to Germany and Turkey. It was a step which would ensure their hold over the Arabian Peninsula. For Turkey of course it meant even more—it would be a vital artery which would ensure Turkey's hold over the Islamic world.

For Britain, it was an ominous move which would raise a major hurdle on its path of complete domination of the Middle East. The Government of India, which was the nerve centre of the British Empire in the East was deeply disturbed, and its policymakers were fully awake to the emerging scenario.

Earlier, in the year 1908, Sultan Abdul Hamid of Turkey had appointed Shareef Hussain Ibne Ali as the grand sheriff of Mecca (this ornamental office was held by the descendants of the Prophet of Islam and its main responsibility was the custody of holy places of Islam). It was around this time that Lord Kitchener was appointed the British agent in Cairo. His earlier rich experience as an administrator in India and deep knowledge of the affairs of the Muslim world were destined to play a critical role in the affairs of the Middle East in the years to come.

Kitchener was fully aware that by virtue of holding the office of the Caliph of Islam, the ruler of Turkey enjoyed considerable influence over Indian Muslims. He was disturbed by the prospects of a possible tie up between Turkey and the revolutionaries in India whose strength was gradually increasing with the passage of time.

In the next few years, Lord Kitchener succeeded in working out a number of treaties between the Government of India and minor Arab chieftains who ruled areas, including Aden, Muscat and Bahrain.

In the year 1913, a new element took shape in the chessboard of Arabian politics. Abdul Aziz Ibne Saud ended Turkish occupation of a segment of the Arabian Peninsula by capturing the province of AI Hasa. It was the beginning of the end of Turkey's hold over Arabia but at that time it hardly caused a ripple.

In February 1914, Ameer Abdullah, the younger son of the Sheriff of Mecca had a secret meeting in Egypt with Lord Kitchener, who was then stationed in Cairo. The brief conversation, however, confirmed Kitchener's earlier suspicions that all was not well between the Sultan of Turkey and his appointee the Sheriff of Mecca, father of Ameer Abdullah. This historic meeting would ultimately prove to be the turning point in Great Britain's grand strategy for the Middle East.

In Europe, the war clouds were gathering fast and Kitchener realised that he had to move fast to dismantle Turkey's hegemony over Arabia and its hold over the Islamic world.

In the months ahead, Lord Kitchener, the brilliant strategist that he was, using his astute diplomatic skills, set in motion a chain of events which would not only influence the course of World War I, but would ultimately lead to the creation of a new country—the Zionist state of Israel.

It was a period of world history which may have faded from public memory in recent years but certainly deserves to be fully understood in today's world marked by a bitter never-ending conflict in the Middle East. Kitchener, as we know, was a brilliant strategist and what he sought was, as far as he was concerned, understandable and fully justified. He was striving to save the British Empire, which he passionately believed should continue to shine in the centuries ahead. Kitchener was in a limited sense an honest man, completely sincere to the cause which he held close to his heart. The fact remains, however, that he exploited his newfound friendship with the Sheriff of Mecca to purely promote the short-term British interests in the Middle East. He hatched a devious plan based upon half truths, deceit and falsehoods designed to bring perpetual misery for the peoples of Arabia.

Kitchener succeeded in luring the Sheriff of Mecca on the false assurance of establishing an independent Arab State in the event of a likely victory of the allied powers in World War I. After the victory, he broke this solemn pledge without the slightest compunction. This act of moral depravity can be considered as a prime example of a bizarre 20th century colonial morality.

It was all done ostensibly for *the freedom of the Arab people.* It was done for *justice and truth.* It was done, as we are now quite aware, for all the high-sounding values which the West has arrogantly appropriated.

So grossly blatant was the British Government's policy of deceit in the months which followed Kitchener's meeting with the sheriff's son that even unbiased Western observers have not failed to accept the enormity of this deceit and betrayal.

On one hand, Great Britain made several assurances, both oral and written, assuring complete freedom to the people of Arabia. Simultaneously, the British Government worked out secret agreements with France and Russia for dividing the entire Arabian Peninsula between the allied powers in gross violation of accepted norms of international diplomacy.

Historians including pre-eminent Western historians have noted that the British and American Governments had repeatedly asserted during the Balkan and World War I that 'Turkish sovereignty would be respected' once peace returned. On 5 January 1918, British Prime Minister Loyld George announced that the allied powers 'would not challenge the maintenance of the Turkish Empire'.[24] On 8 January, the American President Wilson publicly made a similar assurance. What happened in the months ahead was a shocking betrayal of these promises.

Francis Robinson, noted British historian, records:

> But in October 1918 Turkey was overcome by Allenby's armies. Soon after Constantinople was occupied by the Allies, the British Prime Minister, hotly supported by the Archbishop of Canterbury, began to use the language of the crusades, and in August 1920 by the Treaty signed at Sevres, the Sultan was reduced to the status of a British puppet and the Ottoman Empire shared out between Britain, France, Greece, Italy and the Arabs.[25]

As events would unfold in the next few months, it was this policy of deceit based on hypocrisy which would lead to the Balfour Declaration and ultimately the creation of the state of Israel, carved out from the very heartland of the independent United Arabia promised to the Arabs by Great Britain.

It is pertinent to point out here that shortly before World War I had begun, the British Government had rewarded Lord Kitchener for his remarkable success in the Middle East, by appointing him secretary of state for war. After the outbreak of the War, the Sultan of Turkey, sensing the advantage of eliciting the support of the Islamic World, by a formal declaration of jihad sought the cooperation of the Sheriff of Mecca for endorsing this religious decree. Little did the Sultan know that Shareef Hussain was already in the final stages of working out a secret formal agreement with the Government of Great Britain.

On 23 May 1915, in a formal agreement with the Sheriff of Mecca, the Government of Great Britain had agreed to the

[24] Judith M. Brown, *Gandhi's Rise to Power: Indian Politics 1915–1922* (London: Cambridge University Press, 1972), p. 193.

[25] Francis Robinson, *Separatism Among Indian Muslims—The Politics of the United Provinces' Muslims 1860–1923* (New Delhi: Oxford University Press, 1994), p. 291.

demand for an independent Arabia covering the entire Arabian Peninsula in return for the support by the Arab people in the war against Turkey. This agreement was referred to as the Damascus Protocol. Little did the Sheriff of Mecca know that even while the words of this protocol were being drafted, the Government of Great Britain was in the process of working out a secret agreement with the unsuspecting French, an agreement which totally violated the Damascus Protocol in letter and in spirit. Under the Damascus Protocol, Great Britain promised to give *full independence* to all the Arab countries falling in the Arabian Peninsula. Even while the Arabs were rejoicing over the final end to Turkish rule, the Government of Great Britain was negotiating a landmark agreement with France. Under this agreement, later known as the Sykes Picot Agreement, which was formalised in April 1916, the Government of Great Britain had worked out a complete dismemberment of the Arabian Peninsula by ruthlessly splitting the territories inhabited by the Arab people since time immemorial. This piece of paper which fully exposes one of the biggest diplomatic frauds by a civilised country in the 20th century may have never seen the light of the day had not the Bolsheviks seized power in what was till then Czarist Russia. However, as if this political chicanery was not enough, barely three years later on 2 November 1917, the Government of Great Britain through what was referred to as the Balfour Declaration pledged its commitment for the creation of the Zionist State of Israel in the heart of the territory of the Arabs.

Prominent Indian Nationalists, including Mahatama Gandhi and Jawarlal Nehru, later the Prime Mister of India, would in the years ahead express their shock and dismay at what they considered as a shameless example of duplicity and international deceit by the Western powers. After the shocking exposure of the secret Sykes- Picot pact became public thanks to the new rulers of Russia, even unbiased leaders of some Western countries, such as J. Ramsay MacDonald who rose to be the first Labour Party Prime Minister of England in 1924, were forced to admit that the West had indulged in the worst form of subterfuge in betraying the Arabs by creating the state of Israel carved from Arab land. Extending from Egypt to Burma, the Government of Great Britain had created a problem which even a century later remains unresolved and is a festering wound in today's globalised world.

In its eagerness to win over the support of religious figures like the Sheriff of Mecca and later his arch enemy Abdul Aziz Ibne Saud, the Government of Great Britain had no compunctions in exploiting deepest religious sentiments and using religion for their own narrow short-term gains.

In the summer of 1916, the forces of the Sheriff of Mecca with the secret help of the Government of Great Britain launched their secret plan for the armed overthrow of Turkish rule in Arabia. Despite attempts by Western analysts to describe this revolt as a mass uprising against Turkish rule, there are first-hand accounts by highly esteemed Indian Muslim theologians-turned-freedom fighters who were trapped in the sanctuary of the holy land. Maulana Hussain Ahmad Madani, who was a witness to those momentous events, has recorded that despite all the efforts of British secret agent Colonel T.E. Lawrence, popular sentiments against the Ottoman Empire and the then Caliph of Islam were quite negligible. He had also mentioned how the British government cut off food supplies in an attempt to starve the local populace and thus compelled them to raise the banner of revolt. Maulana Madani writes:

> Food supplies to Hijaz were cut off. The last consignment of food shipment to Hijaz reached in the month of Safar 1334 Hijri. Since the food supplies were completely cut off, prices soared and people began to starve. Due to the protest of Indian Muslims, Fairozi Aganboat sailed from Calcutta with a few thousand sacks of rice in the month of Jamadi Al-Saani 1334 Hijri. That too was forcefully offloaded at the port of Aden. It was allowed to reach Jeddah only after the political influence of the Ottoman Empire completely diminished from Hijaz.[26]

The people of India and Arabia have traditionally enjoyed a close association from centuries. The advent of Islam added a new dimension to these historic ties. By the 8th century AD, Islam had spread to almost all regions of the old world. However Arabia's connection with India occupied a very special place. By the 12th century, the Indian subcontinent was home to the largest population of Muslims anywhere in the world. Equally relevant was the fact that after India came under Mughal rule,

[26] *The Prisoners of Malta*, Note 11, p. 45.

Islamic theologians from India substantively grew in stature all over the Muslim world. They were acknowledged for their scholarship even in Arabia, the cradle of Islam.

The above high drama which took place in Arabia marks one of the key turning points in the history of the 20th century. While most Western historians tend to dismiss this series of events as a minor event on the World War I stage, Indian historians by and large, also tend to over look the significance of what took place in Arabia in that stormy phase of the 20th century. There are certain unanswered questions connected to the conflict in the Middle East. The roots of the West Asian conflict are not just of academic interest, for they are of considerable relevance even today. The oil-rich Middle East is still the most explosive place on earth nearly a century after the events described above.

In hindsight, it may be said that had the potentates of Afghanistan and Arabia not succumbed to the ploys of the Western powers at this pivotal juncture, the history of the 20th century would have taken a different turn. There is, to put it bluntly, something rotten in the behaviour of Oriental potentates, especially Muslims, in the 19th and 20th century. The East clearly cannot escape its own moral responsibility for the oppression of its peoples.

By and large, the Muslim world has been painfully slow in introducing *ijtihad* (reform based on independent reasoning), thus depriving their own people of the fruits of mass movements and democracy. Nothing symbolises the Muslim world of the 20th century more than the proliferation of pro-West despots in the Muslim world.

6

The Ulema and the Partition of India

During the Mughal era, the ulema did play some role in the affairs of the state, but it was in essence a non-political role. The Mughal rulers in all their wisdom thought it prudent to restrict the clergy to affairs of religious faith. Since the time of Emperor Babur, the Mughals grasped a very fundamental element of governance in India—to rule a vast country with such diverse faiths and cultures, one had to imbibe the essence of *sarv dharm samman* (equal respect and freedom to all religions).

Akbar, as we know, laid down the principles of religious tolerance as a state policy. He developed the concept of *Sulhi-kul* (absolute peace) that was to serve as a guide for both the state and inter-community relations in society. One fundamental principle of this policy was that the State was separated from any religion. It was the bounden duty of the State to protect all religions without prejudice and partisanship. The policy of *Sulhi-kul* was the guiding lamp for all Mughal rulers and except for a temporary partial lapse during the reign of Aurangzeb, this policy shaped the religious policy of all Mughal rulers until the very end of the empire. Under this policy, the ulema had a very limited political role. They were limited to religious and charitable activities. A greater part of India was inhabited by ancient tribes whose customs were totally alien to those of the ruling class. The rulers, wisely enough, left them with total freedom to follow their ways of life.

As the sun was finally setting on the Mughal Empire in the mid-18th century, a power vacuum started growing.

The threat of colonial rule led to the rise of a number of revivalist movements within the Muslim society. The ulema acquired a growing space in the affairs of the State and they began to display their growing clout by issuing fatwas on issues directly related to public affairs and governance.

The role of the ulema in the early 20th century has to be viewed in this light. Western historians and of course some prominent Indian historians also suggest that the role of the ulema in India's freedom struggle was motivated largely by their *religious opposition* to the Christian missionary tirade against Islam. This viewpoint cannot obviously be lightly brushed aside. It is however too simplistic and calls for dispassionate scrutiny.

The simplistic explanation was understandably challenged by a large body of historians. Ironically, the strongest opposition to this view has come not from Indian historians but primarily from some of the most learned Western historians who have, during the past few decades, accessed large original sources in Persian and Urdu to assert the central point of this thesis—a dominant section of the Indian ulema was drawn to India's freedom struggle because of what has been described as 'colonial injustice and failed promises made by the Empire'. To this body of historians belong Barbara D. Metcalf, Gail Minault, Francis Robinson, Petar Hardy and David Gilmartin. Amongst the present-day Indians whose work on the role of Muslim organisations in India's freedom struggle has deservedly drawn acclaim is Mushirul Hasan.

According to these scholars, the role of the ulema in the freedom movement, including the call for Khilafat, should not be seen as the fallout of a pan-Islamic yearning. Rather, the use of pan-Islamic symbols in the call for Khilafat should be viewed as an attempt to forge *composite nationalism.*

> Muslim self-assertion, in the Khilafatist view, thus did not conflict with Muslim collaboration in Indian nationalism; it actually made it possible. The Khilafat leadership genuinely wished to assist the freedom movement, but their nationalism was based on the premise of Indian Muslim unity, a highly problematic premise, but no more problematic between 1919 and 1924 than the idea of Indian national unity itself. The Khilafat leaders sought to create Indian Muslim unity just as the Congress leaders sought to mitigate the differences within their own movement. These quests were not identical but they may be viewed as parallel rather than contradictory.[1]

When the call for partitioning India gathered momentum in the 1940s, the larger body of the ulema led by Maulana Hussain Ahmad Madani stoutly resisted it. On the other hand, there was a smaller but no less significant group of ulema led by one of

---

[1] Gail Minault, *The Khilafat Movement—Religious Symbolism and Political Mobilization in India* (Delhi: Oxford University Press, 1982), p. 3.

his colleagues from Deoband, Maulana Shabbir Ahmad Usmani, who stoutly championed the cause for partition.

This work is primarily centred on the narrative of Maulana Madani because he epitomises the forgotten heroes of India's freedom movement. This is all the more a very glaring omission, because even highly respected Western scholars acknowledge his role as one which is comparable to that of the tallest of the Congress leaders.

> One could tell Maulana Madani's story as one of a heroic, but ultimately failed, battle. The Partition, after all, did take place, and it happened at enormous and enduring cost (Chapter 6). Although one recent biographer ranks Maulana Madani's impor-tance with Nehru and Gandhi (Goyal 2004), he is in fact today little known. His Indian admirers, however, above all those who follow his sectarian Deobandi orientation and belong to the Jamiat Ulama-i-Hind, claim him as an inspiring example of a 'freedom fighter' who faced multiple incarcerations, campaigned for a united India, and stood for the creation of a secular state. Recent publications, like the biography just noted, have sought to make Maulana Madani a focus of Indian pride in the wake of anti-Muslim rhetoric and violence that has challenged the very presence of Muslims in India.[2]

The abortive international plot for an armed uprising in India spearheaded by the India-based *Junood Allah was* a landmark in India's 100-year-old struggle to attain freedom from British rule.

Raja Mahendra Pratap, one of the main protagonists of this fascinating saga, was bitterly disappointed by the failure of his Mission Kabul. *The Silk Conspiracy* may have failed in its immediate objectives but even in failure it left behind some vital lessons for future generations. Raja Mahendra Pratap, as mentioned earlier, represented the America-based Ghadar Party and Maulana Sindhi was the interlocutor for the ulema.

For more than a half-a-century, the British had left no stone unturned in embittering relations between Hindus and Muslims. They succeeded to a certain extent in their designs as was evi-dent by the rise of groups representing Hindu nationalism like

---

[2] Barbara D. Metcalf, *Makers of the Muslim World: Husain Ahmad Madani—The Jihad for Islam and India's Freedom* (Oxford, England: Oneworld Publications, 2012), p. 8.

the Hindu Mahasabha and later by the spectacular revival of the All India Muslim League, both different sides of the same coin. Ironically both these assemblages which were born and thrived under British patronage during the 1920s ultimately appropriated the mantle of 'true patriots and champions of democracy' once their British patrons departed (The Muslim League had of course come into existence in 1906 but remained more or less a paper organisation for more than two decades till it finally became a mass organisation in the 1930s.).

The strong coalition between the Hindu–Sikh led Ghadar Party and the jihadi *Junood Allah* had however clearly established that both the two major communities of India did at that point of time possess the foresight and vision to forge a strong alliance to fight a common foe. But many Congress leaders close to the Hindu nationalists like Lala Lajpat Rai were not enamoured of such ventures. They contended that any move to bring in Afghanistan and above all Turkey would once again draw India under the influence of the Islamic world. These fears may have been largely unjustified but there was a certain history behind them.

Maulana Sindhi, despite the betrayal of Ameer Amanullah, continued to stay in Kabul. He set up a *Hindustani University* with the objective of providing higher education in the fields of science and arts. The doors of this institution were open to *all humanity*. The medium of education was Hindustani—an amalgam of Urdu and simple Hindi. However, the Afghan authorities were not enamoured of this move because they felt that Maulana Sindhi was using this university for the fusion of Afghan identity with the broader Indian identity. Maulana Sindhi finally decided that the time had come for him to abandon his base in Kabul.

Back in India, a majority of India's ulema including Maulana Abdul Bari of the Firangi Mahal Theological School at Luknow had been backing the Ottoman fatwa in support of the call for jihad against the British. Maulana Azad, as mentioned earlier, was one of the ideologues behind the *Silk Conspiracy*. For his involvement in this conspiracy, Azad spent the next four years in jail at Ranchi. It was only after Gandhi's call for non-cooperation that the Indian ulema, including Maulana Mahmud-ul Hasan, Maulana Abdul Bari and Maulana Azad, agreed to dilute their stand and gave up their call for jihad in favour of the more moderate call for Khilafat.

In the years which followed, Raja Mahendra Pratap relentlessly pursued his efforts to build a consensus with friendly foreign powers to help in India's struggle against foreign rule. Travelling all over Asia and Europe, he kept winning over friends for supporting India's freedom struggle.

Last Days of Maulana Mahmud-ul Hasan

Maulana Mahmud-ul Hasan received a hero's welcome on his return to India from the Malta jail. Amongst those who were present to receive him at the Bombay port was Mahatma Gandhi. But all his admirers who had gathered to welcome him were taken aback by his emaciated appearance. His health had obviously been shattered during his protracted detention. He was, however, still in high spirits. He did not allow his frail health to come in his way and once again plunged into the thick of the national movement, which was entering a critical phase.

Soon, however, he realised that he had not much time left as his health continued to decline. But still he played a pioneering role in launching the nascent Khilafat Movement. During his last few days along with the Ali Brothers, Dr Mukhtar Ahmad Ansari, Hakim Ajmal Khan and Abdul Majeed Khwaja, he infused a revolutionary spirit at the MAO College at Aligarh. He successfully persuaded the Aligarh Group to support the call for non-cooperation with the British government at the MAO College at Aligarh. He was the grand old man who led the split in the Aligarh Group leading to the establishment of the Jamia Millia Islamia which began at Aligarh but later shifted to Delhi at the instance of Mahatma Gandhi.

India's Prime Minister in Exile: Maulana Barkatullah Khan

For his role in the Silk Conspiracy, British intelligence reports had described Mohammad Barkatullah Khan as the most 'dangerous amongst the conspirators'. Also known as

'Maulana Barkatullah Bhopali', he continued to organise subversive activities against the British Raj even after the failure of the Silk Conspiracy.

Acting in collusion with Raja Mahendra Pratap, he kept touring foreign lands trying to establish a network of Indian revolutionaries. Both of them tried to hatch yet another adventurous plot when they sought to elicit the support of the newly formed Soviet regime for an armed uprising against British rule in India.

They held secret parleys with the supreme leader of Soviet Russia, Valdmir Lenin. The meeting did not bear any immediate results but did lay the foundation of the close friendship between independent India and the USSR about four decades later. Sadly, the contribution of these two stalwarts in building bridges between the two countries remains all but forgotten.

The Moscow Connection

It so transpired that for a few months after the foiled plot in Kabul, Raja Mahendra Pratap and Barkatullah Khan lay low. They then drew up a plan for slipping through the Russian border. It was a desperate plan because Russia was in a state of turmoil and there were reports that if discovered they could be killed. They delayed their departure till the summer of 1917 and stayed as state guests to the governor of Khanabad in Afghanistan who was sympathetic to their cause. The governor whose name has not been mentioned by the Raja in his memoirs risked the displeasure of King Habibullah who had by then become fully committed to the British government.

It was during this period that King Habibullah was assassinated. He was succeeded by King Amanullah, who immediately took steps to revere the pro-British policies of his predecessor.

This sudden turn of events provided yet another opportunity to the two mavericks, who seized the chance with both hands. They immediately set up yet another ambitious plan for arranging a secret deal between Soviet Russia and the new Afghan King. This proposed entente between the two countries would be aimed against the common enemy—Great Britain.

It was a period of momentous change all over the globe, especially Europe. The biggest change obviously was the emergence of the Soviet regime in the State of Russia. The new Soviet regime was keen to have friendly ties with the State of Afghanistan. For the Indian revolutionaries, this was just the opportunity they were waiting for.

Raja Mahendra Pratap received an invitation from the Commisar of Russian Turkestan. The Raja wrote:

> I was invited to tea by the Commisar. But he called me away in an adjacent room and began to cross-examine me through an interpreter. 'But why so many Afghan soldiers came with you to the opposite bank of the river?' 'They are not so many, they are only a dozen soldiers who have been accompanying me ever since I left Kabul', I answered. 'You were trying to come in contact with the Czarist and the Kerensky's governments?' 'Yes, why not, I was hoping to have friendly relations with our Northern neighbour.' In some such words, the cross-examination was proceeding when I saw that the Commisar got agitated. Some funny remark of the interpreter made me angry too. We were on the brink of a scene when someone intervened and explained that the whole fault was of the interpreter.[3]

From Russia, Raja Mahendra Pratap went to Germany to meet the Kaiser and apprise him of the events of the past few months.

> In a special carriage I come to Potsdam. Robed in the Bukhara silk, I am standing face to face with H.M. Kaiser Wilhelm the Second, for the second time. Kaiser looks much older than when I saw him last in 1915. His head shakes a little. His voice is clear. We talk about my trip to Afghanistan and back. Kaiser presents me his autograph.[4]

After King Amanullah came to power, he immediately launched hostilities against the British rulers of India. Raja Mahendra Pratap sensed a fresh opportunity and decided to have another meeting with the Russian rulers.

---

[3] Raja Mahendra Pratap, *My Life Story 1886–1979*, Vol. 1, edited by Dr Vir Singh (Delhi: Originals, 2004 edition), p. 56.

[4] Ibid., p. 57.

We met Mr Lenin. The details were arranged by Mr Karakhan.
Prof. Vosnesensky fixed up everything for us. We accompanied
Mr Suritiz to Cabul. I got one German and one Austrian war
prisoners to help me. I picked them up from a German restaurant
in Central Asia. A special train brought us to the Afghanistan
frontier. We reached Herat. Last when I came here in 1915 I
was the first person of our mission, now my role was to act as
the second best to the Soviet diplomat. Strange coincidence was
that now in 1919 the same governor was there once again whom
we met there four years before. At Cabul I properly introduced
the Soviet Mission to H.M. King Amanullah Khan.[5]

Raja Mahendra Pratap and Maulana Barkatullah had by then
become so dangerous in the eyes of the British that there was
no chance of their returning to the homeland. They kept moving all over the globe, painstakingly building a wide network of
Indian freedom fighters.

Maulana Barkatullah, like his close friend Raja Mahendra
Pratap, ranks amongst one of the most colourful personalities
of India's freedom movement in the 20th century.

Early Years

Maulana Barkatullah was born in the city of Bhopal in central
India in the year 1859. After completing his primary education, he joined the prestigious Sulaimania seminary in Bhopal
for Persian, Arabic and Islamic studies. After gaining a high
level of proficiency in the above subjects, he decided to study
English. In the year 1883, he took up service at the Christian
Missionary School at Jabalpur. Shortly later, he left for Bombay
for further studies in English. In the year 1890, he left for
England. For a short while, he taught Oriental languages at
the Liverpool College, where he came in touch with some of the
leading lights of the country's freedom movement like Gopal
Krishna Gokhale and Shyamji Verma. These meetings were to
change his life forever. He lost interest in every other field of
life and henceforth his entire life was that of an exile, totally

---

[5] Ibid., pp. 59–60.

committed to the cause of uprooting British rule from India. Very soon, he developed differences with Gokhale because he considered him too mild.

In 1899, Barkatullah went to the US, where he came in touch with a group of Indian revolutionaries. Shortly later, he left the US for Japan, where he established a small cell for Indian revolutionaries. In Japan, he worked as an editor for a newspaper, *The Islamic Fraternity*, which had been launched by an Egyptian revolutionary.

The British government came to learn of this venture and then used diplomatic pressure with the Japanese government to force down the closure of this publication. The Maulana was thus rendered jobless in a foreign land. With the help of some friends, he arranged for a passage to the US. This proved to be yet another turning point in his life. There he came in contact with some Indian revolutionaries of the Ghadar Party. This group then made all the arrangements for the Maulana to establish base in Europe, which was seething with subversive activities as the war clouds gathered.

His main associates in this period were Champak Raman Pillai, Raja Mahendra Pratap, Lala Hardayal, Maulana Obaidullah Sindhi, Bashir Ahmad and Rahmat Ali Zakariya. Obaidullah Sindhi was the contact man for the jihadi *Junood Allah* and Hardayal was the pointsman for the Ghadar Party. Raja Mahendra Pratap was a binding force which glued together this disparate group of revolutionaries.

After the Silk Conspiracy failed Barkatullah, he shifted base to Berlin and with the help of Champak Pillai, established a new organisation.

According to Professor Abdul Ali, Department of Islamic Studies, AMU:

In July 1925, he was appointed as president of Indian Independence Party which was financed with Bolshevik funds, and published an Arabic paper entitled al-Islah. He was also a member of the seven-man delegation led by Pandit Jawahar Lal Nehru to the anti-imperialistic conference held at Brussels in February 1927, and delivered an illuminating speech in support of India's freedom strugle. His speech was very well received and appreciated. The Maulana attended the conference as a representative of the Ghadar Party, while Pt. Nehru participated in it as a representative of the Indian National Congress. Pt. Nehru has also mentioned in his book The Story of My Life about his meeting with the Maulana at the Conference.[6]

Maulana Barkatullah can be considered one of the most remarkable and colourful figures in the history of India's freedom movement. On one side he was a deeply religious Islamic scholar who was ready to wage jihad for the cause of Islam; on the other side, he was very moderate in his approach towards people belonging to other faiths. But the over arching force of his personality was his fierce commitment to Indian nationalism. His role model in life was the Prophet of Islam, who he firmly believed was an embodiment of the principles of 'religious tolerance and peaceful co-existence'.

In his paper on the life of Maulana Barkatullah Professor Abdul Ali writes:

Maulana Barkatullah lived a very hard life of struggle. He was hotly pursued by members of the British Intelligence Department, as a consequence of which he came face to face with death several times. Towards the close of his life he became a diabetic patient. He remained a bachelor, and devoted his life fully to the cause of his nation in all sincerity and honesty. He rather over tasked himself and suffered a continuous deterioration of his health till he breathed his last on 27th September, 1927 in San Francisco where he had gone to attend a meeting of the Ghadar Party.[7]

On his deathbed in San Francisco, Maulana Barkatullah summed up his entire life story thus:

I struggled hard throughout my life in a very honest and sincere manner for the sake of the freedom of my country. It was indeed fortunate of me that my humble life was dedicated to the service of my nation. Today at the time of my departure while I regret that my efforts could not become successful during my lifetime, I feel contended that millions of people have now joined the struggle for the country's freedom, who are truthful honest and adventurous.

---

[6] Abdul Ali and Zafarul Islam (ed.), *Role of Muslims in the Freedom Movement of India*, Seminar Papers (Aligarh: The Institute of Islamic Studies, Aligarh Muslim University, 2007 edition), p. 140.

[7] Ibid., p. 142.

I am, therefore, departing as a satisfied person by putting the destiny of my beloved country into their hands.[8]

India's first provisional government set up in exile, of which the Maulana was an integral part, did not succeed in achieving its objectives but Maulana Barkatullah did succeed in setting up a platform for Indian nationalists which became the foundation of later-day movements like the Khilafat Movement and ultimately the establishment of the Indian National Army by Subhash Chandra Bose. Maulana's contribution to India's freedom movement may not have received due recognition, but the fact remains that he could well serve as a role model for nationalism in today's troubled times.

Maulana Barkatullah lived barely for a decade after the dismantling of India's *provisional government* in exile, but his close associate Maulana Obaidullah Sindhi was destined to play a much longer innings. After the failure of the Kabul Mission, Maulana Sindhi shifted his operational base to Moscow in the year 1922. His biographer Naimullah mentions that in Moscow, he spent several months as the 'spokesman of the Congress Party'. He spent a lot of his time in studying the Socialist pattern of government and its possible implementation in India. It was an interesting phase in his life. Here was a Muslim cleric who was now trying to acquaint himself with the semantics of Communism. His main focus was to amalgamate the teachings of the 18th century scholar Shah Waliullah, who leaned heavily on an anti-West discource combined with the anti-colonial thrust of Socialism. He drew up an anti-colonial political programme which he unveiled during his three-year stay in Turkey after leaving Russia. From Turkey, he shifted to Arabia, which was then under the rule of the House of Saud. For the next 12 years, he stayed in Arabia, mostly studying emerging political thought in the West and the Muslim world.

In 1939, Maulana Sindhi returned to India after a gap of about a quarter of a century. The India to which he returned was quite a different country from what he had left. The ulema, who had been at the forefront in politics, had by 1939 been pushed to the sidelines by modernist leaders like Mohammad Ali Jinnah. The leadership of the Muslims had by then fallen in the hands

[8] Ibid., p. 143.

of upper middle class lawyers, journalists and landed gentry, who were all deeply disturbed by the socialistic trends in the Indian National Congress. The *zamindar* class in the populous and politically crucial states of UP and Bihar were deeply concerned about their fate if the agrarian reforms propounded by the INC were implemented.

Dr Tarachand, in his monumental *History of the Freedom Movement in India*, comments:

> Unfortunately he arrived in India too late. By 1939 the Muslim League had established its hold over the Muslim community and the Ulema were fighting a losing battle. His advanced and unconventional views on religion and his domineering temper irked the orthodox and the conservatives and seriously undermined his influence. Nevertheless, both because of the part he played in the early years of the struggle and his strikingly modern outlook his ideas deserve attention.

He immediately plunged into the role of a social activist. His objective was to establish a forum within the Congress which would propagate socio-economic policies as envisaged by the 18th century reformer Shah Waliullah. He also started working on a proposal for establishing two wings of the Jamiat Ulema-e-Hind. The first wing would focus its activities on promoting the social reforms within the Muslim community based on the ideology of Shah Waliullah Dehlvi. This organisation would form the bedrock of social reform within the Muslim community. The second wing would align itself with the Indian National Congress for helping the Muslims play their due role in the political system of the country. His biographer Naim Ullah Khan mentions:

> The Maulana undertook a tour of the country despite his failing health. Perhaps he apprehended that time was running short and so he was desperately trying to complete his mission. He was preparing the masses for any revolution and wanted that they should not be taken unaware.[9]

---

[9] Naim Ullah Khan, 'Political Ideas and Role of Maulana Obaidullah Sindhi,' PhD thesis, Department of Political Science, Aligarh Muslim University, Aligarh, 1981, p. 190.

On 12 July 1940, he was asked to inaugurate the Congress Committee office in district Thatta in the state of Sindh. Naim Ullah Khan writes:

While inaugurating the conference of the district Congress he hoped that India would surely come out successful in its effort to liberate the motherland for which Indians have already suffered so much. He said that he was extremely happy that he had been invited to inaugurate the District Congress Committee in the historical town of the Sindh province because of three reasons:

a) He loved Sindh as his fatherland where he also had spent his early childhood.
b) He loved the town where the conference was taking place as it had been a seat of learning of many scholars of repute belonging to the Shah Waliullah School of thought.
c) He loved the Congress organisation which had been successful in achieving an honourable status of a national party in the world body politics. He also felt proud of its membership with which he had a very long association. He stated that he belonged to the National Congress and the National Congress belonged to him but at the same time he wanted to express his views without blindly accepting all the Congress policies. He affirmed that if the programme of the Jamna-Narbada-Sindh Sagar Party was accepted and adopted by the Congress, he would be able to make the Congress more popular. All that he could do at the moment was to put before them his political ideas and experiences.[10]

Maulana Sindhi started a fresh drive to strengthen the bonds between Hindus and Muslims in his home state of Sindh. But he was distressed by the approach of some hardliners within the Congress Party, including Sardar Patel. He felt that instead of weakening the Muslim League in Sindh, the politics of confrontation adopted by such hardliners was in fact driving the Muslims into the arms of the Muslim League.

He made another appeal to Jawahar Lal Nehru whom he considered as a promising leader not to insist on the continuation of Civil Disobedience Movement at that time. He even pleaded with him to make some kind of settlement with Jinnah. He

---

[10] Ibid., p. 191.

expressed his willingness to prepare a line of action which could bring Jinnah and Nehru together. He was confident that the collective leadership of Gandhiji and Jinnah could make a considerable headway in the cause of India's freedom. At the end of his address he also appealed to Subhash Chandra Bose to give up the Civil Disobedience Movement in Bengal and follow Mahatma Gandhi. He wanted that all the forces engaged in the task of India's freedom should join hands and adopt a uniform policy for the attainment of national independence.[11]

Maulana Sindhi's efforts to formulate a political ideology based on the synthesis of Vedic Hinduism and Islamic Sufiism was a singular effort. In today's politics, devoid as it is of any ideological content, his approach of evolving a syncretic ethos in Indian politics cannot be underestimated.

Aziz Ahmad in his critical analysis of Maulana Sindhi writes:

He said that all humanity was bound by a unity—the unity of thought. The Quran also represented this unity as do the other religions. It is, therefore, not exclusively meant for Muslims but for all peoples. He believed that the Quran was the final scripture of all the religions. Its aim was the establishment of a virtuous society which should train people to become worthy members of the human family. Righteousness of the individual society and humanity is the goal of Islam. What unites man is, therefore, religion and what separates is its contrary, i.e. irregularities.[12]

The Maulana bitterly opposed Jinnah's call for creating Pakistan:

He appealed to the Muslims to find out the solution of their problems within the Indian framework and any scheme for their welfare should be initiated from within the Indian National Congress. He emphatically stated that the proposed Muslim state would not be able to solve the problems of the Muslims and he was, therefore, averse to its very idea.[13]

Maulana Sindhi was a visionary leader. He predicted that a Muslim state as envisioned by the Muslim League would neither

[11] Ibid., pp. 198–199.
[12] Ibid., p. 201.
[13] Ibid., pp. 219–220.

be stable nor would it serve as a panacea for the problems of the Indian Muslims.

The Maulana's ideology was a unique synthesis of Marxism and Islam:

> Jehad which literally meant a 'holy war' could be fought on different fields and with different kinds of weapons such as sword, pen, the human heart or fearless expression. Marxist revolution was the atheistic counterpart of the theistic jehad. He said that jehad was like a surgical operation on an inflammatory sore. Its neglect would amount to the neglect of essential self defence and self preservation, especially in a world hostile to Islam. At another place he redefined jehad as essentially the control of one's passions, forbearance and deference of death and thus equated it with passive resistance and 'ahimsa'.[14]

On 24 August 1944, three years before India gained independence, the Maulana breathed his last. His last few years had left him a troubled man. Like so many other Muslims who were in the forefront of the freedom movement and who did not believe in the sectarian approach of the Muslim League, Sindhi was disappointed by the ambivalent approach to politics which many senior Congress leaders adopted. It was fortunate that he did not live to see the ease with which most Congress leaders succumbed to the proposal for the Partition of India.

The Khilafat Movement and Maulana Hussain Ahmad Madani

The 20th century Khilafat Movement in India has been described as a campaign by a dominant section of the Indian Muslim elite to galvanise the entire community through religion and cultural symbols for preserving the institution of the 'Ottoman Caliphate' as a symbol of Islamic unity. Through religious symbolism, it also sought to mobilise the Indian Muslims for participating in the national movement and strengthening anti-British sentiments.

---

[14] Ibid., pp. 226–227.

It was in its essence a quest for pan-Indian Islam rather than a pan-Islamist movement.

The Khilafat Movement was led primarily by clerics of the Firangi Mahal Theological School of Lucknow, and later by those belonging to the Deoband School. The leading architect of this movement was Maulana Abdul Bari of Firangi Mahal. Two persons belonging to the New Aligarh school of thought— Hakim Ajmal Khan and Dr Mukhtar Ahmad Ansari—were the main pivots for spreading this movement. It was these two who drew Gandhi to the movement (after the collapse of the Khilafat Movement, these two stayed on with Gandhi to become two of his closest associates). The movement, however, gathered strength only after the Ali Brothers and the Deoband ulema Maulana Mahmud-ul Hasan and Maulana Hussain Ahmad Madani joined hands.

Let us however return to the story of Maulana Mahmud-ul Hasan and his protégée Maulana Hussain Ahmad Madani.

A hero's welcome was given to Maulana Mahmud-ul Hasan, Maulana Madani and their two colleagues on their return to India after spending more than three years in the prison of Malta. It was 8 June 1920 when their ship landed in Bombay. It was one of the most joyous periods in the history of India's freedom struggle. The atmosphere was resonating with a genuine bonhomie between Hindus and Muslims. The Khilafat Movement was gathering strength. All top Congress leaders, including Mahatma Gandhi, strongly supported the Muslims in their movement against the British for dismantling the centuries-old institution of the Caliphate resting with the throne of the Ottoman ruler.

Mahatma Gandhi and other senior Congress leaders were waiting with garlands on one side. Prominent Muslim clerics from all over the country had also turned up in large numbers for the memorable occasion. For most of them, the very thought of embracing or just catching a glimpse of their beloved *peer* Maulana Mahmud-ul Hasan promised to be a moment of rapture!

At the other end, there stood a smaller group of a welcoming party. They were senior officers from the Intelligence Department. With them there were three civilians. On seeing them, Maulana Madani immediately recognised one of them as a businessman of Indian origin from Jeddah in Arabia. His name was Bahauddin. The Maulana knew that he was close to the British authorities and always acted as their interlocutor. The second man he did not recognise. But this gentleman who had quite an imposing presence quickly introduced himself as the prince of the state of Bhawalpur. The Prince immediately took aside Maulana Madani and with great reverence urged him to use his good offices to persuade his *peer* Maulana Mahmud-ul Hasan not to fall in the trap of the Khilafat leaders and Gandhiji. He suggested that instead of getting involved with the Khilifatists, Maulana Mahmud should now spend the evening of his life in the peaceful climes of Deoband, where the seminary was eagerly awaiting the arrival of its patron. As soon as the Maulana Mahmud-ul Hasan realised what was transpiring, he calmly addressed Bahauddin and in no uncertain words conveyed to him that his commitment to the cause of Khilafat was 'final and irrevocable'.

As word of Maulana Mahmud-ul Hasan's unequivocal support to the Khilafat Movement trickled out of Bombay and spread all over the country, it had an electrifying effect on Congress Party workers. It was the dawn of a short but historic phase in the history of Hindu–Muslim relations in the 20th century India.

Maulana Mahmud-ul Hasan's decision to plunge into the cauldron of active politics after his release from the Malta prison propelled his favourite pupil Maulana Hussain Ahmad Madani to the centrestage of the Khilafat Movement.

Two very important socio-political outfits had come into existence in the year 1919 – the All India Khilafat Committee and the Jamiat Ulema-e-Hind (Party of the Indian ulema). Till this stage, Maulana Madani's role in India's freedom struggle was revolving around his deep reverence for his *peer* and mentor Maulana Mahmud-ul Hasan. It was the role primarily of a devoted pupil of a revered teacher. But the return to India changed his entire perspective of colonialism.

His biographer Barbara Metcalf writes:

> Hussain Ahmad Madani's Indian ties were deep, to be sure, but his ties to the Hijaz and his two surviving brothers were deep as well. In the end, it was his bond to Maulana Mahmudul Hasan that proved critical in his decision. In the course of the trip, he agreed that he would stay in India because his revered elder said he needed him to aid in the completion of the hadith commentary

that he had started during internment. This decision underlined the depth of his scholarly commitment and spiritual bonds at a time when his nationalism had not yet taken practical shape. In the end, he did not pursue the scholarly project at all, but almost immediately turned to the Islamic teaching and political activism within India that would subsequently fill his life.[15]

Metcalf further writes:

Husain Ahmad's politics challenge assumptions that Islamic political actors are invariably rigid or trapped in some 'medieval' past, even as they do not fit easily into contemporary definitions of liberal democracy.[16]

The inaugural session of the All India Khilafat Conference was held at Delhi in November 1919. Apart from all the top Muslim leaders from the Congress and Muslim League, it was attended by leaders like Gandhi, Jawaharlal Nehru and Hindu radicals like Madan Mohan Malviya and Swami Shradananda. But amongst the top Muslims, the only opposition to the Khilafatists came from none other than Mohammad Ali Jinnah. His contention was that in a secular polity, there was no place for ulema to take part in politics.

The inaugural session of the All India Khilafat Conference will be remembered primarily for the spellbinding address delivered by Maulana Hasrat Mohani, a young revolutionary from Muhammadan Anglo Oriental (MAO) College, Aligarh. His address created a deep and long-lasting impression on Gandhi, who, as earlier mentioned, was one of the participants. Maulana Mahmud-ul Hasan, who had by then, earned the title of *Sheikh-ul-Hind* (spiritual leader of India) by the ulema, had already placed his seal of legitimacy on the Khilafat Conference. He had, prior to the inaugural conference, issued a fatwa categorically justifying the call for non-cooperation with the British government in all fields of life. Even before the Non-Cooperation Movement launched by Gandhi had been accepted by the country, *Sheikh-ul-Hind* had, with all the authority which he carried, announced that it was incumbent on all true Muslims to

---

[15] Barbara D. Metcalf, *Husain Ahmad Madani: The Jihad For Islam and India's Freedom* (Oxford, England: Oneworld Publications, 2009), p. 72.

[16] Ibid., p. 73.

withdraw from all Government-supported institutions including schools, colleges and official departments. He called upon all true Muslims to discard all foreign-made goods and to use only goods made in the country.

It was this spirit of *swadeshi* and the call to boycott all foreign-made goods which found resonance in the Khilafat Movement. Gandhi was fully aware that if the MAO College responded to the call of the Khilafatists, it would mark a major victory for the non-cooperation drive. In Maulana Mahmud-ul Hasan, he found an able ally.

On 11 October 1920, Mahatma Gandhi along with Maulana Mohammad Ali, who had been released from jail shortly earlier, arrived at Aligarh. Earlier Maulana Mahmud-ul Hasan and all the top leaders of the Khilafat Movement had also arrived to witness what later turned out to be one of the most remarkable milestones in Hindu–Muslim relations during India's freedom movement.

Gandhi and most of the outstation Khilafat leaders were camping at Habib Bagh, the sprawling bungalow of Abdul Majeed Khwaja, one of the close disciples of Gandhi and a leading light of MAO College Old Boys' Association (This building presently houses the Academic Staff College of the Aligarh Muslim University).

The next day on 12 October 1920, Gandhi and Maulana Mohammad Ali had been invited to speak on the Non-Cooperation Movement at the MAO College Students' Union. This assembly at the MAO College Students' Union was under close scrutiny of the British government. The Viceroy was hopeful that the Trustees of the College who were campaigning for the upgradation of the MAO College into a full-fledged university would not allow the college community to fall prey to the designs of the Khilafatists. The government was enthused by the refusal of the Banaras Hindu University authorities led by Pandit Madan Mohan Malviya to respond to the call of Gandhi to join the Non-Cooperation Movement just a few days earlier. They were quite hopeful that the Loyalists at Aligarh would also defy Gandhi.

But destiny had willed otherwise. The stirring call by Gandhi followed by the electrifying oratory of Maulana Mohammad Ali received an overwhelming response at the Students' Union of the MAO College.

On 13 October, another historic meeting was held at MAO College.

> The hall was packed to its full. There was a big crowd in the verandah outside and even on the ground below them. Syed Noorullah described atrocities committed in the Punjab, explained the Khilafat question and appealed to non-cooperate with the government.
> A. Aziz, a barrister asked what would the students do after leaving the College and it was said that they would do Khilafat work. He asked again about the scheme of constructive work and Maulana Shaukat Ali replied that even in the absence of that scheme, Musalmans should not hesitate to sacrifice all upon religion. He asked again what would happen to the Hindu University, Maulana Mohammad Ali replied that Khilafat is the religious duty of the Muslims, the question, therefore, is irrelevant.
> 'Gandhi said he supported the Khilafat Movement because if Islam is in danger, then Hinduism shall also face a danger. Gandhi announced that despite Malviyaji's opposition, he would go to Benares and appeal to the students....'.[17]

Following these tumultuous happenings, the college Principal Dr Ziauddin declared the college closed. The students however refused to vacate the hostels. The situation was tense. Police was posted all around the campus. The fear of violence was palpable.

The Khilafatists led by Maulana Mohammad Ali decided that the only way to avoid bloodshed of innocent students was to part ways instead of confrontation. Thus was born the Jamia Millia Islamia.

The first person to bless the Jamia was none other than Maulana Mahmud-ul Hasan. On 29 October, a meeting was held at the Jama Masjid of the MAO College. It was presided over by a leading Islamic theologian of the country Maulana Abdul Bari of the Firangi Mahal School at Lucknow. But it was Maulana Mahmud-ul Hasan who was the patron saint of the Jamia Millia. The responsibility of nurturing the Jamia during its early years was left entirely in the hands of Maulana Mohammad Ali, Abdul Majeed Khwaja, Hakim Ajmal Khan and Dr Mukhtar Ahmad Ansari.

---

[17] S.M. Tonki, *Aligarh and Jamia Fight for National Education System* (New Delhi: People's Publishing House, 1983), p. 51.

In December 1921, the All India Congress convention was held at Ahmedabad. In the absence of the President C.R. Das, the session was presided over by Hakim Ajmal Khan. The Ahmedabad session was marked by the radical call for *total freedom* or *Swaraj* given by the youthful Maulana Hasrat Mohani who had earlier been expelled from the Aligarh College. (He had been actively involved in the Silk Conspiracy Case but had been arrested at an early stage while on his way to Kabul in 1916. Three years later, Mohani and other conspirators in the Silk Conspiracy, including Maulana Mohammad Ali, were released from jail.)

Maulana Mohani's stirring call for *Swaraj* was undoubtedly way ahead of the times as even Gandhi and other top Congress leaders were, at that stage, not prepared for such a radical step.

Maulana Mohani was not deterred by the refusal of the Congress leadership to accept his hardline approach. He was a man with a multifaceted personality. In his avatar as a revolutionary poet, the Maulana hid another face—a humanist who was an ardent devotee of Lord Krishna. He had penned several poems reflecting his deep love for Lord Krishna. Every year on the day of the festival of Janmashtami, the Maulana would visit Mathura, the birthplace of Lord Krishna as a mark of his deep love for the deity.

For the Indian ulema led by the likes of Maulana Mahmud-ul Hasan, the period starting from 1920 was a remarkable phase. It was an era which was never again to be repeated in the 20th century India. The Muslim ulema had arrived at a close understanding with Hindu divines under the patronage of Mahatma Gandhi. As was inevitable, this bonhomie was too good to last. Faced by the prospect of an open revolt by both Hindus and Muslims, the British government hatched a sinister plot to divide the two major communities of India on religious grounds. The birth of the Hindu Mahasabha followed shortly later by the Tableegh Movement in the Muslims can be traced to the British government's policy of encouraging differences between Hindus and Muslims. As events unfolded, it was clear that both Hindus and Muslims had swallowed the bait.

The *raison d'etre* behind the Khilafat Movement was the anger in the Muslim world against the West for trying to dismantle the institution of the Caliphate which for centuries rested in the

ruler of the Ottoman Empire. Muslims all over the world were
exercised over British attempts to demolish the Ottoman Empire
while systematically trying to end the Caliphate which was, in
a sense, the endearing symbol of Islamic religious identity. For
the world of Islam, it was almost like ending the papacy for the
Catholics.

The ground under the feet of Khilafatists however slipped
away when Kamal Ata Turk came to power in Turkey in the
aftermath of the World War II. It was Ata Turk who dealt the
final blow to the Caliphate as he strongly felt that this institution
had outlived the purpose for which it had come into existence. He
strongly felt that the Caliphate had become a decadent institution and was largely responsible of dragging back the Turkish
people from the path of modernisation and progress. For the
Indian Khilafatists, it was a deathblow.

It was during this period that violence broke out in the coastal
areas of Malabar. For all purposes, it was a peasant revolt
against the repressive measures of the landlords. A majority of
the peasants largely comprised Mopla Muslims and most of the
landlords were Hindus. The British government perceived this
situation as tailor-made for serving their objectives. This was the
beginning of a sinister phase in Hindu–Muslim relations which
lasted for nearly a decade.

Both for the Muslim ulema and Gandhi, it was a period of
introspection and in fact of catharsis.

Would the decision to mix politics with religion ultimately
prove to be correct?

The same Maulana Mohammad Ali who was placing Gandhi
on the highest pedestal had turned into his bitter critic. What
exactly went wrong?

Mohammad Noman in his *Muslim India, Rise and Growth of
All India Muslim League*, sums it up thus:

> Strictly speaking the activities of the Mussalmans were mainly
> guided by Khilafat organisations, and the leaders were mostly
> from the Jamiatul-Ulama which had also organised itself into a
> body and had started holding regular sessions every year. These
> Ulamas for the first time realised what political leadership meant.
> The Khilafat was presented before the Mussalmans as a purely
> religious question and as such their help was necessary. But they
> did not cease to function after that but began to assert themselves
> in the body politic of the country as a factor to be counted and even

its president claimed the superiority of the Jamiat over all other Muslim organisations or Conferences in India and declared that in times to come it would present a unique position in the world so as to lead Muslim opinion in religious matters, but as politics and religion were inseparable in Islam, the Jamiat was also willing to give a lead on political issues. This notion of religion and politics is today the cause of many of our troubles.[18]

Years later, Jinnah would proudly proclaim that while he stood for 'modernisation', the ulema who were supporting the Congress were 'reactionaries'. He predicted that these votaries of 'nationalism' would ultimately pay a heavy price for their follies.

What ultimately went wrong with Jinnah's Pakistan dream and what was the fate of the Khilafatist ulema in India are interlinked issues whose answers are of critical importance in the 21st century Asia.

This conflict between Westetrn educated leaders of the Muslim League and traditionalist Muslim ulema is summed up by noted historian Ziya-ul-Hasan Faruqi thus:

In short, they were incapable of giving a new interpretation to Islam. In the domain of legal code they were mentally unprepared to scrutinise the provisions of 'Hidayah' and lay down new legal norms as the basis of Islamic law. They were not even true to the traditions of Shah Waliullah in so far as his principle of 'tatbiq' is concerned. This rigid orthodoxy of theirs could not win the support of the western educated Muslims who were trained in an entirely new set of traditions. It was equally unfortunate that the latter, too, while being quite ignorant of their religious traditions, were not in a position to present a synthesis of the old and the new; none of them was intellectually fit to take up the job of a new interpretation of Islam started by Sir Sayyid and 'Islamise' it in the modern frame of reference. As a result, they also failed to produce an Islamic ideology capable of attracting people of all shades of opinion.[19]

In other words, there were serious shortcomings in the approach of both the Muslim League on one hand and the Jamiat

---

[18] Mohammad Noman, *Muslim India, Rise and Growth of the All India Muslim League* (Allahabad: Kitabistan Publishers, 1942), pp. 213–214.

[19] Ziya-ul-Hasan Faruqi, *The Deoband School and the Demand for Pakistan* (Bombay: Asia Publishing House, 1963), p. 80.

Ulema-e-Hind on the other. History has been brutal in its ret-ribution to both. But it is the people of the Indian subcontinent who are paying a price for the short-sightedness of these two Muslim groups.

The Muslim League—as we saw ultimately—bitterly failed in its attempts to create a modern IS which could serve as a role model for the rest of the Islamic world. On the other hand, the Jamiat Ulema-e-Hind leaders were not adequately equipped to draw up a viable alternative for genuine reform within the parameters of Islam which could have helped Muslim masses in facing the challenges posed by the forces of modernisation.

The Mopla riots triggered off a new, bitter phase in the his-tory of Hindu–Muslim relations in the 20th century India. It matters little if one heaps all blame on the British rulers for pouring oil on this fire. The fact remains that Gandhi and his Khilafatist comrades watched helplessly even as the flames of hatred spread like wildfire all over north India.

Maulana Mahmud-ul Hasan died when the Khilafat Movement was about to peak. Despite the storm which broke out, all his friends amongst the Khilafatists remained in his flock. The only exception being the Ali Brothers, Mohammad Ali and Shaukat Ali. But the parting of ways between the Ali Brothers and the Mahatma was a metaphor for the larger fail-ure of Gandhi's vision of a grand alliance between Hindus and Muslims to wage a common war against the colonial West.

Gandhi's efforts of fusing Khilafat and Non-Cooperation were ultimately dubbed as a failure.

But what was the rationale behind this well-intentioned and ambitious venture? In Gandhi's words:

> It is through the Khilafat that I am doing the triple duty of show-ing to the world what ahimsa really means, of uniting Hindus and Muslims and of coming in contact with one and all. And if the non-cooperation movement goes on all right, a tremendous brute-force will have to yield to an apparently simple and negli-gible power. Khilafat is the great churning process of the ocean that India is.[20]

[20] Mushirul Hasan, *Faith and Freedom—Gandhi in History* (New Delhi: Niyogi Books, 2013), p. 126.

It is difficult today to comprehend the mesmeric power which Gandhi had held over the hearts of the Muslim masses during this tumultuous period which lasted right up to the mid-1920s. Even Muslim women from traditional backgrounds were breaking barriers to join the Gandhi-led movement.

Women went as far as far as worshipping Gandhi and putting their babies on his lap. They came in thousands, often removing their age-old veils to see him, and showered their copper, silver, gold ornaments and jewels at his feet. In Panipat, Hakiman, called Hakko, calmly took off her earrings, necklace, bangles, and wristbands for the swaraj fund. In Patna, Begum Mazharul Haque gave away her four choicest bangles made up of pearls and rubies. Gandhi thanked God that He had brought him in touch with the Tyabji family. In Awadh, the gentry cast off their silks and muslins of foreign manufacture. Khadija Phupi (aunt), who was associated with Shah Abdul Haq's much-venerated shrine in Rudauli (Barabanki district), donned khaddar. Nazar Sajjad Hyder, wife of the Urdu journalist-scholar Sajjad Hyder Yildirim, gave up purdah in 1920 and wore printed khadi sarees.[21]

Amongst all the Khilafat leaders, perhaps his most ardent devotee was Maulana Mohamad Ali, a devout Muslim for whom Mahatma was like a *peer*. It was in Maulana Mohammad Ali's house in Delhi that Mahatma chose to hold his fast unto death to articulate his anguish when communal riots broke out near Peshawar in the (NWFP). It was on 8 October 1924 when the entire country stood on the brink of what seemed a continuous Hindu–Muslim confrontation in the whole of India.

To make the event worth its while, Mohammad Ali presented Gandhi, on 8 October 1924, a cow he had purchased from a butcher. Two Muslim physicians stood in constant attendance. On the twentieth day, following 'days of grace, privilege and peace,' friends prayed. On the twenty-first day, Gandhi asked Andrews, the jagatmitra (friend of all the world), to sing his favourite Christian hymn. He was at home with the best things. At the final service a hymn and an excerpt from the Upanishads were read out in the presence of Imam Sahib, Gandhi's co-prisoner in South Africa. Ansari, with his gracious and courteous bearing, offered Gandhi orange juice.[22]

[21] Ibid., p. 133.
[22] Ibid., p. 110.

While Gandhi was ready to offer the ultimate sacrifice for the cause of Hindu–Muslim unity, there was a growing section within the Congress which was becoming increasingly restless due to what they perceived was Gandhi's propensity to succumb to what they saw as Muslim aggressiveness.

> With pan-Islamism becoming increasingly inimical to political democracy, Gandhi was unable to curb the exuberance of its vocal proponents. He tried slowing them down, but without uncovering new relationships and inventing new paths. He encountered multiple sets of groups; his exchanges over conversations during the Moplah riots on 19 August 1921 illustrated that the pan-Islamists were still bound in a thousand chains. The other group from Deoband and Nadwat al-ulama was still busy using the vocabulary of political Islam to dignify their activism and image as custodians of social order.[23]

The breaking point came after the Chauri Chaura violence during the Civil Disobedience Movement. Gandhi decided to call off the movement. The Khilafatists felt a sense of betrayal:

> By suspending Civil Disobedience, Gandhi dropped a bombshell on the Ali brothers and the Muslim religious class. They felt betrayed. They knew not what to do. Instead of remaining true to their anti-colonial ideologies, which was their great strength and to which Gandhi granted much ammunition, they wanted to bask under the sunshine of the Montagu-Chelmsford Reforms and gain concessions for the religious establishment. Other than that, they turned to tabligh and tanzim, an inherently divisive preoccupation, and avoided the route to education and social reforms. The Deobandi ulama took to debating theological issues with the Arya Samaj and the Barelwis, and the Shias. They took a narrow-minded view in engaging with the Shias. They nursed each other's bigotry and with tabarra (Shia cursing the first three Khulafa) and madhe-sahaba (In praise of the Khalifa).[24]

It is true that while most of the Khilafatist leaders tried to rationalise Gandhi's sudden action, Maulana Mohammad Ali was unable to bear the shock. It was as if the very ground

[23] Ibid., p. 139.
[24] Ibid., p. 140.

under his feet had slipped away. From a passionate devotee of Mahatma, he became a bitter critic who had no other desire but to slink in his own corner. Maulana Mohammad Ali arguably, the uncrowned champion of the non-cooperation movement had become a frustrated, bitter man in his last days. It was no doubt a dark chapter in the history of Hindu–Muslim relations in the Indian subcontinent. The British took full advantage of this sharp cleavage between the two major communities, but it is equally true that despite these serious misgivings, the bulk of the Muslim Khilafatists remained steadfast in their loyalty to Gandhi.

It was a love affair which lasted till Gandhi's tragic assassination.

On hindsight, it may be said that the Khilafat Movement was doomed to failure from the very beginning. The very idea of Khilafat rested on the concept of pan-Islamism. Sooner or later, the inherent contractions were bound to surface. Its legitimacy in a modern multi-religious society was inherently questionable. Gandhi was attracted to Khilafat because it was in its essence an anti-colonial movement. He saw it as a legitimate weapon for fighting injustice. But for most of the Muslims, it was much more—it was an issue linked to the fundamental concept of Islamic brotherhood. That it worked for some time was a tribute to the moral leadership of Gandhi and some of the towering leaders within the Khilafatists. If it stumbled and collapsed, then this was primarily a result of the inevitable demise of the Caliphate in Turkey itself. A stage had arrived when the Ottoman Empire had virtually ceased to exist and the concept of 'khilafat' had little relevance in the 20th century.

The fact cannot be brushed aside that there was an influential section within the Congress which did not see eye-to-eye with Gandhi on the issue of Khilafat. The legitimate fears amongst Hindus on the likely fallout of strengthening the pan-Islamists have to be viewed with understanding.

Maulana Hussain Ahmad Madani was amongst those who stood firmly behind Gandhi through those turbulent times although he was not enamoured by the intense articulation by some of the Khilafatists. He was more interested in the task of strengthening and reforming religious institutions of the Muslims.

Immediately after his return from prison at Malta, Maulana Mahmud-ul Hasan had issued a landmark fatwa urging Muslims to totally withdraw from all British institutions and jobs. He also called for a boycott of all British-made goods. A few weeks later on 30 November 1920, the *Sheikhul Hind*, as he was known, passed away. Maulana Madani was not at Deoband when his *peer* departed from this world. The mantle of spiritual leadership of the Indian Muslims had fallen on the shoulders of Maulana Mahmud-ul Hasan's favourite disciple–Maulana Hussain Ahmad Madani.

Maulana Madani was on his way to Calcutta when he received the news of the passing away of his mentor. He immediately broke journey and returned to Deoband but was not in time to attend the funeral of his *peer*. There was now added pressure on Maulana Madani to stay on at Deoband and take over the responsibility of heading the Deoband seminary. But Maulana Madani was made of different stuff—he was determined to fulfil the task (the handling of the Calcutta madarsa which was in a state of neglect) given to him by his *peer* shortly before his demise. He refused to relent and left for Calcutta to take up this mundane responsibility. He remained aloof from the affairs of Deoband and the spotlight of the Khilafat Movement during this period.

> Maulana Madani held fast to his decision, not only to teach at a madrasa but to try to reach Muslims beyond the madrasa with a message of organisation and reform. In Bengal he would set out through the difficult terrain of fields, rivers and creeks, particularly dangerous during the rains, to preach and teach. He would, according to one biographer, arrive in a village and even if only a handful of people turned out, he would 'preach on the sunnat with the joy and enthusiasm as if it were thousands'. He was given credit for influencing some two dozen madrasas in Sylhet to offer a high level of Arabic instruction and to require Qur'anic recitation. He also used his influence to see that the students drilled in 'parade' as volunteers and, using sticks, learned the martial art of 'binaut' (Najmu'd-din Islahi 1951:49). This was typical of the physical culture and discipline that appeared within India and worldwide in the interwar years.[25]

[25] H.M. Seervai, *Partition of India—Legend and Reality* (Bombay: Emmenem Publications, 1989), p. 89.

Maulana Madani's main focus during this phase was the need for reform amongst Muslims. He spoke of the urgent need of creating an organisation which would have a disciplined cadre, trained to protect Muslims and rendering service to the Muslim masses. He advocated a drastic reduction in ostentatious expenditure in weddings and total abolition of dowry.

Maulana Madani believed that Muslims—'poor, unemployed, ignorant, oblivious, few in numbers'—were dangerously weak and that other communities would like to see 'the voice of Muslims gone from the country of India.' For him, those who were ready, as he put it, to conduct a funeral procession for Hindu-Muslim unity had forgotten that their real enemy was the British, and that Muslims themselves needed to awake if they wanted to avoid a very dark future.[26]

In the year 1927, a crisis broke out at the Deoband School following a student strike. At that time, Maulana Anwar Shah Kashmiri was the Principal. He was a leading scholar of his time but he decided that it was time he moved out of Deoband (He headed for Dhabeel in Gujarat where he set up the Darul Uloom).

The managing committee of the Deoband School, with great difficulty, managed to persuade Maulana Hussain Ahmad Madani to return from Calcutta and take up the responsibility of heading the school at this difficult juncture.

Shortly after he returned to Deoband, the Congress set up a one-member committee headed by Pandit Moti Lal Nehru to prepare a report for submission to the British government on political reforms in the country. This was known as the Nehru Report. The report kicked up a controversy amongst the Muslims.

The main features of this report were the recommendation of ending *separate electorates* and reservation of seats in the Legislature. Secondly, it sought *dominion status* for India under British rule as against the demand for *complete independence*, which was being raised by some leaders like Hasrat Mohani.

Muslims were, by and large, opposed to all the three proposals mentioned earlier. The Khilafatists including Maulana Madani were however not in favour of separate electorates because they

[26] Ibid., p. 91.

understood that the time had come for open elections. They however were not prepared to give up on the issue of reservation of seats in the legislature. They also insisted on complete independence from British rule and not the watered down version of dominion status.

Maulana Madani had now been appointed as the president of the Jamiat Ulema-e-Hind and had now become the most important Muslim cleric in India. By virtue of being the foremost ulema, he was now being increasingly referred to as *Sheikhul Islam*—the leader of the Muslims.

Maulana Madani may have reached the pinnacle of his achievements in the sphere of scholastics, but his unwavering commitment to the cause of India's freedom and Hindu–Muslim unity had also earned him the wrath of a radical section of the Muslim political leadership who scoffed at his policy of being a religious leader while simultaneously dabbling in politics.

Those who mocked at him included the Westernised barrister Mohammad Ali Jinnah, who openly displayed his contempt for the clergy while simultaneously championing the cause of Muslim identity politics. Jinnah would never lose an opportunity to show his utter disdain for the Maulvis. Maulana Madani was his favourite whipping boy along with the ubiquitous Maulana Azad.

Another critic of his who lost no opportunity of denigrating Maulana Madani was the iconic Urdu poet and philosopher Mohammad Iqbal. In fact, Iqbal went to the extent of dubbing him as a *non-believer*. For a devout Muslim, this was indeed the ultimate blow.

But Maulana Madani's travails did not end there. He was now beginning to be challenged on his own turf—by a vocal section of the ulema who attacked him by calling him a *stooge of the Congress*. The main attack came from none other than the Islamist Maulana Abul Ala Maududi who later founded the pan-Islamic party the Jamaat-e-Islami.

Maulana Madani bore all these attacks with remarkable fortitude and forbearance.

The British government was quick to seize this opening caused by the differences between the Jamiat Ulema-e-Hind and the critics of Maulana Madani. An ideal opportunity came to the government when the Round Table Conference was held in London in 1931. Gandhi was leading the Indian delegation.

He wanted some Muslims to be a part of the Congress team. Dr Mukhtar Ahmad Ansari was the President of the All India Congress Party. But the British government in including the hardliner Viceroy Lord Willingdon took the convoluted stand that no *nationalist Muslim* could negotiate on behalf of the Indian Muslims—that privilige, according to them, rested solely in the hands of the Jinnah-led Muslim League. It was *divide and rule at its worst*. The Round Table Conference failed and Gandhi returned a dejected man.

Muslim separatist politics was being fanned by the British but, as we shall see, despite all this official patronage, the Muslim masses were still with the Congress.

Maulana Madani was amongst those Muslims who were building an ideological framework for secular Muslim politics.

His detailed letters to some of his protégées provide an in-depth look into his ideological moorings in that critical phase.

In a letter to Hafiz Mohammad Siddiq, he explained:

Thus it is the duty of all Muslims of India that to liberate this country from the hegemony of the British infidels, they should use every possible instrument at their disposal—from boycott to the armed struggle. In view of the current political situation and united Muslim strength, it is the consensus of Ulama and experts that since Muslims do not possess the required strength and power to overthrow the present government, it is the religious obligation of every Muslim to strive against it in a peaceful manner. However, if Muslims at this point of time fight single-handedly against the British, their defeat is certain. And it is also certain that Muslims will have to bear the political and economic consequences of such an act. Thus to make the peaceful agitation against the government successful, it is necessary that other communities living in India also join hands. Due to the united struggle of different communities, when India shall achieve freedom and a new system will be established, Muslims and non-Muslims together shall participate in forming this system. Although the new system would not be totally based on Islamic principles, Muslims will have an effective role in it. How much closer to the Islamic standard can they mould this system now depends upon the Muslims' tact of propagation.[27]

[27] Maulana Syed Mohammad Mian, *The Prisoners of Malta* (*Asira'n-e-Malta*), translated by Mohammad Anwer Hussain and Hasan Imam (New Delhi: Jamiat Ulama-i-Hind in association with Manak Publications Pvt. Ltd., 2005), p. 154.

Explaining his aversion for the colonial policy of the British, he wrote in another letter addressed to Hafiz Siddiq:

Ever since Islam's inception, the British have inflicted losses (so many) on Muslims that no other nation has ever done in history. For more than two hundred years, the British have been systematically destroying Islam. They destroyed the Muslim power in India. They massacred kings and aristocrats. They destroyed Islamic governments and decimated their armies. They introduced currency of their sovereign rule after destroying the Muslims' one, enforced their laws and destroyed the Indian culture, commerce, industry, craftsmanship, education and civilization. Through taxes they looted Indian peasants, made their country rich and India a wretched and bankrupt country. They made Indians, and especially Muslims, helpless, jobless and dishonoured. They sowed the seeds of malicious feelings between Muslims and non-Muslims and stoked the fires of hatred. While on one hand they opposed Islamic laws, on the other they spread the culture of drinks and drugs, debauchery and prostitution. They introduced the law opposed to Islamic tenets, and while describing the department of administration of Islamic law as in contravention of the English laws, they tore down the provision of special law for Muslims. They intentionally encouraged Hindus and employed them in every department and organization, and implemented the culture of interest upon interest. In short, by every available means and ways, they destroyed Muslims in India.[28]

He further continued:

In the declaration of 1858, the Queen Victoria had promised that Britain would not extend its dominion and it was not going to conquer territory any further. But within a small span of 20 years, she got Afghanistan attacked repeatedly and spilled the blood of thousands of innocent Muslims. The British attacked Afghanistan four times and went on usurping the territory of autonomous areas of Muslims such as Suwat, Baeer, and Chitral, and Kohat, territories inhabited by Afridi tribe and Masudi tribe and so on. What crime and barbarism they didn't commit in Baluchistan! Just opposite to what was promised by the Queen, dominion was extended and territories annexed. Residents were enslaved and the freedom-loving Afghans who refused to be subjugated to slavery were done away with swords and bullets.

[28] Ibid., pp. 163–164.

You see the history of your own area. All these happened in areas and countries around India. And the slave Indian army, Indian money and materials perpetrated all these.

Along with it, they destroyed Iraq, Syria, Egypt, Palestine, Somalia, Eastern Africa, Sudan and Burma where Islam was spreading. They subjugated the Ottoman Empire and invaded cities such Hejaz, Jeddah, Mecca, Madina and perpetrated barbaric crimes in cities such as Chinaque, Simarna and Istanbul. Rivers of blood were flown in these cities. And above all, they divided the Islamic countries among European powers. Tripoli, Libya and Adriana etc were given away to Italy, Reef to Spain; Algeria, Tunis, Persia, Morocco etc to France, Central Asian and North Asian countries such as Bukhara, Samarkand, Kirghizstan, Daghestan and Kazakhstan etc to Russia. Bulgaria, Greece, Macedonia, Romania, Albania, Serbia, Montenegro, Croatia and Bosnia, were forcefully made independent from Turkey and went on destroying the Islamic power. History is full of such heart-rending and mind-boggling plays enacted during three hundred years, between 1640 and 1940. And the British government was always the major role player in one act or the other. Now you tell me, which other nation on earth has proved greater enemy of Islam and Muslims than the British?[29]

His views on the future of Hindu–Muslim unity are also elaborated in the same letter:

Hindus were subjects under Muslim rule for a thousand and little more years. It was the British who taught them lessons in hatred and brought them forward (against the Muslims). Thus, you should ponder upon whether you want to destroy and diminish the power of the British or of the Hindus. To keep power and to continue their commerce, it is essential for the British to keep the long strait till the coastal area of Bombay in their custody. They would like to maintain peace on this route so that this vital commercial sea route is not disturbed. And for this reason, it is necessary for them to keep Atlantic Ocean, Bahrein, Red Sea, Indian Ocean, and Persian Ocean in their possession so that the sea and air route from London to India is trouble free. If they fail to maintain centres and warehouses along this route, they cannot achieve their purpose. And thus, the British government subjected all the countries that fall under this route to hardship. For this, Indian soldiers were used. Hindus do not need to enslave these countries and rule over them. Hindus are not powerful

[29] Ibid., p. 165.

today as the British are. Therefore, in the past, present and in the future, the greatest enemy is the British. Regarding Hindus, it can be said that in the future they too could possibly become like the British or even more cruel. But this matter is imaginary at this stage. It is for this reason that the nobles of Islam felt it necessary to destroy British hegemony and get liberated first. For this purpose, the Congress Party was formed and Muslims joined it. And for this purpose, Jamiat Ulama-i-Hind is acting in partnership with them.[30]

Shortly after the return of Gandhi from England, he was arrested on 4 January 1933. The Congress launched another Civil Disobedience Movement to protest against the high-handed behaviour of the government. The Congress Party was declared illegal and all top leaders were arrested. The Congress resorted to a novel method of confronting the government. Every time the top leaders of the Party were arrested, the Party would announce a new team of office bearers. This tactic was very effective as the spate of arrests was having no effect on the movement. The Jamiat Ulema-e-Hind followed the tactic and the same drama was repeated with the followers of the Jamiat.

How could the Jamiat leaders escape the honour of imprison-ment! The Jamiat too resorted to nomination of dictators. On a day fixed for the meeting and protest, the 'dictator' would reach the place and address the gathering. The police would arrive at the scene and baton-charge the procession and the public meet-ing. The dictator, who carried the party flag in the hand, would be arrested. Often it happened that as soon as the dictator was nominated, the police pounced and arrested him. They did not allow the procession or the meeting to take place.

Maulana Hussain Ahmad Madani was the sixth dictator of Jamiat Ulama. In July 1932, corresponding to Rabiul Awwal 1351 Hijri, Maulana's turn came. He took the morning train to Delhi. As per the programme, he was to address the people at Jama Masjid after Juma prayer. The police also boarded the train at Saharanpur. There was a large crowd at Deoband station to greet Maulana, so the police refrained from action. However, at the next Rohana station, the deputy superintendent of police presented Maulana a notice, which was in English. Maulana said he did not know English. The DSP asked for his pen so that

[30] Ibid., p. 166.

he could translate the notice for him in Urdu. Maulana poked fun at him saying that he was asking for a knife from him to cut his throat. The DSP kept quiet and left. Later, when the train stopped at Muzaffarnagar station, the DSP presented to Maulana Madani the translated version of the notice. Maulana saw that the notice was signed by the district magistrate of Saharanpur, and told the DSP that he was away from territorial jurisdiction of the district magistrate of Saharanpur. The district magistrate of Muzaffarnagar was present there. He wrote the notice on his behalf and handed it over to Maulana. Thus, Maulana was taken away from the train and could not reach Delhi. The day passed and another 'dictator' was nominated. Later on, Maulana was released.

This act of Maulana was no less than Jihad as at that time he was suffering from a severe wound on his leg. It was extremely difficult for him to walk even a few steps. The wound had so worsened that others could not bear to see it while dressing was being done. Maulana would be so calm as if it were not his but someone else's wound was being treated.[31]

As the year 1936 began, it was apparent that Mohamad Ali Jinnah was becoming increasingly uncomfortable with the conservative elements mostly from the landed classes within his own party. He started making overtures to the Jamiat leaders led by Maulana Madani who he realised enjoyed popular support amongst the Muslim masses. Maulana Madani was pleasantly surprised by what apparently seemed to be a welcome change of heart and responded positively to Jinnah's overtures. In Maulana Madani's own words which he recorded in a short 40-page booklet:

> Around the year 1936, Mr Jinnah made efforts to revive the Muslim League. He was tired of the conservative elements in the League, and thus he made unity and partnership with the Jamiat Ulama, Ahrar and other progressive parties.[32]

Jinnah had assured Maulana Madani:'Concerning all matters in the State Assembly, the Muslim League will co-operate with the Congress and remain with the Congress.'[33]

[31] Ibid., pp. 151–152.
[32] Ibid., p. 173.
[33] Ibid., p. 173.

This was a key moment in the history of the 20th century Muslim separatism in India. It certainly could have been a turning point in the country's freedom movement. The bonhomie between Jinnah and the nationalist Jamiat leaders lasted several months before the relationship turned sour once again. The breakup came shortly after the election of 1937. It is a phase which has strangely enough drawn scant attention of historians.

The factors which led to this parting of ways, as would unfold later, can be traced to the haughty utterances of some top Congress leaders after the landslide victory in the state elections, especially in the United Provinces. This added to the growing suspicion in the minds of the Muslim League leaders regarding the influence of the Hindu Mahasabha on the Congress leadership. To add to this was the failure of Jinnah to fulfil his commitments to the Jamiat leaders regarding the functioning of the Unity Board which had been established to formalise the joint strategy of the Muslim League and the Jamiat Ulema-e-Hind.

Maulana Madani has narrated the sequence of events thus:

> Mr. Jinnah talked to me for a few hours and impressed upon me his request for co-operation. He said that he was tired of conservative elements in the Muslim League and slowly and gradually wanted to kick them out and replace them with the freedom loving and progressive people, and so, we should join it. I asked him what would happen if he failed to kick them out. He told me that if he failed to do so, he would leave the Muslim League and join the Jamiat.[34]

> Unfortunately, however, in its first session at Lucknow after the electoral success, the League broke its commitment made in its manifesto. Strong efforts were made to induct those conservatives, sycophants and the stooges of the British who were often condemned and about whom we were told that they would be kicked out from the League. Moreover, people knew about these elements who had spent whole lives opposing the national movements and serving the interests of the British government. Mr. Jinnah was told then and there that he had promised to remove these elements from the League, but he himself was making efforts to place them in the party.[35]

[34] Ibid., p. 174.
[35] Ibid., pp. 174–175.

The elections to the state legislatures in the year 1937 were significant for the message they gave: the Muslims of India were with the Nationalist parties led by the Congress. The total number of the Muslim seats in the country was 485. The Muslim League could win only 108 seats. The Congress had contested just 58 seats and secured 26 seats. The rest of the Muslim seats were won by an assortment of Muslim parties.

But for Jinnah the results of the 1937 elections proved another setback in a career marked more by snakes than by ladders. In the Punjab, the unionists swept the board; in Bengal, Jinnah and the League had to accept a coalition led by Huq who did not acknowledge their writ; in Sind they faced an independent ministry; in the N.W.F.P., where almost the entire population was Muslim, the worst humiliation of all, a Congress ministry. In each of the majority provinces, Jinnah's strategy had been repudiated by the voters' choice. In the Muslim-minority provinces, where the League did best, the Congress did much better than anyone had expected, and did not need the League's help to form stable ministries. Despite a measure of argument with Jinnah about the future shape of the centre, the Congress High Command could now plausibly do without the League; understandings with the League were, in the aftermath of the 1937 elections, the expenditure of the expendable. Rejected by the Muslim provinces, the League had nothing to offer the Congress at the centre; so in the provinces where it had won comfortable majorities the Congress saw no reason to dilute its control by giving the League a share of office. The way in which the Muslim vote had split in the elections of 1937 lent some credence to the old Congress line that it was a secular party, ready and able to speak for Muslims, many of whom had entered its camp. Indeed, the Congress now saw the possibility of breaking the grip of rival political groups in the provincial assemblies.[36]

The Muslim League, which had performed relatively better in Muslim minority states, such as UP, was desperate to hide its loss of face by entering into a coalition with the Congress in those states.

[36] Ayesha Jalal, *The Sole Spokesman—Jinnah, the Muslim League and the Demand for Pakistan* (New Delhi: Cambridge University Press, 1994), pp. 35, 38.

The Congress, however, spurned this olive branch.

The Congress decided to have homogenous ministries of its own and chose Muslim ministers from among those who were members of the Congress party. This was the beginning of a serious rift between the Congress and the League and was a factor which induced neutral Muslim opinion to turn to the support of Jinnah.[37]

Maulana Azad in his 'India wins Freedom' wrote:

If the U.P. League's offer of co-operation had been accepted, the Muslim League party would for all practical purposes have merged in the Congress. Jawaharlal's action gave the Muslim League in the U.P. a new lease of life...it was from the U.P. that the league was reorganised. Mr. Jinnah took full advantage of the situation and started an offensive which ultimately led to Pakistan.[38]

The tipping point was reached when none other than Jawaharlal Nehru finally put the seal on the issue by his controversial declaration:

'There are only two forces in India today, British Imperialism and Indian Nationalism as represented by the Congress.'[39]

This imperious rhetoric infuriated Jinnah, whose frustration and fury was rising by the hour.

What was Maulana Hussain Ahmad Madani's response to this embittering of relations between Jinnah and the Congress?

The Muslim League intensified their personal attacks on him. The League leaders understood that perhaps more than Maulana Azad, it was Maulana Madani's opposition which was the biggest stumbling block in their path. Maulana Madani had by this time reconciled himself to the fact that there could be no understanding with Jinnah, who he felt was *not true to his word.*

He responded to the mounting attacks against him by adopting an attitude of calm resignation. He was becoming increasingly aware of the enormous challenge which he and his associates of the Jamiat were facing. There was a certain spiritual core

---

[37] H.M. Seervai, *Partition of India: Legend and Reality* (Bombay: Emmenem Publications, 1989), p. 20.

[38] Maulana Abul Kalam Azad, *India Wins Freedom—An Autobiographical Narrative* (Calcutta: Orient Longmans Private Ltd., 1959), p. 161.

[39] H.M. Seervai, *Legend and Reality* (Bombay: Emmenem Publications, 1989), p. 20.

in him which remained untouched by the rough and tumble of politics. It was this spiritual dimension which was revered by his countless *mureeds* (spiritual disciples). For them, his word was the gospel truth. Clad in the traditional kurta pyjama attire of the clerics of north India he stood in total contrast to the highly westernised Mohammad Ali Jinnah.

His close disciple Maulana Mohammad Mian wrote a booklet *Muijahid-e-Jalil* in which he vividly describes Maulana Madani's simple lifestyle:

> Maulana Madani arose before dawn for the first prayer, followed by an hour of Qur'an recitation and study. He then breakfasted with any guests before teaching the seminary students and carrying out his obligations as principal until noon. After lunch, a short nap, and the noon prayer, he dealt with mail and met additional visitors until the afternoon prayer, and then would promptly return to his hadith classes until the sunset prayer, followed by an hour of supererogatory prayers. He would dine with guests until the time of the night prayer, at which time he would commence a three-hour class on Bukhari Sharif, one of the primary texts of hadith, typically attended by about 250 Indian and foreign students. He regularly performed the extra late night tahajjud prayer and used those quiet hours for zikr as well. Many readers of the pamphlet would recognize even from the schedule that Maulana Madani modeled the life of the Prophet.[40]

On 16 September 1939, the working committee of the Jamiat Ulema-e-Hind met at Meerut and passed a resolution opposing the British government's efforts to involve Indians in the war effort. The resolution, which was the brainchild of Maulana Madani was, in substance, a call for *non-cooperation* with the British war effort.

The address delivered by Maulana Madani on this occasion sums up his entire philosophy. The Maulana defined his approach towards colonialism saying:

> Gentlemen! The current situation places greater responsibility on us that we should make relentless effort so that the entire humanity, especially the people residing in India, is rescued from all sorts of brutality. Not only our slavery is harmful and

---

[40] Barbara D. Metcalf, *Husain Ahmad Madani: The Jihad For Islam and India's Freedom* (Oxford, England: Oneworld Publications), p. 127.

calamitous for us; there are many other nations that are suffering due to this effect.[41]

This was followed by the enunciation of his vision of jihad. He declared:

> When any of you happens to see a wrong being committed, he should stop it by hand; and if he can't, he should oppose it with his tongue. And if he can't do even this, he should disdain from within his heart. This is the weakest form of Ima'n.[42]

Expressing his views on composite nationalism, he stated:

> We, the residents of India, being Indians have something in common that remains along with the religious and cultural differences. It is like our human mélange does not change just because of variance in our visages, differences in our personalities and traits, and differences in our colour and stature. Likewise, our religious and cultural differences do not become hurdle in our national partnership. From the point of view of nationality, we all are Indians. Therefore, to think of the benefit of the country and concern for its protection from any harm is the equal responsibility of Muslims as of any other nation and religious entity.[43]

The Congress Party decided that all Congress-led governments would resign as a gesture of defiance against the British government. The Muslim League, however, decided to offer cooperation to the government. The war had thus become an issue of communal divisiveness.

On 24 March 1940, the Muslim League at its annual session held at Lahore first adopted its proposal for the creation of the state of Pakistan.

The final chapter in the history of India's freedom struggle had begun.

The Quit India Movement was launched by the Congress in 1942. It was a movement of passive resistance.

Maulana Madani plunged into the movement with full gusto, delivering speeches all over the country. The government became

---

[41] Tariq Hasan, *The Aligarh Movement and the Making of the Indian Muslim Mind 1857–2002* (New Delhi: Rupa & Co., 2006), p. 200.

[42] Ibid.

[43] Ibid., pp. 202–203.

increasingly alarmed by the response which Maulana Madani was evoking in the masses.

It was only a matter of time before the government decided to arrest Maulana once again. The sequence leading to his internment is narrated by his disciple and biographer Maulana Syed Mian thus:

> The district unit of the Jamiat Ulama-i-Hind organised a conference at Bachraon village, district Amroha, United Provinces on April 23–25, 1942. Shaikhul Islam had taken the government permission to attend the conference. He invariably spoke the same thing he used to speak at public meetings. Since the policy of the government had changed now, it arranged to obtain a copy of his speech. A case was filed against him and a warrant issued for his arrest. Since it was not advisable to arrest him in Deoband, the administration waited for him to leave Deoband. While on his way to Punjab to attend a 'Unity Conference' on June 24, 1942, Maulana was arrested at Telhari station (situated between Deoband and Saharanpur) around two past mid-night.
>
> The Inspector of Police entered in the bogey and presented him with the arrest warrant. Maulana was detained at the Saharanpur police station for the night. He was sent to Moradabad in the morning. The telegram sent by Jamiat members of Saharanpur to the Jamiat office in Moradabad was handed over to the addressee when Maulana reached Moradabad in police custody and was taken to jail.[44]

The Maulana was given a sentence of 18 months of rigorous imprisonment. His lawyers applied for bail but the district authorities let it be known that if the magistrate did grant him bail he would be re-arrested under the defence of India rules.

He was kept in a solitary cell in Moradabad Jail. It was a cell which was normally designated for those prisoners who were to be executed. It was rumoured that this cell was haunted by the spirits of those had been executed in those premises.

As the Quit India Movement gathered momentum in Moradabad district, the authorities cracked down on the protestors. A large number of arrests were made and all of them were interned in the Moradabad jail. Maulana, however, had some welcome company in his detention cell. Almost all the internees

[44] Ibid., pp. 206–207.

were members of the Jamiat Ulema-e-Hind including its chief organiser Maulana Hifzur Rehman.

In January 1943, Maulana Madani was to be released. However, instead of being released, he was informed that he would be shifted to Naini Jail in Allahabad. All other political detainees were deeply upset on hearing this news:

> All prison mates considered Maulana their guide. Maulana Madani's love and affection so overwhelmed them that for a while they forgot their near and dear ones. Besides Muslims, even Hindus had affection and and reverence for him. The Hindus who loved him were supporters of the Congress. Jail wardens and officers also used to respect him. Many a time, faced with personal problems or difficulties, they would request Maulana to pray for them. They had often witnessed the result of his 'Dua' and their reverence for him increased many fold.[45]

On 24 January, Maulana Madani arrived at Naini Jail. His sadness at leaving his close associates at Moradabad of whom he had grown quite fond was to some extent mitigated by the fact that amongst the large number of detainees at Naini Jail were some prominent Muslim clerics of eastern UP, which included Maulana Syed Shahid Faaqri of Allahabad, Maulana Abdul Qayuom from Lucknow and Maulana Abdul Bari from Gorakhpur.

Shortly after Maulana Madani arrived at Naini Jail, an incident took place which led to quite a stir. It so transpired that one day, the Maulana was indisposed and was unable to present himself for the daily roll call. The Jailer came to know of this and without knowing the exalted status, which the Maulana had in the eyes of his followers all over the country, used insulting language to reprimand Maulana for this minor lapse. The incident led to a furore and was widely reported in newspapers. When the government realised that the situation could worsen, the Jailer was made to tender a public apology. This belated gesture however did not appear to quell the rising tempers of the jail inmates. The Maulana's riled up supporters made it clear that nothing short of the suspension of the Jailer would mollify them. Maulana, however, chose to pacify them.

[45] Ibid., p. 209.

He announced that there was no need to keep the matter on the boil and persuaded them to end their protest.

After spending more than two years in jail, Maulana Madani was finally released on 6 August 1943. The long internment had however taken a heavy toll on his health. He had lost nearly 40 kg weight. Doctors warned him that if he did not take adequate rest and care, his health would worsen.

But this was no time for Maulana to enjoy some well-deserved rest. India's century-long quest for freedom from British rule was reaching its climax. The Maulana and other members of the Muslim clergy associated with the Jamiat Ulema-e-Hind and some Muslim organisations, such as the Muslim Majlis, were growing increasingly restive as they had sensed that their ally—the INC—was succumbing to the pressures of the Indian Muslim League which was determined to partition the country.

It is important to point out that apart from the Muslim League, Maulana Madani was at this stage facing stiff opposition from a growing section of the ulema. From the ranks of the Deoband ulema, Madani was challenged by the renowned scholar Maulana Ashraf Ali Thanvi. His criticism of Madani was academic. The strongest opposition, however, came from a person who was not formally from the ranks of the ulema but who ultimately became the founder ideologue of the 20th century Islamic revivalism—the ultimate Islamist of his age: Maulana Abul Ala Mawdudi. It was he who founded the Jamat-e-Islami in 1941 to confront the pluralistic agenda of Maulana Madani.

Mawdudi was born at Aurangabad in the state of Hyderabad. It is known that he participated in the Khilafat Movement in 1920 and wrote articles in support of the Congress. After the abrupt end of the Khilafat Movement, Mawdudi like Mohammad Ali and some other prominent Muslims moved away from Gandhi. The launching of the *Shudhi* Movement and Gandhi's perceived proximity to some Hindu hardliners within the Congress party led to a metamorphosis of Mawdudi. Within the next 10 years or so, he had become the world's leading proponent for establishing a political order based on an Islamic world order. He also sought to reinvent the concept of jihad. His was an aggressive ethical jihad through which he primarily attacked the modernists belonging to his own faith. His aggressive jihad did not imply use of violence to overthrow hostile regimes.

(His party, the Jamat-e-Islami of Pakistan, after his death, supported a militant version of jihad to rally the Afghan mujahideen in their battle against the Soviet-backed regime in Afghanistan. This bigoted version of jihad took birth during the regime of President Zia-ul Haq of Pakistan. It was nurtured with fatal consequencies in the proliferating madarsas funded by American agencies which served as nurseries for raising jihadi cadres.)

The birth of the Jamat-e-Islami marked an important phase in the history of the 20th century Muslim religious movements in India. But the role of the Jamat-e-Islami only gathered momentum after the creation of Pakistan. In the runup to the freedom of India, it was the Jamiat Ulema-e-Hind which held centrestage.

Historians have somehow failed to highlight one salient feature of this critical phase in Indian history: the nationalist Muslims led by Maulana Madani, Maulana Azad, Maulana Hifzur Rehman and Khan Abdul Ghaffar Khan (the man known as Frontier Gandhi) were the last people in India to accept the partition of India.

Behind this fissiparous history lies a definate pattern—the role of some of those who fought against the move for portioning India till the bitter end has not drawn the attention which it deserved. Their contributions to the freedom movement and the credit which they deserved have been appropriated by others.

On 31 January 1945, a general body meeting of the Jamiat Ulema-e-Hind was held at Saharanpur town. It was chaired by Maulana Madani. This meeting drew up a charter opposing the creation of a Muslim homeland as advocated by the Muslim League.

The Jamiat Ulema-e-Hind's proposals found no takers within the Congress Party as they found some of the suggestions to be impractical. It turned out to be an exercise in futility.

Maulana Madani started hectic consultations with his colleagues to arrive at some compromising solution which would take the winds out of the sails of the League's demands and its growing popularity amongst the Muslim elite. Consequently, all Nationalist Muslim organisations decided to put up a final fight against the Muslim League by calling an All India Conference of leading Muslims, especially those representing the ulema.

On 19 September 1945, about 200-odd Muslim leaders including about 125 of those from the Jamiat Ulema-e-Hind met in a house in old Delhi. This meeting concluded on an impassioned appeal by Maulana Madani to somehow prevent the partition of India. In his speech, Maulana declared:

> Through the scheme of Pakistan, the gulf of aversion is being made. We should try to bridge this gulf. The propagation of Islam should not be confined to one territory. The sacrifices and relentless efforts of our ancestors have established Muslims' rights in every nook and corner of India. To maintain this and, rather than relinquish, to spread it further is our duty today.[46]

It was a very challenging period for Maulana Madani. Some of his close associates parted ways with him to express their disapproval of the Congress Party's approach on the question of Muslim participation in the scheme of things in post-independence India. Amongst the Deoband ulema who left the Jamiat Ulema-e-Hind at this juncture were Maulana Mufti Mohammad Shafi, Chief Mufti of the theological school and Maulana Shabbir Ahmad.

The elections to the state assemblies and the central legislature resulted in a near total victory of the Muslim League in all seats reserved for Muslims. Maulana Madani who had campaigned tirelessly for the Congress candidates in the Muslim seats was deeply upset by the manner in which the official machinery, particularly in the sensitive state of Bengal, had shown bias in favour of the Muslim League. Reacting sharply to these events, the Maulana issued a statement saying:

> There seems a deliberate conspiracy in the government's failure to maintain law and order during the elections. The conspiracy was quite apparent in Bengal. In many incidents, the government machinery openly sided with the Muslim League. A majority of Muslim officials had adopted an approach that made it difficult to differentiate whether they were government officials or workers of the Muslim League. Their approach and actions were such that they make the election results doubtful. For this reason, it is being alleged that at several places bogus votes were inserted into the ballot boxes. Candidates were constricted in their movement

[46] Ibid., p. 246.

from one place to another, which is an essential part of an election campaign. Polling booths became the centre of violence and
hooliganism. Votes were not cast in secrecy. Polling agents of other
parties were intimidated and were not allowed to work properly.[47]

There is strong evidence to suggest that the nationalist
Muslims including, ironically, the Congress President Maulana
Azad himself, felt that even Nehru was falling in line with
the stand articulated mainly by Sardar Patel on the issue of
having a strong centre and diluting the powers of the states.
This approach was adopted despite warnings by leaders such
as Maulana Madani that its ultimate consequence would be
the partition of the country. Azad, along with all Muslim
nationalist groups, was desperately trying to work out some
compromising solution which would force the Muslim League
to reconsider its demand of a separate homeland. Azad is on
record to have stated:

> There is at least one proposal in the Sapru Committee's Report,
> which deserves consideration though it has been overlooked in
> the heat of controversy. The report had visualised a Central
> Government in which Hindus and Muslims would be in equality
> but on the basis of joint electorates. Personally (he) felt that this
> proposal should be considered further.[48]

The Government of Great Britain finally constituted a committee referred to as the *Cabinet Mission* to work out the modali-
ties for granting freedom to India. It was a watershed event in
the run-up to India's freedom. Apart from meeting leaders of the
Indian National Congress, the Cabinet Mission—much to the
disproval of Mohammad Ali Jinnah—decided to seek the suggestions of the nationalist Muslim groups.

These organisations had succeeded in convincing the government that the Jinnah-led Muslim League should not be
considered as the sole spokesman of the Muslims. They sought
to assert that while Jinnah might have enjoyed the overwhelming support from the Muslim elite—the zamindars, business

---

[47] Ibid., p. 241.
[48] H.M. Seervai, *Partition of India—Legend and Reality*, (Emmenem
Publications, Bombay, 1889), p. 42.

class professionals and the urban middle class, the rest of the Muslims including peasants, farmers and the working class were not enamoured of Jinnah. It was this section which formed the majority of the total population but was not a part of the electoral system. Their voice had been snuffed out. The vocal Mulim elite and middle class particularly in states like UP and Bihar had captured the centre stage.

Five prominent Muslims, representing different Muslim organisations, were selected to present the viewpoint of the nationalist Muslims before the members of the Cabinet Mission.

The members of this delegation were Maulana Madani on behalf of the All India Muslim Parliamentary Board, Abdul Majeed Khwaja representing the Muslim Majlis, an umbrella organisation of more than a dozen organisations, Hooseinbhoy Lalji representing the All India Shia Conference and Zahiruddin representing the All India Momin Conference.

Maulana Madani was the main interlocutor on behalf of the nationalist Muslims. He presented a compromise formula before the members of the Cabinet Mission. The highlights of the Madani formula were:

1. Hindu–Muslim parity in the Central Assembly
2. Autonomy to the states
3. No separate electorates

The final recommendations of the Cabinet Mission broadly reflected the suggestions made by the nationalist group.

Significantly enough, both the Congress leadership led by Nehru and Patel on one side and the Muslim League on the other rejected the Cabinet Mission proposals.

The well-known journalist Durga Das, who was an eyewitness to the entire drama of the run-up to the partition, has presented a vivid description of how Jinnah succumbed to the manipulations of a British official who managed to convince him that he should not be tempted by a compromise formula when the British 'were ready to give him a separate Pakistan'. Thus ended what can be described as the last chance to prevent the break-up of India—an abortive stand in which the nationalist Muslims fought almost alone along with Mahatma Gandhi.

The Last Battle

The almost forgotten saga of this heroic attempt is recorded in some letters exchanged between Gandhiji and the above-mentioned Muslim leaders. There are also some personal records and memoirs which trace these events.

This writer's uncle Dr Raveend Khwaja (Rasheed Bilal Khwaja) is a living witness to some of these revealing incidents, as he would often accompany his father Abdul Majeed Khwaja during his visits to Gandhiji.

'Gandhiji realised that the Nationalist Muslims who were representing a large number of social, religious and political organisations led by the Muslim Majlis were getting increasingly frustrated by the apparent failure of the Congress leadership to resist the surge of the Muslim League',[49] recounts Raveend Khwaja

In a letter to Abdul Majeed Khwaja, Gandhiji wrote:

> I wish that Maulana Sahib and certain other friends, particularly Maulvi Hifzur Rehman Sahib, Mufti Kifayatullah Sahib and Maulana Syed Ahmad Sahib, would take the trouble of meeting me here. I would try to clear their doubts. We can all work together and pray to God to show us the straight path of freedom.[50]

The nationalist Muslims were also not comfortable with Sardar Patel's hard line on some issues.

Raveend Khwaja relates one such incident which he vividly recollects.

> It was some time in the year 1946. My father had an appointment with Gandhiji. Since we had arrived early, we were strolling on the path leading to the bungalow where Gandhiji was staying. I shortly noticed that Sardar Vallabh Bhai Patel, who also had an appointment with Gandhiji. On seeing us, Patel greeted my father and moved forward to shake hands with him. To my surprise my father refused to shake hands with Patel and politely told him that he was too hurt by his statement, which had appeared in that day's Hindustan Times pertaining

[49] Interview with Dr Raveend Khwaja by author, December 1914.

[50] Ministry of Information and Broadcasting, *The Collected Works of Mahatma Gandhi* (Government of India: Publication Division), p. 376.

to Indian Muslims. The Sardar was taken aback and did not respond immediately. He indicated that he would discuss the matter later with my father.

A few minutes later, A.M. Khwaja and his son were called in to meet Gandhi, Raveend Khwaja continued: After discussing a few things with Gandhiji, my father told him that it would be better if the remaing discussion took place in front of Sardar Patel Sahib who was waiting outside. Gandhiji immediately nodded his approval. After Sardar Patel was ushered in, my father pointed out to Gandhiji that a statement had appeared that day in which Sardar Patel had been quoted saying that 'the Muslims of India could no longer be trusted'. My father, in a voice choked with emotion, asked Gandhiji, 'With such statements how do you expect the nationalist Muslims to react'. For a few moments Gandhi just kept quiet. Then in a low voice he asked Patel, 'Is this true?' Sardar Patel who was in a very embarrassing position mumbled a few words saying, 'I have been misquoted'. Gandhiji told Patel that his statement was bound to hurt the sentiments of the nationalist Muslims and it would be appropriate if he would clear this misunderstanding.[51]

This exchange between Gandhi and Patel is a minor episode but is a pointer to the uneasy relationship between Patel and the nationalist Muslims. Two years later, shortly after the Mahatama's assassination, it was Nehru who confronted Patel when the latter in his capacity as Home Minister of India issued a circular to all government departments to weed out Muslims as they would pose a threat to the state because of their possible disloyalty to the fledgling country. Nehru is reported to have cautioned Patel that such witch hunting of Muslims could backfire, particularly when India was trying to settle the vexed issue of Kashmir and all such attempts would further exacerbate the bitterness between Hindus and Muslims.

The founder of the pharmaceutical company Cipla, Dr K.A. Hamied in his book *A Life to Remember* also poignantly recounts the dilemma of the nationalist Muslims when it finally dawned upon them that the Congress leadership had succumbed to the demand for partioning the country. Hamied, it may be mentioned, belonged to a staunch nationaist family and had contested the 1936 elections for the Bombay State Legislatue

[51] Ibid., pp. 235–236.

and had defeated the Muslim League candidate. He had started
Cipla the same year. Gandhi was very fond of him and would
visit him whenever he was in town. Hamied writes:

> I went to Delhi to meet Mahatmaji, where I met him with my
> uncle, Mr Khwaja an old and one of the most trusted associates of
> Gandhiji. Among the people present in the shack with Mahatma
> Gandhi was Sardar Patel. I asked Mahatmaji as to how he could
> agree to this partition. I remember the exact words of Gandhiji.
> He replied in Hindustani which I quote:
>   'Who listens to Gandhi now? You must ask Nehru and Patel
> about the partition. The country has been doomed.'[52]

Hamied further writes:

> I asked Sardar Patel as to why for such an important decision
> to divide India, he did not hold a plebiscite, if not of all the
> people, but at least among the Muslims. Sardar Patel replied,
> 'Dr. Hamied, you know very well that all Muslims would have
> voted for Pakistan. Hence I considered that plebiscite amongst the
> Muslims was not necessary'. I replied, 'In the election in 1946, 36%
> of the Muslims voted against Jinnah's Muslim League and your
> contention, Sardar Patel, and Pandit Nehru's that all Muslims
> would have voted for Pakistan is not correct.[53]

As observed by Barbara Metcalf, the nationalist Muslims
were steadfast in their opposition to partition, when all others
had abandoned such efforts.

The Partition of India in 1947 was undoubtedly one of the major
catastrophes to have struck Asia in the 20th century. More than
a million lost their lives and many more were rendered homeless
almost overnight. For nationalist Muslims and all those Muslims
especially in north India who had no intention of leaving their
birthplace, the tragic course of events had an added dimension.
Huddled together in Muslim-dominated areas in cities and small
towns; millions watched helplessly as the leaders belonging to
organisations like the Jamiat Ulema-e-Hind pleaded with them
not to leave India despite the plunder and mayhem.

[52] Ibid., p. 238.
[53] Ibid., pp. 238–239.

In the terrible days following the partition, Maulana Madani was travelling tirelessly all throughout western UP.. in all districts between Saharanpur and Delhi, helping thousands who had been trapped in the ensuing terrible chaos. His life was always in danger. Gandhiji asked Prime Minister Nehru to make special arrangements for his transport and safety. He was provided an armed escort comprising troops from the Gorkha Regiment.

In the city of Delhi, his close disciples had organised a relief camp at Hazrat Nizamuddin locality where they were providing shelter to members of the beleaguered Muslim community residing in that city. The relief camp at Hazrat Nizamuddin adjoining a mosque was managed by Maulana Zakariya, Madani's spiritual heir and Maulana Yusuf, the chief of the Tablighi Jamaat, one of the country's best organised Muslim religious organisations. These leading Muslims would incessantly plead with all those Muslims who wished to migrate to Pakistan not to do so. Their main refrain was, 'All our sacred places are here in Hindustan where our ancestors lie buried and Pakistan will be alien territory for us.'

Letters and speeches of Maulana Madani and his associates during those testing times present a striking testimony to their passionate conviction that the creation of Pakistan would not provide a lasting solution to the woes of the Muslims of the Indian subcontinent.

The last minute proposals offered by Maulana Madani to avert the Partition of the country can be dismissed today as being impractical. What however cannot be denied is his complete sincerity in his opposition to the partition.

The ideal of jihad as envisioned by Maulana Madani is in his own words:

> Muslims today remember only the word 'jihad' but they do not remember that in opposition to rebels against Islam and enemies of the community...patience, forbearance and high ethics were spoken of as jihad-i akbar ('the greater jihad'). In this greater jihad, there is no need of sword or dagger, but only strength, resolve, and action...[54]

[54] Ibid., p. 151.

Delivering an address at Bombay on the issue of violent jihad, the Maulana declared:

'To end such cruelty...is absolutely central to the 'program' of Islam. It is in fact a Muslim's duty to work for this...Any suggestion that this...violence and killing is 'Islamic jihad' is a blasphemous slander that mocks [Islamic] teachings...'[55]

The weeks before the assassination of Gandhi present a remarkable account of Gandhi's commitment to universal love and his passionate espousal of Hindu–Muslim unity. Personal accounts translated into English by those Muslims close to him in those stormy days are scanty. Barring Maulana Azad, whose prolific writings are available to all, we can only search the letters, speeches (all in Urdu) and interviews of those Muslims who gravitated towards him in those days. The present work mainly traces the narrative of the main protagonist Maulana Madani. Others like Maulana Hifzur Rehman, Maulana Syed Ahmad, Abdul Samad Khan (of Baluchistan) and Hafiz Mohammad Siddiq have largely been lost to mainstream history. The accounts of Sufi sages, such as Maulana Abdul Qadir Raipuri and Maulana Mohammad Zakariya, are treasures which still elude the English readership.

Abdul Majeed Khwaja, another active participant in the high drama which took place then also deprived history by failing to put in writing what could have been a compelling account of events. However, his son Raveend Khwaja, who usually accompanied his father in his frequent meetings with Gandhi and also assisted him in his secretarial work, vividly recounts his experiences.

Raveend Khwaja had been captivated with the Mahatma since his childhood days. As a college student, he had campaigned vigorously for the Congress Party in the fateful 1946 elections for the State and Central Legislatures. Interestingly enough, he had a very close personal relationship with two of the main protagonists of this narrative—Maulana Husain Ahmad Madani and Raja Mahendra Pratap. Khwaja says that his first meeting with Maulana Madani 'transformed' his entire life. 'He was a spiritual master who had strayed into politics', recounts Khwaja. His (Khwaja's) relationship with Raja Mahendra Pratap was

---

[55] Ibid., p. 150.

also warm and unaffected. It was a lifelong association with a person who was in fact originally his father's friend.

This writer also recollects his (Raja sahib's) frequent visits to the family house in Aligarh. Raveend recollects Raja Mahendra Pratap as an oft-spoken man full of exceptional kindness and warmth. It was impossible to gauge that for nearly two decades he had travelled all over the globe plotting the downfall of the mightiest Empire of the 20th century.

Now settled in England in his mid-80s, Khwaja is perhaps the only living witness of Gandhi's last but two public darshans at Birla House (believed to be the one in which Godse was amongst the audience finalising his game plan for Mahatma's assassination).

Khwaja vividly describes that fateful meeting and is of the firm opinion that Gandhi's discourse that day 'must have finally persuaded Godse that in his scheme of things Bapu had to be eliminated'.[56]

What exactly did Gandhi say on that day that fuelled the flames of pathological hatred in Godse's heart?

During the last few weeks of his life, Gandhi had been under relentless attack by Hindu extremist elements for what they perceived was *appeasement* of Pakistan on a number of issues, including the transfer of assets. The fact that Gandhi had intensified his quest to rationalise and espouse the commonality between Islam and Hinduism was for these sections like sprinkling oil on fire.

In Khwaja's own words:

If I am not mistaken, it was three days before Gandhji's assassination, when my father, Abdul Majeed Khwaja and I had driven down to Delhi from Aligarh, Khwaja Sahib had an appointment with Gandhiji. The appointment was in the slot immediately before the daily prayer meeting which the Mahatma used to address at Birla House. As we entered the room Gandhiji addressed my father and asked him if the Muslims in Delhi were now feeling secure. Before Khwaja Sahib could reply Gandhiji continued, 'I ended my fast only when Maulana Azad assured me that the riots have stopped.' Khwaja Sahib assured him that things were now well under control in all parts of the country.

[56] Interview with Dr Raveend Khwaja by author, December 1914.

He continued to talk of the situation for several minutes when suddenly he asked my father, 'Tell me Khwaja if in today's prayer meeting I announce that I am a Muslim what will be the response in the country?' For a moment Khwaja Sahib was too taken aback to respond. Then he calmly replied, 'Bapu I think many people will appreciate your sentiments but some may not understand and could get angry.' To this Gandhiji replied, 'I will explain to them what I mean and then perhaps they will appreciate my sentiments. But tell me Khwaja will you also announce that you are a Hindu—I mean what I define as a Hindu?' My father promptly replied, 'Certainly Bapu, at the most some Muslim League persons will abuse me. But I am a bit worried that people may not appreciate what you plan to say.' By this time our appointment was coming to an end. Gandhiji asked us to accompany him to the prayer meeting.[57]

Raveend Khwaja vividly recounts those few minutes which are deeply etched in his memory. He remembers that there were about a thousand-odd people present in that *prarthna* (prayer) meeting. Gandhi and Abdul Majeed Khwaja were seated on a wooden *takhat* (broad bench) and the rest of the audience were squatting on a carpeted floor.

Raveend continues, 'Gandhiji as per his usual practice started off by a short recitation of scriptures from different religions. He then spoke about the crying need for communal amity and mutual love between all sections. Almost abruptly he announced *Main Musalman hoon* (I am a Muslim). There was a hushed silence followed by a sharp murmur. No one raised his voice. Suddenly I noticed that a man who was sitting barely twenty feet from us got up. He was staring intensely at Gandhiji. There was fire in his eyes. He did not utter a word but elbowed his way out of the gathering. I have never forgotten his face till today. A few days later all the country's newspapers were plastered with photographs of this man—Nathuram Godse—the assassin of Gandhi.'

Khwaja says:

After the murmurs subsided, Gandhi continued with his sermon, 'Let me tell you what I mean by a Muslim.' Gandhiji continued, 'It means to me any person who believes in one creator call him

[57] Ibid.

Allah or Ishwar and believes all humanity to be one.' Then turning to Abdul Majeed Khwaja he continued, 'This is Khwaja my
old friend and dedicated freedom fighter. Do you know he is a
Hindu.' Again there was a murmur. When Khwaja nodded his
head to affirm what Gandhiji had said he continued, 'By Hindu
I mean an individual who has stayed in this land for four or five
generations and speaks any of the indigenous languages.'[58]

After the meeting concluded, they bid Gandhi goodbye.
Raveend Khwaja recounts, 'My father told Gandhiji that we
would be visiting him again after four, five days and he warmly
responded saying that he would be looking forward to our visit.
Little did my father know that the next time he sat with Bapu
he would be reciting the holy Quran at his funeral.'

Gandhi's assassination shook India to the core. Khwaja says,
'As far as the Muslims of India were concerned, it was an earth-
shaking moment, because the very existence of what Bapu had
sought to create appeared to be under threat.' It was at this juncture that the Muslim leaders like Maulana Azad and Maulana
Madani turned towards Nehru for saving what appeared to be
a sinking ship. Nehru did not fail them.

'In his final years before his end in 1957, Maulana Madani
spent most of his time in spiritual pursuits. Till his dying day,
he kept reminding Indian Muslims to come to terms with the
Partition of the country and prepare themselves for living in a
secular democratic country,' recalls Khwaja.

There is a very revealing anecdote connected with the
Maulana's final years:

When Hazrat Maulana Madani returned from his final hajj we
came to the station in Lahore for the honour of seeing him (sharf-
i-ziyarat). Among those in relationship with him was Sahibzada
Muhamad Arif, from district Jhang [in Pakistani Punjab], who
accompanied him as far as Deoband. He reports the following
story. On the train, there was also a 'Hindu gentleman' who
experienced a call of nature and went to attend to it. Clearly
unhappy, he came right back. Hazrat Maulana Madani understood what had happened, and immediately gathered some empty
cigarette packets and a jug of water and went and cleaned the
toilet completely. Then he said o the Hindu friend, 'Please go, the

[58] Ibid.

toilet is completely clean. Perhaps because it is night you couldn't see it properly.' The youth said, 'Maulana, I saw the toilet was completely full.' But he got up and went, and found the toilet completely clean. He was much moved and with great conviction ('aqida) said, 'Your honor's (huzur) kindness (bandanawazi, cherishing of servants) is beyond comprehension.[59]

Ironically enough, his memory was pushed into oblivion. Otherwise Maulana Madani would certainly have served as a role model for the 20th century Islam.

Paying tributes to the Maulana in his monumental *History of the Freedom Movement in India*

Dr Tara Chand writes:

His was an intellectual approach to the problems of society and state. This is amply proved by his writings on India's politics and economics and on international affairs.

On religious matters his knowledge was both in depth and breadth extraordinary. But it is amazing how a Maulavi had gathered a vast amount of information on the political and economic history of India and on the international relations of the western powers with Islamic countries.[60]

Then again Dr Tara Chand says:

His unequivocal stand on the political problem of India and his outright support to the Congress drew him into many controversies.

Among them the one which provoked the bitterest dispute related to his advocacy of Hindu-Muslim unity. He held that the people of India irrespective of religious differences ought to form a united nation in order to secure independence and pursue policies of common welfare. In a speech he stated that the modern nations were constituted on the principle of territoriality and not race or religion.[61]

---

[59] Maulana Syed Mohammad Miann, *The Prisoners of Malta* (Asira'n-e-Malta), translated by Mohammad Anwer Hussain and Hasan Imam (Delhi: Jamiat Ulama-i-Hind in association with Manak Publications, 2005 edition), p. 173.

[60] Tara Chand, *History of the Freedom Movement in India*—Volume Three (New Delhi: Publications Division, Ministry of Information and Broadcasting, Government of India, 1972), p. 258.

[61] Ibid., p. 259.

Even as India was grappling with the reality of having lost the Mahatma before it could fully savour its freedom, its sibling neighbour Pakistan was also going through the birth pangs, albeit in a different manner.

The last days of Pakistan's founder Mohammad Ali Jinnah have largely remained shrouded in mystery. This was not because of any sinister plot but primarily because Jinnah was in a certain sense a very private man and was too proud to compromise on his privacy. He was suffering from ill health since a long time but was adamant not to permit his family and doctors to probe the cause of his debilitating condition beyond a certain point.

Jinnah's illness was known only to his immediate family, the topmost government officials and his personal medical staff. In short, it was a well-kept state secret. But there is a certain critical importance in fully understanding Jinnah's turmoil, both physical and mental, in his final days.

A first-hand account of his last days is now available in a book, *With the Quaid-i-Azam During His Last Days*. The author Lt Colonel Ilahi Bakhsh was Jinnah's physician in his last days and based his account on his personal diary.

This monograph was first published in 1949, shortly after Jinnah's demise. The author was then in government service and was under pressure to publish a very watered down version of the original manuscript. The reasons are obvious—the newly founded state of Pakistan could ill afford any controversy over the last days of its own founder. This book, even in its diluted version, was relegated to the dustbin of history there, where it remained unnoticed till 1978. The Quaid-e-Azam Academy then reprinted the monograph but it remained largely unnoticed till 2011, when a leading publisher, realising its importance, finally published it for the larger public domain. This edition is of critical importance for historians not because of the published contents of this work but because of what was in the author's mind at that time but had to be omitted, for 'reasons of state'. Now the truth is finally out through the preface of this edition written by Nasir Ilahi the late author's son. Nasir, a resident of the US, shifted there permanently with his other siblings shortly after the premature death of his father in 1960.

In his preface, Nasir Ilahi states:

> Yet another puzzling aspect, that gave considerable pause to the
> author, was that after what the doctor felt was an 'almost miracu-
> lous' response to the treatment, something that the patient was
> able to sustain for a number of weeks, did the patient appear to,
> quite unexpectedly, gradually sink into a state of listlessness and
> 'baffling depression' (p.39). A careful examination could reveal no
> physical cause for this sudden change. It occurred that when the
> patient had been in Quetta for a few weeks, having been brought
> down from the higher altitude of Ziarat to lessen the strain on
> his lungs, and just before serious thought was given to a move
> to the even lower altitude of the city of his birth, Karachi. In a
> most poignant and emotional moment, which takes the doctor
> by surprise, the patient confides in him, telling him that while
> he wanted to live when the physician first visited Ziarat, 'now,
> however, it does not matter whether I live or die' (p.39).[62]

What exactly was the cause of this depression suffered by
the founder of Pakistan within months of the realisation of his
dream state?

We have Nasir Ilahi's version based on his father's written
and unwritten text:

> It should be noted here that, based on information available to
> Dr Ilahi Bakhsh's eldest son, M Humayun, that there was an
> initial version of this book which the author had submitted to
> the Pakistan government for review (as he was a government
> employee), but which regrettably does not exist any longer. The
> author was required to delete certain passages from the book as
> they were considered to be politically inappropriate and sensitive.
> Essentially, these included, inter alia, information based on
> the author's close personal relationship with the Quaid, which
> suggested that the patient was unhappy after some difficult
> meetings with his close political allies who he felt were depart-
> ing from the cardinal concepts of the state of Pakistan that he
> had begun to visualise. These concepts, included in some of the
> Quaid's important speeches of the time, emphasised the guiding
> principles of equality, justice, and fair play for all the citizens of
> the new State. It is believed that the author took the view that

---

[62] Ihahi Bakhsh, *With the Quaid-i-Azam During His Last Days* (Karachi:
Oxford University Press, 2011), p. xvi.

the Quaid's reaction to these emerging political differences, and his possible perceptions about the lack of support or them, may have been one of the factors that contributed to the onset of the Quaid's depressed state.[63]

These carefully drafted words should remove all doubts about what was always whispered regarding the Mohammad Ali Jinnah's last few days but never publicly acknowledged by the establishment in Pakistan.

The details of Jinnah's final days go beyond the ambit of this work. What is however of critical importance to history is the fact that in his final days, the founder of the modern world's largest theocratic state discovered what should now be an axiom for the 21st century world: any modern state based entirely on religious identity and animosity cannot survive the burden of its inner contradictions. Far from being a unifying factor, religion in Pakistan had become a major factor in generating internal discord.

That Pakistan has forgotten the deep torment of its founding father in his final moments is so obvious by the present fragile state of that troubled nation. The growing space occupied by doctrinaire Islamists leading to a polarised state is much too far from the vision of its founding father. What is possibly even more dismaying for the 21st century world is that India too appears to be willing away the legacy of tolerance and accommodation for which its founding father laid down his life.

---

[63] Ibid., p. xvii.

Photo 1: Maulana Mohammad Ali Johar, Leader of the Khilafat Movement

Photo 2: Maulana Hasrat Mohani, Prominent Freedom Fighter and a Second-generation Leader of the Aligarh Movement

Photo 3: Dr Mukhtar Ahmad Ansari (circa 1926), Noted Gandhian and Prominent Leader of the Khilafat Movement

Photo 4: Raja Mahendra Pratap during His Travels in Asia

Photo 5: Raja Mahendra Pratap with Prime Minister Indira Gandhi (circa 1960)

Photo 6: Maulavi Barkatullah, Werner von Hentig, Raja Mahendra Pratap, Käzm Orbay and Walter Röhr (from left to right, circa 1915)

Conclusion: Colonialism and Jihad in the 21st Century

I perceived in this moment that when the white man turns tyrant it is his own freedom that he destroys.

—George Orwell, *Shooting an Elephant*

Often wars, mass murders and empire building go hand in hand. Together they have been part of a game that has repeatedly been played upon mostly unsuspecting, if not totally innocent, people. Sadly, down the ages this has turned out to be so in the name of one cause or the other that history may well justify as pangs of civilizations' birth or realization of freedom. The 11th-century wars between Christian powers and Muslim rulers were conveniently called Crusades by the West for it becomes easier to take fancy to *crusade*, rather than war. And it takes as noble a soul as the late George Orwell to say what figures at the top of this chapter. This at once pays tribute to Englishmen's collective sagacity and virtues and also chastises and serves a warning on them about losing their best possessions in the hubbub of maintaining an empire as has been the case with Orwell in far off Burma. Anyway, the colonial context nearer home would be taken up later towards the second or last half of this account since much before that a myth was born that Christendom took to Crusades *to liberate* the holy city of Jerusalem from the *satanic Muslim rule*. It was in this tradition that years later, famed classicist Dante in his magnum opus *Divine Comedy* painted Islam in the vilest colours. Thus, a clash of kings that took place purely for political and economic gain was chronicled by the West as a clash of two religions. And like an old habit, it continues to be the same wont behind so many battles fought ever since to this day.

It is a myth which has sustained for centuries and until this belief is not demolished and a new perspective accepted, lasting peace will, in all probability, elude the 21st century world.

As another year—2014—is poised to lapse into history, a vitriolic rhetoric of hate and revenge is being played vis-à-vis Middle East. A minor Syria-based militant Sunni Muslim outfit, born shortly after the West's *war against terror*, a sequel to 9/11, has mutated into a Frankenstein called IS. Beneath the mystery of its origins lie clandestine misadventures of American intelligence agencies aided and abetted by its client states in the Middle East. Its original purpose was to help the West in toppling the unfriendly regime of President Bashar Al Asad. The Asad regime was always on the radar of the Americans because of the Iran–Syria–Lebanon–Hezbollah axis, which had always been a major threat to Israel. The fact that the Al Asad ruling clan had always had a notorious track record of genocidal activities directed against Sunnis had come very handy to the USA and Israeli intelligence agencies. The Maliki-led government of Iraq did the rest by persecuting Sunnis in that country. This provided additional motivation to its victims to join with the IS.

Today the IS is in the throes of waging a brutal war against its fellow Muslim rival militias, primarily Shia groups and the hapless Kurds. Throwing all canons of civilized behavior to the wind, the IS goes merrily around raising the bogey and war cry for jihad. The Saudi State and the Salafi–Wahabi official religious establishment are making painstaking efforts to distance themselves from the IS. This is more so since IS is also being identified whether rightly or wrongly with a virulent strain of Salafi ideology. Saudi Arabia's leading clerics and theologians have issued a joint appeal condemning the IS for indulging in wanton destruction and abusing the name of jihad. The Saudi State's abhorrence for militant Islam is understandable. Since the past decade, the ruling House of Saud has been living under the shadow of a mortal threat to its very existence by such militant groups. Ironically, while they themselves faced such existential threats, they have felt no compunction in funding such militant groups externally whenever it has suited their self interests. Historically, the Saudi ruling family's grab of power is itself based on rebellion and violence against the Ottoman rule as part of British colonial policy.

The irony of the situation cannot be lost on the world. Saudi Arabia is the staunchest ally of the West in its war against terror, along with Jordan and Egypt. The Salafi–Wahabi ideology is the dominant force in the religious establishment both in

Saudi Arabia and Egypt. This group has played a pivotal role in toppling Egypt's first democratically elected President by allying itself with the military junta, which is strongly allied with the US military and Arab petro-monarchies.

Yet, strange as it sounds, all the militant Sunni groups in that region are in the eyes of the world identified by their Salafi–Wahabi ideology, without any mention of their patronage by Western-backed friendly dictatorships. Obviously, there is a missing link in this strange jigsaw puzzle.

The answers to these troubling questions are complex and any attempt to reduce issues to black and white or search for simplistic explanations will serve little purpose.

The fact is that with all the resources and intelligence inputs at their disposal, the West and in a way the rest of the world has scant information of the ideological moorings or the social roots of the IS. Western analysts are realising a bit late that even if the army of the IS is defeated by sheer military might, the possible mutations of this organization could still pose a serious threat to the US and its allies in the future. This is truly a frightening proposition. The IS through its propaganda machinery is deliberately seeking to identify itself with a militant strain of Salafiism. But what exactly is the ideology of this group?

It is true that Wahabism and its offshoot Salafism are religious doctrines marked by intolerance, myopic dogmatism and bigotry. But there is scant evidence in classical Salafi texts, if any at all, to explain the virulent behaviour of its adherents in modern times. The answer lies not in the scriptures of this school of thought but in the historical narrative of the people of that area. The answer also lies in the political compulsions faced by them in the wake of nearly a century and a half of colonial intervention on their lands.

The origins of the Salafi ideology can be linked to the 19th-century Islamist reformer Al Afghani who, as we know is the founding ideologue of modern-day political Islam. But Al Afghani's pan-Islamism had no place for religious war. It was directed mostly against ulema and corrupt Muslim rulers and of course against imperialism. This was almost a very secular form of Islamisation which was very accommodative towards nationalism and of course other religions, including Hinduism and Christianity. It was however Rashid Rida (1865–1935), the Libyan-born scholar, who drew some inspiration from Al Afghani, but ultimately chartered his own course by preaching an ideology known as Salafism. The roots of the word 'Salafi' means 'one who honors one's righteous ancestors'. It was Rida who first raised the issue of an ideal IS. This concept rested not on jihad but a broader vision of providing succour to *all humanity* on the basis of the *pure Islam*, such as which existed during the time of the Prophet and his associates.

The original Wahabi texts also relate to the idea Salafism, in the sense that Wahabis also seek to draw inspiration from *pious ancestors* against the form of Islam practiced by corrupt ulema. But what is clear is that Rida's Salafiism does not at all share the rabid bigotry which marks the original Wahabism of the 18th century. This school of Wahabism which flourished in Saudi Arabia after 1785 was virulently intolerant of any form of dissent. The Wahabis' main targets were those Muslims who did not conform to their form of belief. In 1927, when the Wahabi inspired Abdul Aziz finally became the King of Arabia, he had his hands full in controlling his fellow Wahabis who unleashed terror on any Arab Muslim who differed with them. It is important to note that the Wahabi-inspired House of Saud could never have come to power without the full support of Great Britain and the Allied powers (This support of Great Britain for the Wahabi chieftains was nothing new. In the year 1866, when the Wahabi chief Abdullah, son of Faisal Ibni Turki, was in serious trouble, he sought the help of Great Britain and a treaty of friendship was signed between the two. The symbiotic relationship between the Wahabis and the West has a long history.)

King Abdul Aziz was not a man without wisdom and he managed to ensure that the Wahabi–Salafi variant of Islam, which prevailed in his kingdom took a slightly moderate hue. Nevertheless during the century-long rule of the Saudi dynasty, there has been a systematic attempt to promote the Wahabi school of thought throughout the Muslim world. This has been accompanied by an eradication of historical monuments connected with Islam.

The particular variant of Salafism which is attributed to the founders of the present-day Syria's IS has however to be examined according to the existing paradigms in that region. Noted anthropologist and one of the leading analysts of contemporary Islamic movements in the Middle East, Professor Alireza Doostdar of the University of Chicago states:

'The view that one particular religious doctrine is uniquely extremist won't help us to appreciate the cycles of brutality that feed on narratives of torture, murder and desecration.'[1]

Tracing the roots of the IS and Western media reports on recent developments in the Iraq–Syria region Doostdar writes:

> The problem with these statements is that they seem to assume that the ISIS is a 'causa sui' phenomenon that has suddenly materialized out of the thin ether of an evil doctrine. But ISIS emerged from the fires of war, occupation, killing, torture, and disenfranchisement. It did not need to sell its doctrine to win recruits. It needed above all to prove itself effective against its foes.
>
> In Iraq, the cities that are now controlled by ISIS were some of those most resistant to American control during the occupation and most recalcitrant in the face of the newly established state. The destruction that these cities endured seems only to have hardened their residents' defiance. Fallujah, the first Iraqi city to fall to ISIS, is famous for its devastation by the US military during counterinsurgency operations in 2004. It still struggles with a legacy of rising cancer rates, genetic mutations, birth defects, and disabilities blamed on depleted uranium in American munitions.
>
> In Mosul, many of those who joined ISIS last summer had been previously imprisoned by the Iraqi government. They numbered in the thousands and included peaceful protesters who opposed Prime Minister Nuri al-Maliki's increasingly authoritarian rule.[2]

The harsh truth is that the emergence of the IS is a direct consequence of the colossal blundering of the armies of the American Empire in the post- 9/11 scenario. As the war to liberate Iraq from Saddam Hussain was moving ahead, reports started filtering out from war-torn Iraq regarding the brutalities of the American armed forces. These reports included accounts of how American troops had frequently chosen to savage Iraqi prisoners and had with scant compunction to civilized war-time behaviour gone out of the way to pour vitriol on religious sentiments. Stories of how the Quran had been deliberately desecrated started circulating. A territorial war of clout, power and pelf with an eye on oil resources, contracts and deals had been turned into

---

[1] Alireza Doostdar, 'How Not To Understand ISIS,' 13 October 2014, https://divinity.uchicago.edu/sightings/how-not-understand-isis-alireza-doostdar (accessed on 11 may 2015).

[2] Ibid.

a religious war. What is worse, it has been dehumanized and allowed to degenerate into a melee where lumpens have overtaken the system to call the shots.

There are other local geo-political factors which have contributed to the rise of the IS and these seem to have escaped the notice of the West. The simmering tension between Syria and Turkey over river water disputes is just one example.

There was also no presence of the militant Al Qaida in Iraq till 2003 when the West chose to dismantle the Saddam Hussain regime on the false pretext of weapons of mass destruction. The Saddam regime will be remembered in history for its notoriety but the mayhem which followed after the country's 'liberation' by the US suggests that the cure was worse than the disease.

Jihad and the West

To uncover the historical roots of the so-called jihad between the followers of Islam and the Christian West, we will have to travel back with an open mind to a period over a thousand years back. The scene of the conflict is again the holy city of Jerusalem.

Islam and Christianity share a common belief in monotheism. For the devout Muslims, the Christians are one of the *people of the book*. According to the Islamic tradition, the first person to acknowledge and recognize the fact that the Prophet of Islam heralded a divine message was a Christian monk—Bahira. It was he who told members of the sceptic Quraish tribe (to which the future prophet belonged) that Mohammad (peace be upon him) would, according to the scriptures which Bahira possessed, 'one day carry the mantle of prophet-hood'. All the Abrahamic religions—Judaism, Christianity and Islam—share and equally revere all the prophets who followed Adam's descent on the Earth. Yet, these are the religions which wage religious wars with each other. They also share another common trait unlike other religions of the East—self-righteousness. They are obsessed with the belief of being the *chosen people.*

To put it in plain words, theological differences are not the root cause behind the wars between Muslim rulers and Christian kingdoms—it is the vanity, pride and quest for territory.

The prophet-hood of Jesus and the spiritual purity of Virgin Mary are amongst the basic historical traditions of Islam. Muslims accord reverence and respect to Mary, the Mother of Christ equal to that which they accord to the mother of their own prophet. It is incumbent on every Muslim to address Jesus Christ and his Mother Virgin Mary with the prefix Hazrat as a mark of deep reverence. Christianity for Muslims is a vital milestone in the history of divine tradition on earth. There is just one point of difference between the followers of Islam and Christianity—the divinity of Christ. Muslims consider him like they regard their own Prophet—an ordinary mortal who carries a divine message. Muslims refuse to recognize Christ as the son of God. The Quran is perhaps the only holy book which repeatedly reminds its readers that God has been sending prophets and holy scriptures to the people since the time of Abraham.

The followers of Christianity, however, do not share this reverence for the Prophet of Islam. For Christians, Islam is a 'religion spread by the sword' and by a person who was an anti-Christ.

It is an undeniable fact of history that military power played an important role in spreading the Arab Empire but this territorial ascendancy took place after the demise of the Prophet. The Quranic injunctions regarding jihad and war which were enforced during the life time of the Prophet can even today serve as a model code of conduct during a state of war. So too is the concept of *shahadat* (martyrdom in the cause of God).

When the Prophet of Islam began his mission by preaching the divine revelations; his own people became his bitterest foes. He was subjected to the worst types of persecution and humiliation by members of his own tribe, the Quraish. He bore all the insults, assaults on his people and torture with unbelievable fortitude and patience. He answered them with compassion, perseverance and deliverance. At a later stage when his life was at stake, he accepted the principle of taking up arms in self-defence. It is this covenant of defensive war which is used for denigrating Islam by its opponents and also by its adherents for justifying their temporal wars by ascribing religious motives.

The Quranic injunctions for waging war are based on the notion that one should not hesitate to wage war when one's existence or faith is challenged. There are however stringent norms both for justifying the need to wage war and also on the method of treating the vanquished foe. The Quran strongly directs the believer to seek the path of peace.

It is also true that there are several references in the Quran urging the followers of the faith to wage war. All these directives are in a specific perspective and come in a particular reference to the situation prevailing at that time. If these injunctions are torn out of context, they can be misinterpreted.

For more than half-a-century, the successors of the Prophet, the four Caliphs, scrupulously followed the directives of their leader on the issue of waging war in letter and spirit.

The fourth Caliph of Islam, Hazrat Ali, was arguably the spiritual heir of the Prophet. He was the Prophet's cousin and also his son-in-law. Both Sunnis and Shias revere him, but for the Shias he is the supreme heir of the Prophet. He is also the founding father of Sufism. There is a wealth of writings pertaining to this phase in Islamic history. These are in the form of letters and directives by Hazrat Ali on issues related to the guiding principles on matters of governance in Islam.

For Sunni Muslims, both Hazrat Ali and the second Caliph Hazrat Omar served as iconic role models for Muslims during times of war and also for treating conquered people.

The following is the translation of one such letter by Caliph Hazrat Ali to the Governor of Egypt Malik Ashtar:

> Bear in mind that you do not throw away the offer of peace which your enemy may himself make. Accept it, for, that will please God. Peace is a source of comfort to the army; it reduces your worries and promotes order in the State. But beware! Be on your guard when the peace is signed; for, certain types of enemies propose terms of peace, just to lull you into a sense of security only to attack you again, when you are off your guard. So you should exercise the utmost vigilance on your part, a place no undue faith in their protestations. But, if under the peace treaty you have accepted any obligations, discharge those obligations scrupulously. It is a trust and must be faithfully upheld and whenever you have promised anything, keep it with all the strength that you command, for whatever differences of opinion might exist on other matters, there is nothing so noble as the fulfillment of a promise. This is recognized even among the non-Muslims, for they know the dire consequences which follow from the breaking

of covenants. So never make excuses in discharging your respon-
sibilities and never break a promise; nor cheat your enemy. For
breach of promise is an act against God, and none except the
positively wicked, act against God.[3]

The directives (as mentioned earlier) of the fourth Caliph of
Islam, who is regarded as the first Imam by the Shia sect, are
of considerable importance if we wish to understand the foundations of the Islamic revolution which swept across Asia and
Europe between the 8th and 12th centuries.

It also true that immediately after the demise of Hazrat Ali,
there came a brief phase in Islamic history when the temporal
leaders were guided more by political consideration and very
often compromised on guiding principles of statecraft. The
Islamic Empire continued to spread and its armies, reaped
conquest—its leaders often displaying scant concern for the
original guiding principles and instead succumbing to the tribal
traditions against which the Prophet had campaigned.

Professor John L. Esposito of the Department of Religion and
International Affairs at the Georgetown University has summed
up the Crusade Wars (1095–1453) thus:

Two myths pervade Western perceptions of the Crusades: first,
that the Crusades were simply motivated by a religious desire to
liberate Jerusalem, and second, that Christendom ultimately
triumphed.

Jerusalem was a sacred city for all three Abrahamic faiths.
When the Arab armies took Jerusalem in 638, they occupied
a center whose shrines had made it a major pilgrimage site in
Christendom. Churches and the Christian population were left
unmolested. Jews, long banned from living there by Christian
rulers, were permitted to return, live, and worship in the city
of Solomon and David. Muslims proceeded to build a shrine,
the Dome of the Rock, and a mosque, the al-Aqsa, near the area
formerly occupied by Herod's Temple and close by the Wailing
Wall, the last remnant of Solomon's temple.[4]

---

[3] Hazrat Ali, *Good Governance: A Divine Document—Directives for Good
Governance*, translated from Arabic by Allama Rasheed Turabi (Pakistan: Turabi
Centenary Publications, 2008), pp. 29–30.

[4] John L. Esposito, *Islam—The Straight Path* (New York: Oxford University
Press, 2005), p. 58.

He also clarifies some other myths about the Crusades by stating:

> The contrast between the behaviour of the Christian and Muslim armies in the First Crusade has been etched deeply in the collective memory of Muslims. In 1099, the Crusaders stormed Jerusalem and established Christian sovereignty over the Holy Land. They left no Muslim survivors, women and children were massacred. The Noble Sanctuary, the Haram al-Sharif, was desecrated as the Dome of the Rock was converted into a church and the al-Aqsa mosque, renamed the Temple of Solomon, became a residence for the king. Latin principalities were established in Antioch, Edessa, Tripoli, and Tyre. The Latin Kingdom of Jerusalem lasted less than a century. In 1187, Salah-al-Din (Saladin), having re-established Abbasid rule over Fatimid Egypt, led his army in a fierce battle and recaptured Jerusalem. The Muslim army was as magnanimous in victory as it had been tenacious in battle. Civilians were spared; churches and shrines were generally left untouched. The striking differences in military conduct were epitomized by the two dominant figures of the Crusades: Saladin and Richard the Lion-Hearted. The chivalrous Saladin was faithful to his word and compassionate toward non-combatants. Richard accepted the surrender of Acre and then proceeded to massacre all its inhabitants, including women and children, despite promises to the contrary.[5]

Colonialism essentially was driven by economic interests and Imperial designs. The initial phase in the 18th century religious fervour had little or no role in powering the European Colonial powers in their thirst for worldly riches. But very soon the Christian missionaries were consumed by an overwhelming desire to civilize the heathen Easterners. These missionaries became a critical element in strengthening the hegemony of the colonial powers in their subject states in the East. It was in the early 19th century in India that the native Hindus and Muslims decided to offer the only serious challenge to British hegemony over India. This was the only time when the Muslims who were the dominant power in India for 600 years took resort to jihad to confront the British. Invading armies of Muslim Sultans from Afghanistan, Persia and Mongolia may have occasionally

---

[5] Ibid., p. 59.

raised the bogey of religious wars to justify their conquest in North India, but these attempts were always half-hearted and few. These invasions were always for territorial gain and not religious wars.

Unlike this, the history of the East India Company and subsequent rule by the British Crown mainly combined trade and commerce and ran to be a far deeper domination where the role of Evangelization was also too pronounced to be missed by any observer. Yet, the US had no role in the Colonialism of the 18th and 19th centuries. Its role as a neo-colonial power actually began in the aftermath of the World War II. This was what was known as the Cold War.

For just about a quarter-of-a-century after the end of the World War II, there was a marked decline in the level of hostility between the West and the Muslim world. It was the era of cold war between Soviet Russia and the West. There were little signs, if any at all, to foretell any impending clash between the two civilizations.

But by the end of the 1970s, things began to change. The first distinctive change was the Islamic Revolution in Iran. It was primarily a movement for democracy by people yearning for a breath of freedom against one of the most oppressive regimes of that era. Instead of respecting the aspirations of the people of Iran against the despotic regime of Shah Raza Pehalvi, the Government of USA chose the path of short-term expediency and continued to assist the Shah and his brutal regime. As frequently happens in such situations, the oppressed people took refuge under the leadership of the most charismatic figure who appeared on the horizon—Ayatollah Khomeni. He led Iran to Islamic revolution strangely from the safety of far off Paris where he had taken asylum on being exiled. This revolution sent a chilling message all over the Middle East—that militant Islam is the only way for the oppressed people of this region to get rid of Western backed despotic tyrannical regimes.

The second development was in the 1980s. This time Pakistan and neighbouring Afghanistan came handy. The US funded and actively backed madarsas with militant ideologies in Pakistan for fighting their proxy war against the Soviet backed regime in Afghanistan. This was achieved by the partnership between the fundamentalist General Zia-ul-Haq and the US. It marked the birth of the modern-day terrorism in the third world. It was a Himalayan blunder by the government of the US in the second half of the 20th century.

Today, nearly half-a-century after America's neo-colonial misadventure, the West could well be facing the most serious threat to its hegemony in the Middle East. For the embittered despairing Arab youth, there is a role model that rose from the ashes of the anti-Soviet jihad in Afghanistan led by Osama Bin Laden. In hindsight, it will be worth recalling that in the early 1980s when the US started stoking the rebellion against the pro-Soviet regime in Afghanistan, they had a very viable opinion of arming the local tribal warlords in Afghanistan. Powerful chieftains like Gulbuddin Hekmatyaar and the legendry Ahmad Shah Mehsud were quite capable of taking on the pro-Soviet regime of Afghanistan. But the US intelligence agencies, wishing to take no chances, deliberately sought to give a religious colour to this conflict by inducing the services of the Kingdom of Saudi Arabia to this war. None of the Saudi Princes were willing to leave their lives of comfort and luxury to join this holy war. Laden—then a mere Saudi entrepreneur—stepped out alone amongst the hordes of consequential Arabs in the wake of the dreams of martyrdom flaunted by Americans. It was the birth of a legend scripted and nurtured by the US intelligence agencies. Instead of secular leaders like Ahmad Shah Mehsud, the Afghan people had a new role model and a new political force fired by faith to look up to in the shape and form of Taliban.

In its obsession to preserve and protect the State of Israel, the West trampled upon the hopes and aspirations of several generations of Arabs. By propping up despotic regimes and tin pot dictators loyal to it throughout Middle East instead of allowing genuine democratic aspirations of vast majority of Arabs to find their roots and flourish, the US has prepared fertile ground for extremist ideologies to grow and prosper in the entire region.

Today, there is a segment of Muslim youth spread all over the globe that abhors the crass materialism of the West. They perceive that materialism has been clouding deeper issues related to human spirit and conscience. The simmering discontent and bitterness over Palestine has robbed sanity from the minds and hearts of Arab youth. The spiritual and temporal establishment within the Islamic fold is somehow too apathetic to play a meaningful role in regenerating hope, or reorienting the belief system to shape a badly needed renaissance throughout the Muslim world. The bankruptcy of Muslim leadership the world over seems to have no answers to the growing crisis. A sense of bewilderment and helplessness seems to have taken a stranglehold amongst the Muslim intelligentsia the world over.

There is no denying the fact that Islam's failure to throw up a genuine movement of reform and the ability to reinvent itself according the challenges posed by a globalised world are major stumbling blocks for millions of Muslims right from Arabia to all other parts of the world. In fact, during the past one and a half centuries, almost all major reform movements within Islam have been prompted by revivalism. In India, the only genuine movement of religious and social reform amongst Muslims was the one started by Sir Syed Ahmad Khan in the 19th century. This is also referred to as the Aligarh Movement. Sir Syed's attempt for religious reform stands out not just in the Indian subcontinent but in a way all over the Muslim world. Sir Syed's Islamic liberalism was, however, not pursued by most of his successors. Indian Muslims whole heartedly embraced his reform in the field of education but found it expedient to push aside his attempts in the field of religious reform. His stress on scientific inquiry and large hearted tolerance was never really adopted by a majority of the Muslim intelligentsia. It no doubt remains a moot point that whether Sir Syed's propensity for wholeheartedly imbibing western values during the final phase of his life served any meaningful purpose or whether it thwarted his social reform movement.

What matters today is whether Muslims are able to shake off the denial mode which seems to be preventing them from genuine introspection on the issue of political, social and religious reforms. To live and to live fully in a globalised world and pluralistic societies without compromising on the core beliefs and the essence of Islamic teachings remains a moot point before them.

The question arises: Is the situation irretrievable? Or is the 21st century going to witness another version of the Clash of Civilizations?

To avert this and bring back a semblance of peace and sanity to the Middle East, the US has to put an end to its interventionist policies. Acts of aggression by American and Israeli forces on Arab territories in utter violation of the UN charter and the guidelines of the International Court of Justice have to come to an end. The complete impunity with which the Western alliance has chosen to invade the skies and oceans of sovereign nations further reinforces the notion of the Arab people that American machismo when on the boil knows no confines. This perception will have to be changed in the minds of sane and not so sane segments spread across the shores.

This should be followed by an engagement between Islam and the West. Since the state actors have failed to initiate a meaningful dialogue between the East and the West, civil society, rights groups, lawmen and laymen have to step in and mull together to find a way forward and move on from confrontation to consultation and from strife to peace.

This ought to be more so since whenever democracy tries to kick off in Middle East, the West and its local cohorts try to snuff it out as it happened recently in Egypt. And this has also been largely the case with the *Arab Spring* for it held the promise to signal an era of dialogue, democracy and resumption of peace throughout the region.

Lost Roadmap of Post-colonial Third World

BS is an acronym for British Standard. The great George Orwell is no more to bemoan its loss vis-à-vis public life and its conduct though it is used in trade like the ISI or Indian Standard Item has been in vogue back home, courtesy the vanishing tribe of Brown Sahibs of yore. Yet, the deep colonial backdrop through which India and Pakistan became independent dominions determined their role to set modern standards within their confines so impeccably that it can well be emulated beyond by the less fortunate parts of the post-colonial Third World.

Sadly, this remains today a collegiate fancy. First look at the creation of Pakistan. It has neither fulfilled the aspirations of the Muslims in the area where it exists nor has it by any stretch of imagination served the broader interests of the Muslims of the subcontinent. It has created more problems than it has solved. The reason for its failure is that no modern state with a multi-religious and multicultural population can excel unless it evolves a polity which guards the interest of all sections of society. The founder of Pakistan, Mohammad Ali Jinnah, understood this well albeit too late but his successors remain blissfully oblivious about so stark a fact. The more the Pakistani State gave in to the demands of small yet vociferous, belligerent fanatics of its polity, the more their demands grew. Under the patronage of the US, the pocket dictators like General Zia-ul-Haq nurtured religious fundamentalism. The results are there for all to see. India under Gandhi and Nehru chartered its own course and the pitfalls have so far been skirted. Today Pakistan is itself one of the worst victims of acts of terrorism. India in sharp contrast is the world's not only largest democracy but also an island of relative peace.

Yet, for the Indian Muslims, the 1980s and 1990s were periods of great despair because of highly emotive tussle around the Babri Mosque and Ram Temple and the issue of changes in Muslim Personal Law following the Shah Bano Case. Large-scale communal riots in this phase scarred the sensitivities of both Hindus and Muslims and also tarred India's image as a modern progressive State. The role of the Muslim leadership in this period was also questionable. It lacked maturity and was reactive instead of being wise and foresighted. But with the advent of the 21st century, the Indian Muslims by and large showed signs of maturing out. Gone are the days of identity politics leading to strident shrill cries of 'Islam in danger' so characteristic of the earlier decades. Indian Muslims have finally been coming of age.

It was in this scenario that in the summer of 2014, a new political dispensation came to power in India.

The rise of the right wing Bhartiya Janta Party which stands for strident Hindutva has once again raised grave apprehensions in the minds of the Muslim minority. During the first six months of its tenure, the new Government has done precious little to allay such fears. In fact the sporadic communal riots which took place through the run up to the Parliamentary polls and also through subsequent months after the new Government assumed office have exacerbated such fears. It is difficult for any nation to embark upon a path of all round progress if more than one-fourth of its population remains in a constant state of fear. Since suspected perpetrators of violence in communal riots in western UP in 2013 have sadly been rewarded and publicly feted, this does not auger well. It remains a moot question whether the new dispensation will address such concerns or allow the situation to drift into a state of confrontation. If India is to now take its rightful place as one of the most powerful nations in the world, a disciplined and friction-free society is essential.

India has the second largest population of Muslims in the world. It could well have provided the most fertile soil to the Salafi–Wahabi school of thought which is the fastest growing sect of its kind in the Muslim world, thanks mainly to the patronage by the Saudi ruling elite. But this has obviously not happened. This is primarily because 99 per cent of Indian Muslims belong either to the Sunni–Deobandi (Waliullahi) sect which follows the Hanafi school of thought or the Sunni Barelvi sect or are Shias. All three of them are passionate devotees of the Prophet of Islam unlike the Wahabis who seek to diminish the significance of the Prophet. These three sects are the biggest barrier to the rise of the radical Wahabi ideology not only in India but all over South East Asia. Pakistan and Afghanistan saw the rise of the Wahabi sect in the 1980s only because of the bogey that 'Islam is in danger' so craftily engineered by the dictatorial regime of General Ziaul Haq. It was this stratagem which touched the deepest fears and sensitivities of the peoples of the two countries. So long as such deep rooted fears are not allowed to be nurtured in India, there are scant prospects that Islamic extremism will gain a foothold in this country

Majoritarian trends, however, through the early days of the new regime could open old wounds and rekindle bitter memories of the 1980s and 1990s when India was rocked by major communal confrontations. If the simmering apprehensions within the Muslim community do not subside and their concerns are not adequately addressed, it could foster isolationist tendencies within the community. This estrangement of the Muslim community with the mainstream politics could seriously impair the major development plank of the new regime which needs an environment of peace and rule of law. The new government has shown that it has the will and ability to deliver on industrial development and infrastructure growth. It remains to be seen how determined it is to ensure that India does not fall victim to the sectarian violence and lack of religious tolerance similar as is the case in the neighbourhood.

Bibliography

English Translations from Original Urdu Works:

Ansari, Ishrat Husain. *1857 Urdu Sources*. Translated by Ishrat Husain Ansari and Hamid Afaq Qureshi. Lucknow: New Royal Book Co, 2008.

Ansari, Ishrat Hussain and Qureshi, Hamid Afaq. *1857 Urdu Sources* (Translations). Lucknow: New Royal Book Co, 2008.

Hazrat Ali. *A Divine Document—Directives for Good Governance*. Translated from Arabic by Allama Rasheed Turabi. Pakistan: Turabi Centenary Publications, 2008.

Khan, Sir Syyid Ahmad. *Tarikh Sarkashiy-e-Dhilla Bijnor* (History of Bijnor Rebellion). Translated by Hafeez Malik and Morris Dembo. Delhi: Idarah-i Adabiyat-i Delli, 2009.

Manglori, Tufail Ahmad. *Musalmanon Ka Roshan Mustaqbil* [Towards a Common Destiny: A Nationalist Manifesto]. Translated by Ashraf Ali. New Delhi: People's Publishing House, 1994.

Mian, Maulana Syed Mohammad. *Asira'n-E-Malta* [Prisoners of Malta]. Translated by Mohammad Anwer Hussain and Hasan Imam. Delhi: Manak Publications Pvt. Ltd., 2005.

Nadwi, S. Abul Hasan Ali. *Islam and the World*. Translated by Mohammad Asif Kidwai. Lucknow: Academy of Islamic Research & Publications, 1982.

———. *Khandang-i-Ghadar and Naunaga* [1857 Classics-1]. Translated by Qureshi. H.A. Lucknow: New Royal Book Company, 2007.

Original Urdu Works:

Gilani, Maulana Syed Manazir Ahsan. *Sawaneh-Qasmi* (volumes 2 & 3). Deoband: Department of Nashr-o-Ashaat, Darul Uloom.

Lari, Dr Ahmar. *Hasrat Mohani—Hayat aur Karname*. Lucknow: Uttar Pradesh Urdu Academy, 1973.

Madani, Maulana Husain Ahmad. *Naqsh-e-Hayat* (autobiography). Deoband: Maktaba Sheikh-ul-Islam, 2007.

Qureshi, Saleem. *Attharah Sau Sattawan Ke Ghaddaron Ke Khutoot*. New Delhi: Anjuman Taraqqi Urdu Institute of Third World Art and Literature, 2001.

Unpublished Research Material:

Buddhani, Gulzar N. *The Role and Contribution of the Aligarh Muslim University in Modern Indian Islam* (1877–1947) (PhD thesis). Manchester: University of Manchester, Department of Near Eastern Studies.

Khan, Naim Ullah, *Political Ideas and Role of Maulana Obaidullah Sindhi* (PhD thesis). Aligarh: Department of Political Science, AMU, 1981.

Books:

Ahmed, Akbar. *The Thistle and the Drone—How America's War on Terror Became a Global War on Tribal Islam*. Noida: HarperCollins Publishers India, 2013.

Ahmad, Mohiuddin. *Saviours of Islamic Spirit Series—Saiyid Ahmad Shahid— His Life and Mission*. Introduction by S. Abul Hasan Ali Nadwi. Lucknow: Academy of Islamic Research and Publications, 1975.

Ahmad, Qeyamuddin. *The Wahabi Movement in India*. Calcutta: Firma K.L. Mukhopadhyay, 1966.

Al-Badawi, Mostafa. *Man & the Universe—An Islamic Perspective*. Amman, Jordan: Wakeel Books, 2002.

Antonius, George. *The Arab Awakening—The Story of the Arab National Movement*. New York: Capricorn Books, 1965.

Asad, Mohammad. *The Road to Makkah*. New Delhi: Islamic Book Service, 2000.

Azad, Maulana Abul Kalam Azad. *India Wins Freedom—An Autobiographical Narrative*. Calcutta: Orient Longmans Private Ltd., 1959.

Bakhsh, Lt. Colonel Ilahi. *With the Quaid-i-Azam during His Last Days*. Foreword by Fatima Jinnah. Karachi: Oxford University Press, 2011.

Bandopadhyaya, Shailesh Kumar. *Muhammad Ali Jinnah*. Patna: Khuda Bakhsh Oriental Public Library, 1996.

Bhattacharya, Sabyasachi (ed.). *Rethinking 1857*. New Delhi: Orient Longman Pvt. Ltd., 2008.

Chatterjee, Partha. *The Black Hole of Empire—History of a Global Practice of Power*. Ranikhet: Permanent Black, 2012.

Datta, V.N. *Maulana Azad*. New Delhi: Manohar, 1990.

Desai, Mahadev. *Maulana Azad*. Foreword by Mahatma Gandhi. Delhi: Shiva Lal Agarwala & Co. Ltd., 1946.

Ernst, Carl W. *Rethinking Islam in the Contemporary World*. Edinburgh: Edinburgh University Press, 2004.

Esposito, John L. *Islam—The Straight Path*. New York: Oxford University Press, 2005.

Fisher, Michael H. (ed.). *Themes in Indian History—The Politics of the British Annexation of India 1757–1857*. New Delhi: Oxford University Press, 1993.

Forrest, G.W. *The Indian Mutiny 1857–1858*. Delhi: Low Price Publications, 1902.

Grewal, J.S. *Muslim Rule in India—The Assessments of British Historians*. Calcutta: Oxford University Press, 1970.

Grewal, J.S. *Medieval India: History and Historians*. Amritsar: Guru Nanak University, 1975.

Hamied, K.A. *An Autobiography—A Life to Remember*. Bombay: Lalvani Publishing House, 1972.

Hasan, Mushirul. *Faith and Freedom—Gandhi in History*. New Delhi: Niyogi Books, 2013.

Hasan, Tariq. *The Aligarh Movement and the Making of the Indian Muslim Mind—1857–2002*. New Delhi: Rupa & Co., 2006.

Hopkirk, Peter. *On Secret Service East of Constantinople—The Plot to Bring Down the British Empire*. London: John Murray (Publishers), 2006.

Howe, Stephen. *Empire—A Very Short Introduction*. Oxford: Oxford University Press. 2002.

Hunter, W.W. *The Indian Musalmans*. Introduction by Bimal Prasad. New Delhi: Rupa & Co., 2004.

Hussain, Zahid. *Frontline Pakistan—The Struggle with Militant Islam*. Lahore: Vanguard Books, 2007.

Islam, Zafrul. *Role of Muslims in the Freedom Movement of India*. Edited by Abdul Ali (Seminar Papers). Aligarh: Institute of Islamic Studies, 2007.

Jalal, Ayersha. *The Sole Spokesman—Jinnah, the Muslim League and the Demand for Pakistan*. New Delhi: Cambridge University Press, 1994.

Jalal, Ayesha. *Partisans of Allah—Jihad in South Asia*. Lahore, Pakistan: Sang-e-Meel Publications, 2008.

Joshi, P.C. (Ed.). *Rebellion 1857*. Foreword by Irfan Habib. New Delhi: National Book Trust, India, 2007.

Keppel, Arnold. *Gun-running and the Indian North-West Frontier*. Lahore: Pakistan. Sag-e-Meel Publications, 2004.

Khan, Sayyid Ahmad. *An Account of the Loyal Mahomedans of India*. Patna: Khuda Bakhsh Oriental Public Library. Tips Enterprises, 1998.

Kumar, Ram Narayan. *Martyred but not Tamed—The Politics of Resistance in the Middle East*. New Delhi: Sage Publications India Pvt. Ltd., 2012.

Lelyveld, David. *Islamic Reform and Revival in Nineteenth-century India*. New Delhi: Yoda Press, 2008.

Llewellyn-Jones, Rosie. *The Great Uprising in India 1857–58—Untold Stories Indian and British*. New Delhi: Supernova Publishers & Distributors (P) Ltd., 2010.

Malleson, G.B. *The Indian Mutiny of 1857*. New Delhi: Rupa & Co., 2006.

Metcalf, Barbara D. *Husain Ahmad Madani: The Jihad for Islam and India's Freedom (Makers of the Muslim World)*. Oxford, England: Oneworld Publications, 2012.

Metcalf, Barbara D., Ahmed, Rafiuddin and Hasan, Mushirul. *India's Muslims— An Omnibus*. New Delhi: Oxford University Press, 2007.

Minault, Gail. *The Khilafat Movement—Religious Symbolism and Political Mobilization in India*. New Delhi: Oxford University Press, 1982.

Mishra, Pankaj. *From the Ruins of Empire—The Revolt Against the West and the Remaking of Asia*. England: Allen Lane—an imprint of Penguin Books, 2012.

Moosvi, Shireen (Ed.). *Facets of the Great Revolt 1857*. New Delhi: Tulika Books, 2008.

Muhammad, Shan. *The Indian Muslims—A Documentary Record 1900–1947*. New Delhi: Meenakshi Prakashan, 1980.

Muhammad, Shan. *Successors of Sir Syed Ahmad Khan—Their Role in the Growth of Muslim Political Consciousness in India*. Delhi: Idarah-i Adabiyat-i Delli, 1981.

Muhammad, Shan. *The Growth of Muslim Politics in India (1900–1919)*. New Delhi: Ashish Publishing House, 1991.

Muhammad, Shan. *Muslims and India's Freedom Movement*. New Delhi: Institute of Objective Studies, 2002.

Mujeeb, M. *The Indian Muslims*. New Delhi: Munshiram Manoharlal Publishers Pvt. Ltd., 1995.

Nayar, Pramod K. (Ed.). *The Penguin 1857 Reader*. New Delhi: Penguin Books, 2007.

Prasad, Bimal. Pathway to India's Partition. Volume 1: The Foundations of Muslim Nationalism. New Delhi: Manohar, 2001.

Pratap, Raja Mahendra. *My Life Story 1886–1979*. Edited by Dr Vir Singh. Delhi: Originals, 2004.

Ray, Niharranjan. *Nationalism in India*. Aligarh: Aligarh Muslim University, 1973.

Ray, Santimoy. *Freedom Movement and Indian Muslims*. New Delhi: National Book Trust, India, 2011.

Rizvi, Syed Sifarish Hussain. *Partition—End Product of the Trend*. Patna: Khuda Bakhsh Oriental Public Library. Produced by Tips Enterprises, 1998.

Robinson, Francis. *Separatism among Indian Muslims—The Politics of the United Provinces' Muslims 1860–1923*. Delhi: Oxford University Press, 1994.

Robinson, Francis. *The 'Ulama of Farangi Mahall and Islamic Culture in South Asia*. New Delhi: Permanent Black, 2005.

Robinson, Francis. *Islam and Muslim History in South Asia*. New Delhi: Oxford University Press, 2009.

Roy, M.N. *Historical Role of Islam—An Essay on Islamic Culture*. New Delhi: Critical Quest, 2006.

Seervai, H.M. *Partition of India—Legend and Reality*. Bombay: Emmenem Publications, 1989.

Siddiqui, Mohammad Yasin Mazhar. *Shah Waliullah Dehlavi—An Introduction to His Illustrious Personality and Achievements*. Aligarh: Institute of Islamic Studies, 2001.

Taylor, P.J.O. *Chronicles of the Mutiny & Other Historical Sketches*. New Delhi: HarperCollins Publishers Pvt. Ltd., 1992.

Taylor, P.J.O. *A feeling of Quiet Power—The Siege of Lucknow 1857*. New Delhi: Indus, 1994.

Taylor, P.J.O. *A Star Shall Fall: India 1857*. Noida: HarperCollins Publishers, 1995.

Tonki, S.M. *Aligarh and Jamia Fight for National Education System*. Foreword by A. Rahman. New Delhi: People's Publishing House, 1983.

Troll, C.W. *Sayyid Ahmad Khan—A Reinterpretation of Muslim Theology*. Karachi: Oxford University Press.

Wolpert, Stanley. *Jinnah of Pakistan*. New Delhi: Oxford University Press, 1985.

Index

About the Author

Tariq Hasan is an Aligarh-based journalist, who began his career in journalism (1975) as a correspondent for *The Pioneer* (Lucknow). He has worked with *The Times of India* for more than two decades, and prior to this with *The Patriot* (New Delhi). He is presently associated with the Press Trust of India (PTI) and has been reporting on the Aligarh Muslim University (AMU) for more than a quarter of century now.

Hasan has written extensively on Muslim issues. His critically acclaimed book, *The Aligarh Movement and the Making of Indian Muslim Mind* (2005), was well received all over the Indian subcontinent.

Hasan has served as the president of India's nominee to the AMU Court for more than three years. His other field of interest is environment affairs, especially wildlife.

Born in the year 1946, he received his early education at St Mary's High School, Mumbai, and completed his high school education from St Joseph's Collegiate, Allahabad. He joined AMU in 1965 and obtained his Bachelor's degree in Engineering. However, after a short stint in the engineering industry, he returned to his childhood passion—journalism.